Cricket and Nationhood in the Twenty-First Century

Cricket and Nationhood in the Twenty-First Century

Identity Projects in Uncertain Times

Edited by

SOUVIK NAHA

OXFORD
UNIVERSITY PRESS

OXFORD
UNIVERSITY PRESS

Great Clarendon Street, Oxford, OX2 6DP,
United Kingdom

Oxford University Press is a department of the University of Oxford.
It furthers the University's objective of excellence in research, scholarship,
and education by publishing worldwide. Oxford is a registered trade mark of
Oxford University Press in the UK and in certain other countries

Published in the United States of America by Oxford University Press
198 Madison Avenue, New York, NY 10016, United States of America

British Library Cataloguing in Publication Data

Data available

Library of Congress Control Number: 2024932393

ISBN 9780192889287

DOI: 10.1093/9780191982576.001.0001

Printed and bound in India by
Replika Press Pvt. Ltd.

Contents

Contributors

Ashwin Desai is Professor of Sociology, Director of the Centre of Social Change, and the SARChi (South African Research Chairs Initiative) Chair for Social Change based at the University of Johannesburg. His research interests include sports, political economy, and social policy. He has published well over a hundred peer-reviewed journal articles, books in chapters, and books. His latest works include the co-authored *Durban's Casbah: Bunny Chows, Bolsheviks and Bioscopes* and the single-authored *Of Fathers, Sons and Timeless Tests: Wicket Tales from Kingsmead*. In 2023, the Human Sciences Research Council awarded a medal to Professor Desai in the **Established Researcher Category** for his lifelong dedication to researching ways to view, understand, and uplift the day-to-day lives of ordinary human beings.

Tom Heenan lectures in Australian and Sports Studies in Monash University's School of Languages, Literatures, Cultures and Linguistics. A frequent commentator in the Australian and international media, he has written widely on sport as a columnist for *The New Daily*, as well as for Fairfax and News Corp publications, *The Conversation*, and *Outlook India*. With David Dunstan he has co-authored a biographical study of the Australian cricketer Sir Donald Bradman, titled *Bradman: Episodes in a Life* (2015), as well as the internationally acclaimed essay, 'Don Bradman: Just a Boy from Bowral', in the *Cambridge Companion to Cricket* (2011). With Dunstan, he has also written on Australia–India cricket, and with Salma Thani on the influence of Arab money on European football. He also has an interest in journalism and the media. His research interests include sports and business history, international relations, and globalization.

Ben Hildred has a PhD in Anthropology from Durham University, UK for a project titled 'Cricket in Post-War Sri Lanka: An Ethnographic Study of Sport and Reconciliation'. His previous work has explored how sport creates meaning for the individual by focussing on the role of cricket in configuring notions of personhood, identity, and the self.

Ali Khan is Associate Professor of Anthropology and Dean of the Mushtaq Ahmad Gurmani School of Humanities and Social Sciences at Lancaster University Management School (LUMS), UK. Ali Khan has an MPhil and a PhD in Social Anthropology from the University of Cambridge, UK. Prior to joining LUMS, Ali Khan spent over ten years working for the World Bank and the International Labour Organization.

Roy McCree is Senior Fellow at the Sir Arthur Lewis Institute of Social and Economic Studies (SALISES), Jamaica. He first worked at the Institute as a graduate research assistant from 1991 to 1995, when it was still the Institute of Social and Economic Research (ISER). He has been a full-time member of staff there since 1996. His research interests have covered the areas of sport, culture, race relations, policy evaluation, and social policy in particular relation to the issues of youth, community development, suicide, social capital, and gambling. He has a special interest, however, in the study of sport and its social, political, economic, cultural, and technological significance in the development of modern society.

Souvik Naha is Senior Lecturer in Imperial and Post-Colonial History at the University of Glasgow, UK. He has a PhD in History from ETH Zurich, Switzerland and held a Marie Skłodowska-Curie Actions fellowship at Durham University, UK. His recent book is *Cricket, Public Culture and the Making of Postcolonial Calcutta*. In addition, he has co-edited several journal special issues including 'FIFA World Cup and Beyond: Sport, Culture, Media and Governance' (2017), 'Global and Transnational Sport: Ambiguous Borders, Connected Domains' (2017), 'Ethical Concerns in Sport Governance' (2018), 'Moments, Metaphors, Memories: Defining Events in the History of Soccer' (2019), and 'Cricket in the 21st Century' (2021). He edits three journals: *Sport in Society*, *Sport in History*, and *Soccer & Society*.

Greg Ryan is Professor and Proctor at Lincoln University, New Zealand. His most recent book, co-authored with Dr Geoff Watson and published in 2018, is *Sport and the New Zealanders: A History*—the first comprehensive social history of New Zealand sport from Māori origins to the present. He has also published various academic and popular press articles and chapters on sport in New Zealand, authored three other books, and edited two. He is currently researching various aspects of Māori sporting contact with the British Empire and also writing a social history of beer and brewing in New Zealand.

Goolam Vahed did his undergraduate degree at the University of Durban-Westville, South Africa and PhD at Indiana University, USA. He teaches in the Department of History at the University of KwaZulu-Natal, South Africa and has written on various aspect of the history of Indians, Muslims, and cricket in South Africa. His most recent work is *Chota Motala: A Biography of Political Activism in the KwaZulu-Natal Midlands*.

Stephen Wagg has been Professor of Sport and Society at Leeds Beckett University, UK since 2008 and has been writing on the politics and history of sport since the mid-1980s. He edited *Cricket and National Identity in the Post-Colonial Era: Following On*, published by Routledge in 2005, and his book *Cricket: A Political History of the Global Game, 1945–2017* (Routledge, 2017) was shortlisted for the Cricket Writers' Club Annual Award in 2018.

Claire Westall is Senior Lecturer in the Department of English and Related Literature at the University of York, UK. Her forthcoming book is *The Rites of Cricket and Caribbean Literature*. She is also co-author of *The Public on the Public* (2015) and co-editor of *Prison Writing and the Literary World* (2020), *Cross-Gendered Literary Voices* (2012), and *Literature of an Independent England* (2013). She has edited special issues of the *Journal of Postcolonial Writing*, one titled 'Resistant Resources/Resources of Resistance' and the other 'The Worldiness of Cricket and Its Literature'. Her next sports-linked project will be a book about cricket and world literature.

Introduction

Uncanny Belongings: Affective Nationalism, State Power, and Cricket in the Twenty-First Century

Souvik Naha

An Age of Uncertainty

In 2010, noting the global political convulsions of the two preceding decades, historian Tony Judt called the twenty-first century 'an age of insecurity'. Judt defined insecurity as a paralysing fear of 'change', 'decline', 'strangers', and an 'unfamiliar world' that subverted the social and liberal democratic idea of a civil society.[1] The commitment to diversity, equality, and tolerance, he argued, had been a double-edged sword. State-led faith in justice and human rights seemed to work well in culturally homogenous countries in which 'strangers' were invisible and not perceived by most of the population as a threat or to have benefitted from state largesse. On the contrary, in multicultural countries, social conflicts and rifts deepened around the growing awareness of equality, equal opportunity, and the empowering of the marginalized. While some people have embraced the idea of systemic change and an egalitarian community, others have trenchantly opposed putting these concepts into practice.

One can trace the historical roots of this dilemma to the rejuvenation of the concept of civil society in the 1970s. The new civil society emerged across the world to varying degrees of efficacy and magnitude as a counterbalance to state-led economic and political modernization, intending to give the common people more voice and autonomy in the process.[2] Although the idea was to challenge institutions and ameliorate the condition of traditionally deprived and marginalized people, civil society often disregarded popular opinion. Instead of the majority's view, it often

Souvik Naha, *Introduction* In: *Cricket and Nationhood in the Twenty-First Century*. Edited by: Souvik Naha, Oxford University Press. © Oxford University Press 2024. DOI: 10.1093/9780191982576.003.0001 represented a self-righteous and elitist sense of the greater good and pro-gress.[3] Its nature varied depending on specific needs for action, while some non-Western trajectories emerged independent of its Western ideals. While the key imperative for most Western civil societies was the recognition of cultural difference and multiculturalism, the existence of these values was a serious problem for a postcolonial state like India that needed to triumph over its boundless diversity of identities for building nationhood.[4] The increasing interdependence of the world through trade and communication has facilitated the connection between distinct, gen-erally sanctimonious, ideologies of identity and power and has also made their clash inevitable and a global problem. This conflict has emerged ra-ther emphatically in the twenty-first century as the flaws of democracy have been writ large in some of the world's largest and most politically influential countries, many of which play cricket.

This book is a history of this unsettling present—the global drifts in identity politics, state power, capitalism, nationalism, and nationhood in the twenty-first century. It examines this contemporary history through the pedagogic optic of cricket, which is the 'national' game in almost every country, however few, that takes it seriously. It argues that cricket is a 'deep play' element in global society and has generated the contexts and tools for constructing, promoting, displaying, and legitimizing nation-alism and national identity in these countries spread across the world.[5] Followers drawn to nationalist or nationalized identifications channel national optimism and articulate national aspiration through cricket. As a political project that defines (inter)national and global collective and self-identity, cricket is intricately entangled with various territorial and emotional epitomes of belonging, attitudes, and involvement. It there-fore provides a vantage point for understanding the modern world, rep-resented in this book by South Asia, Australia, western Europe, southern Africa, and North America.

The chapters in this book collectively examine three connected aspects of contemporary identity projects. First, they discuss movements fo-cussed on equal rights and opportunities for historically marginalized racial, ethnic, and gender categories that have gathered momentum in many countries. The growing awareness of equality shows that the public have risen to the 'cosmopolitan challenge', in the words of sociolo-gist Ulrich Beck, by appreciating diversity and prevailing over self/other dichotomies.[6] Second, they consider the impulses of exclusionary nationalism for strengthening the nation-state, far-right activism, and toxic forms of chauvinism that have deepened across the globe. More borders have closed than visa regulations eased between countries in recent years. Symbolic boundaries have divided citizens of a country, leading to violence that often has the state's support. In general, scholars have explored the turn of events through a variety of factors from the failure of neoliberalism to the endemic nature of violence.[7] Third, they ponder the implications of the largescale integration of a network of interdependencies into a world economy. Transnational capitalism has enabled the circulation of ideas and artefacts beyond borders and promoted cultural convergences. The power of the market in shaping culture and aesthetics at both global and local levels is not wholly independent from state policies.[8] The tension between the political and consumerist needs of the state and the people plays a significant role in the circulation of cultural resources. The exponential growth of media and communication since the 2000s has contributed to the mass reckoning of these three global tendencies.

The State of Democracy

Are inequalities implicitly tolerated? In *The Society of Equals*, Pierre Rosanvallon argued that a vast majority of people are aware of inequality and injustice, but very few of them demand political changes to make things right. Equality comes not from accepting social differences or reducing economic disparity, but from a social bond created by similarity, independence, and citizenship.[9] Rosanvallon outlines an idea of generating equality through 'singularity, reciprocity, and commonality', in which the concept of singularity is rather telling. As opposed to insularity, singularity is the acknowledgement of a person's distinctive characteristics that engenders reciprocity by recognizing difference as a building block of society. Several democratic countries have arguably embraced singularity and reduced discrimination based on difference in identity. This has produced positive changes in state policies and public attitude towards women, queer communities, and racial and minority ethnic groups. At the same time, the accommodation of differences has also led to political fragmentation. Members of the public have been anxious about the nation-state's dissolution because of the shift in government's policy from acculturation to multiculturalism.[10] Certain political regimes have legitimized discontent against women and LGBTQ+ people. Some minority ethnic and religious groups who have ordinarily co-habited the same territory for sometimes thousands of years, with numerically superior groups, allegedly do not conform to majoritarian visions of nationhood.

Old identities that were stable for centuries have transformed and new identities have emerged in the hyperglobalized world since the mid-twentieth century, while the definition of identity is always in flux.[11] Many people continue to oppose identities that do not have the support of their scriptures or traditions. Yet, the freedom of making life choices, openness about sexuality, acceptance of people into previously denied professional roles, and opportunity irrespective of specific identities seem to have increased in the twenty-first century. People across the world have rallied in protests, often for months, asking governments to redress wealth inequality, the minimum wage, job precarity, religious persecution, systemic racism, environmental abuse, and so on. These dissident voices have braved crackdowns and alerted wider society to problems.[12] Policymaking is still criticized as a bastion of masculinity and social privilege that one needs to be able to benefit from the struggle for equality of the sexes. These ideals, often slammed as liberal, can be trivial for a vast majority of people for whom the government's equality initiatives have had small purchase.[13]

The efforts of various governments to assimilate minority ethnic groups under the rubric of citizenship demonstrate a similar contradiction. The policy of respecting rather than erasing difference has produced inconsistent results. What minorities desire and what their adoptive countries are willing and able to provide are sometimes delicately balanced, if not incompatible. While the nation-state undertakes massive, expensive plans for minority improvement, their police continue to harass specific communities more than others.[14] Welfare policies that overlook the internal differences and class segments among racial and ethnic communities end up being inefficient and redundant. The diversity ideology has reduced but not minimized communitarian inequality.[15] Social movements too have often been undermined by various factors such as their leaders yielding to political opportunities or resorting to misdirected protest tactics. Indeed, people are apprehensive of depletion of their privileges while making space for others. It should not come as a surprise that experiments with cultural pluralism and social justice have not met with the desired success, with some scholars arguing that European state-sponsored integration policies were ill informed and doomed from the very beginning.[16] Just as identities at the periphery are being consolidated, are the cleavages of identity also deepening by the day?

The answer to this question is context driven, scholarly explorations of which have mostly been focussed on Western liberal democracies. The tendency among many scholars to practise the West as a stand-in for the world and the non-Western modernity as an imitation of the West—a disposition increasingly in decline—had deflected attention from the West's internal contradictions for a long time. These issues started coming to the fore as late as the 1990s.[17] The 'narrow provincialism' of the discussions on 'populist movements, authoritarian leaders, and a visible fragility of liberal institutions', as Partha Chatterjee provocatively argues, tends to neglect the prevalence of similar structures in African and Asian countries for ages, primarily as a legacy of colonial rule.[18] In recent years, several stable democratic governments, most notably the UK, have surrendered to populism in a manner befitting neophyte nation-states with little experience and control over power and public sentiment. For Chatterjee, postcolonial democracies like India have operated with a carefully curated governmental populism that strategically favoured one class above the other. This opportunistic strategy of mobilizing support for one's party or ideology, conspicuously endemic in India as well as many other nations, was camouflaged in the West. In the twenty-first century, the lore of the primordial nation and the problems wrought by singularity and reciprocity have become convenient conduits of its expression.

Before the French presidential election in 2017, far-right National Rally (then known as National Front) leader Marine Le Pen declared, 'The time of the nation state is back.'[19] The nation-state had not really disappeared. According to some of the world's most influential politicians, it had been losing its meaning, purpose, and power for some time. The nation, they say, must be rebuilt in the image of its primordial identity, which is variously race, ethnicity, religion, and language.[20] In an interview with the *Financial Times* in 2019, Russian president Vladimir Putin insisted that the so-called liberal idea had 'outlived its purpose.'[21] He and many other heads of states have not been averse to breaking international laws for their country's benefit. Some of them, like Donald Trump, have antagonized the world in their efforts to restore their countries' greatness, while democracy has meant little for some others unless it strengthened their idea of the nation. Disdain for liberal values and support for violence abound in election speeches, rally slogans, and everyday conversations. In India under the right-wing Bharatiya Janata Party, 'left-liberal' is an umbrella term for critics of the national government, coined in utter disregard for the massive difference between left and liberal ideologies.[22] These demagogues and their supporters criticize the idea of equality as a politically correct and henceforth untenable concept.[23] The decline of the nation is perceived rather than reflected in most cases. Yet, the idea of decline is most often conveniently blamed on various aspects of modern liberal and socialist thought such as equality, secularism, internationalism, and multiculturalism. Some scholars have identified in the eye of the storm a populist moment catalysed by unfulfilled demands.[24] One Nation in Australia, New Zealand First in New Zealand, the African National Congress in South Africa, the Sri Lanka People's Front in Sri Lanka, and so on have been practising populism with varying degrees of success.

In addition to a widespread anxiety about the changing structure of society, a fear of one's country being subsumed under an undesirable identity—or worse, compromising its symbols of sovereignty—has emerged. National identity has a strong foundation of community feeling that creates boundaries against outsiders, protecting the nation against potential devolution. Any movement of subversive ideas across the boundary, a change in political economy, or an unexpected class experience can cause panic in the community.[25] Right-wing and conservative thoughts are usually blamed for perpetuating a politics of division and differentiation, but the political content of this disaffection is not always their handiwork. In fact, for complex multicultural entities like India and the UK, the architectonics of national identity encompass several, often contradictory, political commitments that render the idea of national identity fragmented, if not illusory.[26] Self-designated progressive, liberal, and left-wing regimes too have deported migrants en masse, suppressed dissident voices, erected trade barriers, and continued profitable commercial relations with countries with poor human rights records. In short, the politics of identity born out of lived experiences and brushes with ideological speeches or texts is transient and shapeshifts as all other forms of politics do. Will this lead to more durable states of exception springing up across the world?

Amidst the reinforcing of borders and doubts over social inclusion, the movement of capital and manufactured products seems to be the least affected of global connections. Modern citizen-consumers, particularly in the West, have facilitated the corporatization of the world economy and the emergence of a transnational capitalist class.[27] The socialist challenge to inequalities generated by capital accumulation having failed spectacularly, most democratic nation-states have chosen either restrained, welfare-focussed capitalism or a hollow declaration of anti-capitalism. Critics have blamed neoliberalism for the slow-down of economic growth in the West. On the contrary, several Asian countries have revitalized their economy by adopting a hybrid form of neoliberalism with clever power-sharing between the state and the market.[28] Some scholars see neoliberalism as a predatory form of capitalism that has waged a war on democracy and driven up social and economic disgruntlement by normalizing inequality in everyday life.[29] It has spawned a transnational capitalist class by internationalizing financial resources. The market controlled by this class offers the consumers of their merchandise critical cultural resources articulated through advertisements for building their identity around the product. This method not only ensures loyalty and yearning for the specific product but also strategically devolves and reinvents identities. As the transnational capitalist class is allegiant to the market of more than one nation-state, it packages cultural products such as sport in a way that serves both global citizenship and regional fervour, as well as traditional and countercultural demands. It produces nationalism and national identity as it deems favourable to position its product. Such consumer-orientated branding has the potential to formulate perceptions of what a nation is meant to be. Therefore, the twenty-first century presents a perplexing social portrait in which empowerment and disenfranchisement of the people can be traced to the same political and economic root. Where does people's choice feature in the economic control room of global societies? Has the limited statist form of capitalism won over the market, or is the nation still capable of determining the limits of privatization and welfare?

Cricket and Contemporary Nationhood

At the time of writing, international and transnational sports federations and sports leagues have not usurped the nation's traditional function as an organizer of sporting teams and competitions in the broad-gauge manner surmised in the 1990s. Instead, national governments are perennially in transaction with these institutions, leveraging their political and financial power to retain control. They are sometimes sanctioned for exerting unfair influence on the governance of sport. FIFA banned several countries such as Chad, Guatemala, India, Kenya, Nigeria, Pakistan, and Zimbabwe in the 2010s for excessive political interference in football administration. More importantly, sport followers draw extensive inspiration from their national or regional contexts to give meaning to sporting encounters. Therefore, sport cannot be purely framed as a national or global endeavour.[30] Just as sport broadens the possibility of inclusion by enabling formerly marginalized groups, it is used as a tool of exclusion. British Conservative MP Norman Tebbit courted controversy in 1990, claiming in an interview with the *Los Angeles Times* that the loyalty of South Asian immigrants to their countries of origin was weakening British nationhood. He infamously invoked the cricket test, in which 'which side do they cheer for?' determined their right to live and work in Britain. In 2014, he conceded that the performances of several British Asian cricketers now encouraged generations of British-born Asians to feel part of the nation. He also supported a national Asian Cricket Award.[31] A variant of the Tebbit Test is routinely invoked to gauge the loyalty of Indian Muslims when India plays against Pakistan. Recently, when an Indian fan tweeted that he enjoyed 'watching English and Australian batsmen more than these Indians', the Indian captain Virat Kohli bellowed back, 'Why are you living in our country and loving other countries? . . . I don't think you should live in our country and like other things. Get your priorities right.' The sentiment hardly differed from Tebbit's expectation of seamless integration into a totalizing society. Such comments unlock a key political dynamic of the modern world—the relapses of modern democracies from 'world-building' into 'nation-building'. The nation has indeed ruptured globalizing discourses with a vengeance.

Set against this context of the 'age of insecurity', in which contrasting ideologies co-exist and receive immense public visibility and concern, this book studies the game of cricket to broaden the understanding of how internationalism, populism, diversity, exclusion, assimilation, and corporate interests shape nations in the twenty-first century. Several important studies have addressed the relationship between sport, nationalism, and politics, considering how sport has led both region-centric identity formation and some of the global campaigns for equity and equality for disadvantaged people.[32] There is a larger body of work on how sport reflects and performs various aspects of imperial, colonial, ethnic, romantic, cultural, populist, and corporate nationalisms.[33] Scholars have also keenly observed the rise of global ties and networks in sport, producing a number of studies focussed on the circulation of sport codes, migration of athletes, organization of mega events, and consequent transnational and cosmopolitan manifestations of sport.[34] This is the first book, however, that combines interdisciplinary perspectives to navigate contemporary global power relations, identities, and political philosophy.[35] The focus on a single sport provides a coherent analytical tool unlike in other relevant books that consider several sports that are characteristically contrasting. Since every sport has its own history and logic of production and consumption, studying several sports together can lead to incompatible and conflicting conclusions. A single-sport book can capture its subject in greater complexity and lend more credence to comparative and global studies.

The eight chapters in the book thematically intersect in their analysis of modern nation-states. Greg Ryan's chapter on New Zealand, Goolam Vahed and Ashwin Desai's chapter on South Africa, and Stephen Wagg's chapter on England examine the processes and consequences of encouraging formerly marginalized gender, racial, and ethnic groups in cricket for national identity. The ascendancy of the indigenous people and immigrants of colour in New Zealand and England cricket heralds a new age of inclusive policymaking, but the tensions of race and class continue to undermine multiculturalism. The development of Black and 'Coloured' cricket in South Africa started as a fight against inequality but soon turned into political opportunism and vengeance. These chapters show the systemic nature of inequality by charting its transformation into various forms, while also pointing out the efforts to resist the politics of marginalizing people based on their identity.

Ali Khan and Ben Hildred tackle the contentious world of South Asian cricket by interrogating cricket's role in generating nationalist rivalry between India and Pakistan and addressing the challenge of peacebuilding in Sri Lanka. Subcontinental cricket is rife with problems due to the national government's direct involvements and tacit interventions in making the game a public discourse. Khan charts the history of the two decades in which Indo-Pak reconciliation through cricket turned into a quagmire of power politics, mainly due to the rise of religious nationalism in India, resulting in the sport being a weapon for both countries to denigrate one another. In Sri Lanka, as Hildred demonstrates, cricket failed to deliver its promise of national integration since class and ethnicity continue to command local cricket.

Claire Westall, Tom Heenan, and Roy McCree consider the impact of commercialization on English, Australian, and West Indian national identity. The rise of franchise-based cricket leagues that disengage cricketers from countries and birthplaces and turn them into service-providers hired by the highest bidder has generated new forms of territorial loyalty. Australia seems to have surrendered to the lure of revenue generation, but West Indian nationhood is waging a battle of relevance against this irreverent model. These chapters explore the power and importance of primordial ties in the production and consumption of leisure, showing how the different histories of these nations have inspired their citizens to forge altogether different relationships with neoliberal capitalism.

Patriotism, nationalism, and all components in the politics of difference, broadly defined, are constructed, not least in the sporting context. For these concepts to operate, one tradition is replaced by another, the nature of hierarchy changes, and the agents and subjects of change acquire new identities.[36] Cricket provides communities a dynamic space and social capital, enabling them to negotiate their gender, sexual, ethnic, and racial identities in their adoptive settlements. It has been a powerful medium of shaping ethnic and racial identities.[37] National distinctiveness in sport goes beyond fans wearing national colours or chanting in unison. It is created and reinforced by the same politics of belonging that reify citizenship and participation in a national community. This book takes a critical step forward, analysing the broad performative, affective, and representational significance of these conditions.

Notes

1. Tony Judt, *Ill Fares the Land: A Treatise on Our Present Discontent* (New York: Penguin, 2010), 33.

2. See Jean Cohen and Andrew Arato, *Civil Society and Political Theory* (Cambridge, MA: MIT Press, 1992); Paul Hirst, *Associative Democracy: New Forms of Economic and Social Governance* (Cambridge, MA: MIT Press, 1993); John A. Hall, *Civil Society: Theory, History, Comparison* (Cambridge: Polity Press, 1995); Michael Edwards, ed., *The Oxford Handbook of Civil Society* (Oxford: Oxford University Press, 2011).

3. Sunil Khilnani, 'The development of civil society', in *Civil Society: History and Possibilities*, eds. Sudipta Kaviraj and Sunil Khilnani (Cambridge: Cambridge University Press, 2001), 11–32.

4. Shalini Randeria, 'Entangled histories: Civil society, caste solidarities and legal pluralism in post-colonial India', in *Civil Society: Berlin Perspectives*, ed. John Keane (New York: Berghahn Books), 213–242.

5. Philosopher Jeremy Bentham coined the term deep play to describe pursuits that may have high, mostly irrational, spiritual import but little material significance. Anthropologist Clifford Geertz adopted this concept in his now classical analysis of the Balinese cockfight to shed light on the ideological and political underwritings in sport. Geertz concludes that sport stands in for communities and cultures owing to these serious investments. It can make people stake their lives on the outcome, which may seem irrational but it is far from it. Clifford Geertz, 'Deep play: Notes on the Balinese cockfight', *Daedalus* 101, no. 1 (1972): 1–37.

6. Ulrich Beck, 'Redefining the sociological project: The cosmopolitan challenge', *Sociology* 46, no. 1 (2012): 7–12.

7. Heinrich Geiselberger, ed., *The Great Regression* (London: Polity, 2017); Pankaj Mishra, *Age of Anger: A History of the Present* (New York: Farrar, Straus & Giroux, 2017).

8. Robert Keohane, *Power and Governance in a Partially Globalized World* (London: Routledge, 2002); William I. Robinson, *Global Capitalism and the Crisis of Humanity* (New York: Cambridge University Press, 2014).

9. Pierre Rosanvallon, *The Society of Equals*, trans. Arthur Goldhammer (Cambridge, MA: Harvard University Press, 2013), 47.

10. Mark Redhead, *Charles Taylor: Thinking and Living Deep Diversity* (Lanham, MD: Rowman & Littlefield, 2002), 1–2. In this book, Redhead studies Charles Taylor's ideas of 'dialogue society' and 'deep diversity', which Taylor proposed as solutions to Canada's policy towards integrating local communities, immigrants, and non-Christians. Taylor thinks that promoting a sense of dignity of individuals and communities gives them the freedom to belong to the larger society or federated state on their own terms.

11. Margaret Wetherall, *Identity in the 21st Century: New Trends in Changing Times* (Basingstoke: Palgrave Macmillan, 2009).

12. Charles Lindholm and José Pedro Zúquete, *The Struggle for the World: Liberation Movements for the 21st Century* (Stanford, CA: Stanford University Press, 2010); Kim Voss and Irene Bloemraad, eds., *Rallying for Immigrant Rights: The Fight for Inclusion in 21st Century America* (Berkeley, CA: University of California Press, 2011); Chris Zepeda-Millán, *Latino Mass Mobilization: Immigration, Racialization, and Activism* (New York: Cambridge University Press, 2017); Marco Giugni and Maria T. Grasso, *Street Citizens: Protest Politics and Social Movement Activism in the Age of Globalization* (New York: Cambridge University Press, 2019).

13. Shannon N. Davies, Sarah Winslow, and David J. Maume, eds., *Gender in the Twenty-First Century: The Stalled Revolution and the Road to Equality* (Oakland, CA: University of California Press, 2017); Joyce P. Kaufland and Kristen P. Williams, eds., *Women, Gender Equality, and Post-Conflict Transformation* (London: Routledge, 2017).

14. Stevie-Jade Hardy, *Everyday Multiculturalism and 'Hidden' Hate* (Basingstoke: Palgrave Macmillan, 2017).

15. Seyla Benhabib, *The Claims of Culture: Equality and Diversity in the Global Era* (Princeton, NJ: Princeton University Press, 2002); David G. Embrick, Sharon M. Collins, and Michelle S. Dodson, eds., *Challenging the Status Quo: Diversity, Democracy, and Equality in the 21st Century* (Leiden: Brill, 2019).

16. Rita Chin, *The Crisis of Multiculturalism in Europe: A History* (Princeton, NJ: Princeton University Press, 2017).

17. Arjun Appadurai, 'The nine lives of modernization theory', *The Los Angeles Review of Books*, 26 June 2020, https://lareviewofbooks.org/article/the-nine-lives-of-modernization-theory.

18. Partha Chatterjee, *I Am the People: Reflections on Popular Sovereignty Today* (New York: Columbia University Press, 2020), ix–x.

19. Angelique Chrisafis, '"The nation state is back": Front National's Marine Le Pen rides on global mood', *The Guardian*, 18 September 2016, www.theguardian.com/world/2016/sep/18/nation-state-marine-le-pen-global-mood-france-brexit-trump-front-national.

20. The idea of primordial bonds such as kinship or religion has been criticized for not adequately recognizing their flexible, context-orientated meanings. Yet, as Clifford Geertz rightly pointed out, kinship may hold greater significance than most other forms of collective selfhood for a great number of people. It may be perceived as the natural and normal order of things. Any threat to this belief may cause the nation-state to break down. Clifford Geertz, *The Interpretation of Cultures* (New York: Basic Books, 1973), ch. 10.

21. *Financial Times*, 27 June 2019, www.ft.com/video/a49cfa25-610e-438c-b11d-5dac19619e08.

22. Aatish Taseer, 'Does India's right wing have any ideas?', *The New York Times*, 29 November 2016, www.nytimes.com/2016/11/29/opinion/does-indias-right-wing-have-any-ideas.html.

23. The term political correctness became a 'rallying cry of the conservative critics of academia' in 1990s America. As a critique of radical or uncomfortable thoughts promoted by the academic left, political correctness soon became an international buzz-phrase for leftist thoughts concerning equal rights, feminism, affirmative action, etc. The complaint was not purely fabricated given the left's intolerance to criticism, but it was rarely undergirded by logical argument. John K. Wilson, *The Myth of Political Correctness: The Conservative Attack on Higher Education* (Durham, NC: Duke University Press, 1995).

24. Ernesto Laclau, *On Populist Reason* (London: Verso, 2005); Chantal Mouffe, *For a Left Populism* (London: Verso, 2018).

25. Deborah J. Schildkraut, *Americanism in the Twenty-First Century: Public Opinion in the Age of Immigration* (New York: Cambridge University Press, 2011); Elke Winter, *Us, Them, and Others: Pluralism and National Identities in Diverse Societies* (Toronto: University of Toronto Press, 2011); David McCrone and Frank Bechhofer, *Understanding National Identity* (Cambridge: Cambridge University Press, 2015).

26. Sebastian Schwecke, *New Cultural Identarian Political Movements in Developing Societies: The Bharatiya Janata Party* (London: Routledge, 2011); Wendy Doniger and Martha C. Nussbaum, eds., *Pluralism and Democracy in India: Debating the Hindu Right* (New York: Oxford University Press, 2015); Angana P. Chatterji, Thomas Blom Hansen, and Christophe Jaffrelot, eds., *Majoritarian State: How Hindu Nationalism in Changing India* (London: Hurst, 2019); Robin Mann and Steve Fenton, *Nation, Class and Resentment: The Politics of National Identity in England, Scotland and Wales* (Basingstoke: Palgrave Macmillan, 2017).

27. William K. Carroll, *The Making of a Transnational Capitalist Class: Corporate Power in the Twenty-First Century* (London: Zed Books, 2010).

28. Aihwa Ong, *Neoliberalism as Exception: Mutations in Citizenship and Sovereignty* (Durham, NC: Duke University Press, 2006).

29. George Monbiot, *How Did We Get into This Mess? Politics, Equality, Nature* (London: Verso, 2016); Wendy Brown, *In the Ruins of Neoliberalism: The Rise of Antidemocratic Politics in the West* (New York: Columbia University Press, 2019).

30. David Rowe, 'Sport and the repudiation of the global', *International Review for the Sociology of Sport* 38, no. 3 (2003): 281–294; Grant Jarvie, 'Internationalism and sport in the making of nations', *Identities: Global Studies in Culture and Power* 10, no. 4 (2003): 537–551.

31. Edward Malnick, 'Lord Tebbit suggests more British Asians now pass his cricket test', *The Telegraph*, 30 September 2014, www.telegraph.co.uk/news/politics/11131816/Lord-Tebbit-suggests-more-British-Asians-now-pass-his-cricket-test.html.

32. Simon Darnell, *Sport for Development and Peace: A Critical Sociology* (London: Bloomsbury, 2012); Jean Harvey, John Hone, Parissa Safai, Simon Darnell, and Sebastian Courchesne-O'Neill, *Sport and Social Movements: From the Local to the Global* (London: Bloomsbury, 2013).

33. Some of the more important contributions are: J.A. Mangan, ed., *Tribal Identities: Nationalism, Europe, Sport* (London: Frank Cass, 1996); Mike Cronin and David Mayall, eds., *Sporting Nationalisms: Identity, Ethnicity, Immigration and Assimilation* (London: Frank Cass, 1998); Alan Bairner, *Sport, Nationalism, and Globalization: European and North American Perspectives* (Albany, NY: State University of New York Press, 2001); Adrian Smith and Dilwyn Porter, eds., *Sport and National Identity in the Post-War World* (London: Routledge, 2004); Alan Tomlinson and Christopher Young, eds., *National Identity and Global Sports Events: Culture, Politics and Spectacle in the Olympics and the Football World Cup* (Albany, NY: State University of New York Press, 2006); Fan Hong and Lu Zhouxiang, eds., *Sport and Nationalism in Asia: Power, Politics and Identity* (London: Routledge, 2015).

34. Toby Miller, Geoffrey Lawrence, Jim McKay, and David Rowe, *Globalization and Sport: Playing the World* (London: Sage, 2001); Joseph Maguire and Mark Falcous, eds., *Sport and Migration: Border, Boundaries and Crossings* (London: Routledge, 2011); Peter Millward, *The Global Football League: Transnational Networks, Social Movements and Sport in the New Media Age* (Basingstoke: Palgrave Macmillan, 2011); Souvik Naha, ed., *Global and Transnational Sport: Ambiguous Borders, Connected Domains* (London: Routledge, 2018).

35. Michael Silk and David Andrews' edited book on sport and neoliberalism explores, with a focus on the US, how neoliberal power relations have turned sport into a tool of public governance. Michael L. Silk and David L. Andrews, eds., *Sport and Neoliberalism: Politics, Consumption, and Culture* (Philadelphia, PA: Temple University Press, 2012).

36. Liah Greenfeld, *Nationalism: Five Roads to Modernity* (Cambridge, MA: Harvard University Press, 1992); Adrian Hastings, *The Construction of Nationhood: Ethnicity, Religion and Nationalism* (Cambridge: Cambridge University, 1997).

37. Thomas Fletcher, 'Cricket, migration and diasporic communities', *Identities: Global Studies in Culture and Power* 22, no. 2 (2015): 141–153.

1

Viability, Identity, and the 'Browning' of New Zealand Cricket

Greg Ryan

Introduction

For more than a century, cricket was a perfect embodiment of the self-image of New Zealand society as a harmonious and intensely loyal component of the British Empire/Commonwealth in which more than 95 per cent of immigrants came from Britain and Ireland. Even as stirrings of a distinct national identity and eventually dominion status emerged from the early twentieth century, they did so within a reassuring imperial framework underpinned by extensive economic and cultural ties to Britain. Accordingly, cricket was avowedly amateur and traditional with both administrators and followers preferring exchanges with England and deference to Lord's a great deal more than their uneasy relationship with neighbouring Australia.[1]

The Cold War Australia, New Zealand, and United States (ANZUS) alliance precipitated a change to New Zealand's international alignment. This was confirmed by Britain's gradual withdrawal from empire and its membership of the European Economic Community from 1973, which eroded New Zealand's longstanding preferential economic relationship. In parallel, strands of globalization from the 1960s and neoliberal reforms from the mid-1980s introduced a swathe of economic and structural change that shifted New Zealand to a more individually orientated and less collective society, but one with greater wealth disparity than previously.[2] This period also witnessed a dramatic broadening of New Zealand's ethnic composition. A Pākehā (European New Zealander) majority that had existed in relative isolation from indigenous Māori was

Greg Ryan, *Viability, Identity, and the 'Browning' of New Zealand Cricket* In: *Cricket and Nationhood in the Twenty-First Century*. Edited by: Souvik Naha, Oxford University Press. © Oxford University Press 2024.
DOI: 10.1093/9780191982576.003.0002

gradually challenged firstly by more overt biculturalism and later by multiculturalism. The number of people identifying as Māori increased from 8.1 per cent to 14.9 per cent of the population between 1961 and 2013. The population of Pasifika (Polynesian migrants from the Pacific region and their descendants) ancestry also increased sharply on the back of migration from the 1960s to comprise 7.4 per cent of the population by 2013. New immigration legislation introduced in 1987 abandoned the emphasis on obtaining immigrants from 'traditional source' countries such as the United Kingdom in favour of merit selection, business immigrants, and family reunification. The result was a significant increase in Asian immigration, especially from China and later India. All of these transformations were predominantly urban and therefore very visible to the dominant Pākehā population.[3]

Beyond the numerical transformation, concerted Māori protest at the deprivations of colonialism, land dispossession, and economic marginalization emerged from the late 1960s. The establishment of the Waitangi Tribunal in 1975 to investigate and address actions and omissions of the Crown against Māori, and especially its ability to work retrospectively from 1985, was symptomatic of a gradual determination by successive governments to facilitate economic and cultural redress. Legislation enshrined Māori as an official language in 1987, reforms to the electoral system during the mid-1990s greatly increased Māori political representation, and a succession of Treaty of Waitangi settlements have enabled *iwi* (tribes) to enhance their cultural and economic base.[4] While Pasifika peoples, as migrant rather than indigenous, were not afforded the same levels of formal institutional support, the establishment of the Ministry of Pacific Island Affairs (now Ministry for Pacific Peoples) in 1990 reflected a similar determination to meet the needs of a growing but frequently disadvantaged population. Meanwhile, the Labour Government led by Prime Minister Helen Clark from 1999 emphasized multiculturalism and diversity as a key policy platform. Among a wide range of official initiatives were interpreter and language support for new migrants and related support in the employment, housing, education, and health systems. The role of the Race Relations Commissioner, initially established in 1972, was strengthened, and an Office of Ethnic Affairs was created in 2001. Numerous government agencies and departments also created diversity and inclusiveness strategies ranging across ethnicity, gender, and identity.

Similar developments proliferated at local government and community level.[5]

The key question underpinning this chapter is: how has cricket adapted to this changing society? After first considering the major impediments confronting the New Zealand game throughout the twentieth century, the main focus of what follows is on significant demographic and structural changes over the last decade and the success or otherwise of New Zealand Cricket Inc. (NZC) and its provincial affiliates to harness these to the viability of the game at all levels. The chapter also examines the advantages and disadvantages of the emergence of global T20 leagues and the proximity of the Australian Big Bash; the transformation of women's cricket; the slowly growing presence of indigenous Māori and other Polynesian players; and the more pronounced impact of relatively recent migrant groups, especially South Africans and Indians. While most of these trends are by no means unique to New Zealand, they are undoubtedly having a substantial impact on a traditionally conservative game.

A Viable Game?

Judged purely by the performance of its most visible commodity, the men's national team, New Zealand cricket has enjoyed considerable success throughout the second decade of the twenty-first century. In Test matches its winning percentage has increased from 21.3 per cent during the 1990s to 41.1 per cent for the nine years from the beginning of 2011. During the same period in One Day Internationals, victories increased from 37.6 per cent to 53.8 per cent and the team contested the World Cup final against England in 2019.[6] In New Zealand sporting parlance there is no question that the team has 'punched above its weight' on the international stage. Yet there is a case to be made that such results are something of a mirage derived from a lucky alignment of talented players that masks concerning demographic trends in the New Zealand game as a whole. By one analysis, to be discussed in what follows, the primacy of cricket among summer sports is under threat amid a wide range of leisure alternatives and periodic fluctuations in both participation rates and the financial stability of the game at all levels. A more optimistic interpretation points to high rates of participation at the junior level but stresses that the future for New Zealand cricket likely rests with abbreviated forms of the game and with new player constituencies that cricket administrators have been relatively slow to embrace. The question therefore is whether these new patterns of participation will ultimately be able to reinforce the elite level in general and the tradition of Test cricket in particular.

The overarching challenge to the long-term health of New Zealand cricket stems from the small size of the country and hence of the potential pool of players and the revenue generating spectator base. Although it is highly developed, economically prosperous, and politically stable in global terms, and although the population has increased from 3.5 to 5 million in the three decades since 1991, New Zealand is the smallest of the leading cricket nations behind the increasingly struggling member states of the West Indies with around 6.2 million. Among nations with full international status, recently emergent Ireland has an almost identical population.[7] Certainly as a developed country, New Zealand is better able than some of its economically less advantaged counterparts to maximize and resource its elite player pool. But it is equally the case that developed countries offer a much wider variety of recreational and sporting opportunities to fragment the interests of their citizens. On one hand, a pattern of neoliberal economic reforms and restructuring of business and employment practices since the 1980s, such as casualized working hours and weekend trading, has considerably eroded the notion of Saturday as a day off work when almost all cricket was traditionally played.[8] At the same time, increased disposable income for some sections of the population and elements of cultural globalization have challenged the longstanding emphasis on team games of English origin, such as cricket and rugby, and encouraged the pursuit of a much wider range of individual and team sports. The economic and structural changes have also produced a more individualized society in which people are opting out of team sports which oblige them to commit set periods of time to training and playing in favour of solitary and sedentary activities which can be fitted around their own schedule and preferred lifestyle. Gyms and the personal-fitness industry have clearly benefitted from this fragmented environment, as have such activities as mountain biking. It is also evident that the two main reasons young people traditionally took up team sport, to have fun and gain a sense of connection with others, are increasingly being filled by such technologies as interactive online gaming.[9]

A report circulated by Sport New Zealand to national sports organizations in 2019 stated that participation in sport among eighteen- to twenty-four-year-olds had declined by 13.9 per cent during the previous sixteen years, while other accounts suggest that the rate of decline among younger age groups is even higher.[10] Although cricket remains the most popular among summer sports in New Zealand, both in terms of participation and television viewing, the consistent trend of sport and recreation surveys since the 1990s reveals a marked decline in participation and club membership.[11] In 2000 nearly 18,000 secondary school students, mostly boys, were playing cricket. By 2016 the number had fallen to just under 10,000.[12] Among the trend to sedentary activities, there are also contrasting arguments as to the impact of an ever-increasing volume of televised national and international cricket. While there is an argument, as in India especially, that easy accessibility to the game on television constantly inspires new generations of players, it has also been suggested that the shift of New Zealand cricket to pay television in 1998 reduced access among those who are unable or unwilling to subscribe.[13]

From the beginning of the twentieth century, cricket has also been dwarfed by the dominance of rugby union within the New Zealand sporting consciousness, and especially so since rugby embraced open professionalism in 1995. Expanding domestic and southern hemisphere international and franchise competitions and successive victories by the All Blacks in the 2011 Rugby World Cup in New Zealand and the 2015 tournament in the United Kingdom, as well as rapid growth in the women's game domestically and internationally, ensure rugby's centrality within media coverage of sport. Whereas the successes of rugby are expected, and have prompted both invective and national soul-searching when they periodically do not eventuate, those of cricket have been treated more as a bonus to be celebrated at the time.[14]

The ability of NZC to adapt to this rapidly changing environment since the 1980s presents a mixed verdict. The televising of international men's one-day cricket from the early 1980s, and especially events such as the 'underarm' incident with Australia in 1981,[15] garnered strong public interest that was sustained through to New Zealand's very successful co-hosting with Australia of the 1992 World Cup in which they reached the semi-finals. To manage the demands of a rapidly professionalizing game, the previously amateur and volunteer-based New Zealand Cricket Council was transformed during the 1980s. The first full-time chief executive was appointed in 1985. In 1992, the Council was replaced by NZC, which combined the administration of both men's and women's cricket—the first country in the world to do so, although we will see shortly that this may not have been an advantage to the women's game. In 1995 a new Board was established to replace the previous Board of elected provincial association representatives with one comprising independent members appointed for their mix of business and cricket expertise. This structure drew a clearer distinction between strategy, governance, and day-to-day management and was better able to engage with the corporate demands of professional sport.[16] The on- and off-field success of the 1992 World Cup was also taken to suggest that one-day cricket was the future of the New Zealand game. For the 1992–1993 season NZC officially sanctioned Action Cricket, a twenty-overs-per-innings format that allowed for two games on the same day—the visionary nature of which was scarcely appreciated at the time. The following season they introduced a second round to the domestic one-day competition and began to significantly reduce the amount of domestic first-class cricket played. From 1991–1992 to 1995–1996 the one-day programme doubled while first-class cricket was reduced by a third. From 1995–1996 the one-day game was condensed still further with Cricket Max—a format developed by former New Zealand batsman Martin Crowe in which each team had two ten over innings and an opportunity to double the value of runs by hitting the ball straight into a 'Max Zone'. A concerted marketing and 'branding' campaign from the early 1990s also saw the national team recast as firstly the 'Young Guns' and later the 'Black Caps', a sobriquet that has entered common usage despite an initially frosty reception.[17]

But these and other changes did not sustain success or public confidence. Despite the growth in participation at all levels of cricket from 59,234 in 1990–1991 to 81,489 in 1994–1995, NZC did not initially put in place any coherent development programme to sustain and manage this growth.[18] Consequently, as the national men's team generally struggled on the field throughout the 1990s and became embroiled in periodic player behaviour controversies and changes of coach off it, the public became antagonistic to branding strategies that were perceived as an attempt to disguise poor performances. As attendances at one-day internationals dwindled, sometimes to less than one third of those during the early 1980s, NZC re-evaluated its preoccupation with the one-day game during the late 1990s. Cricket Max never found a secure niche, was reduced to a pre-season event, and eventually fizzled out in 2002. There was a renewed emphasis on first-class domestic cricket.[19]

The first decade of the new century revealed a familiar pattern of decidedly mixed fortunes at the elite level and antagonisms within the running of the game. The nadir was undoubtedly the players' strike during 2002 when what were essentially justified demands for improvements in pay and conditions by the Cricket Players Association (CPA) entirely failed to generate sympathy from a sporting public disillusioned with the performance of the national men's team.[20] Thereafter, although some genuine international stars emerged such as Brendon McCallum, Ross Taylor, and Kane Williamson, international performances tended to fluctuate regularly between good and mediocre. In response, NZC engaged a succession of coaches, talent development managers, and analysts, including some from non-cricket backgrounds, described by one journalist as 'a carousel of curious appointments'. But a survey of professional and semi-professional players in 2012 revealed that 64 per cent of them were 'not aware of, and do not understand, how the NZC high-performance programme works'.[21] Former players also criticized parochial rather than national interests among the provincial cricket associations and an apathetic and disengaged administration which appeared not to grasp the global transformation of cricket consequent to the dominance of the Indian market in particular.[22]

Especially under Brendon McCullum's captaincy, significantly improved international results did feed public interest, no more so than in New Zealand's co-hosting with Australia of the 2015 World Cup in which the two countries met in the final. But in other respects, the financial largesse that descended on world cricket from the mid-2000s with lucrative broadcasting deals, and especially the establishment of the Indian Premier League (IPL) in 2008 and other T20 leagues soon after, can be seen as a rather mixed blessing for New Zealand cricket beyond the international level. From 2006, NZC developed its own T20 competition but one that has become decidedly secondary to the Australian Big Bash League (BBL) and latterly the Women's Big Bash League (WBBL) played at the same time. The BBL, as with the IPL, most other T20 leagues, and a plethora of domestic and international cricket from around the world, has received full coverage on New Zealand pay television since its inception. But at the same time, and as a clear reflection of the small New Zealand market and the broadcast and sponsorship resources available, substantial coverage of New Zealand limited-over competitions only developed from the 2018–2019 season. Consequently, the New Zealand competitions have struggled to draw large crowds. While the public can be satisfied with a greater volume of televised cricket than ever before, an impressionable generation of potential players are less likely than those in other countries to find their inspiration and role models in local settings.[23] It follows from this dearth of coverage and spectator engagement that the six major cricket associations are largely dependent on NZC disbursements for their survival. In turn, NZC runs on a four-year revenue cycle which is heavily dependent on the International Cricket Council (ICC) and revenue from certain lucrative tours, such as India, to offset lower public interest in others.[24]

In 2019 NZC initiated the 'One Cricket' project overseen by former international player and NZC chief executive Martin Snedden to broaden participation in the game at all levels and especially to retain and grow youth participation. Although Sport New Zealand had long regarded cricket as the 'exemplar' for recruiting players at junior level and numbers had increased markedly in the wake of the 2015 World Cup, underpinning an overall increase to nearly 150,000 registered players throughout New Zealand, those at secondary school level were showing a rate of decline greater than other team sports, with an average of thirty-two teams dropping out of secondary school cricket each year since 2015. According to NZC, the decline stemmed from a growing perception among young people that cricket took too long to play, was expensive, was only played on a Saturday, and contained long periods of inactivity for individual players. Snedden's focus, derived from similar initiatives in Australia, was therefore aimed at fostering abbreviated and hybrid forms of the game and 'age plus stage' rules to make junior cricket a more inclusive experience which would encourage players to continue with the game as they get older. The approach includes shorter pitches to reduce the bowling of wides, therefore keeping the ball in play for longer; a reduction in team sizes and a requirement for all players to bat and bowl; and experiments with dual-pitch formats where teams made up of eight players played two games at the same time—six players fielding on one pitch while the other two batted on the other as the opposing team did the same. At secondary school level and beyond, a number of regions have also developed mid-week and twilight competitions to shift the emphasis from the weekend.[25]

Following the lead of a number of provincial rugby unions, there has also been debate about removing all representative cricket below the under-fifteen age group and shifting the emphasis from talent identification to a broader programme of skill development. Dissenters, and especially those from some elite schools that have traditionally dominated junior representative teams, argue that rule changes and the removal of representative incentives erode interest in the game. But Snedden replied that while it was important not to alienate committed coaches and volunteers, the dissenters 'base their arguments entirely on the effect it has on kids they perceive to be the most talented'. However, evidence suggested that talent identification at junior level is unreliable and exclusion of other players based on perception of a lack of talent at that age is detrimental to cricket as a whole. 'The conversation we are having with our members is that we don't believe it's the right thing to be playing rep cricket at that level. We put significant resource into rep programmes for under-13s that should be put into something else. The amount of junior rep cricket played around the country risks burnout. It's not just burnout of kids, it's burnout of parents, too.'[26]

Growing the Women's Game

Attracting girls is another significant dimension of the player retention strategy. Notwithstanding a sharp increase in participation by girls at junior level since 2011–2012, 90.5 per cent of clubs did not have girls-only teams and 57.6 per cent of clubs did not offer cricket for girls at all. Consequently, in 2016 only 4 per cent of all female players were adults compared to 23 per cent of males.[27] While acknowledging that cricket still had to have traditional pathways for players aspiring to representative or international honours, Snedden also suggested that the structure of the game available for most girls needed to change. 'Girls do not want to play traditional cricket. When you think about it there was not a lot of thought that went into the way the girls' game was delivered when it started off. For girls it is to have fun and they really enjoy it.'[28] This approach also feeds off more fundamental changes. The promotion of women's sport has been a focus area of government sport and recreation policy since the mid-1980s, aligning with a period in which women appeared to be making significant progress towards legal, social, and political equality in New Zealand. At the end of 2001, the prime minister, attorney-general, governor-general, chief justice, and chief executive officer of New Zealand's leading telecommunications company were all women.[29] While this progressive shift slowed during the following two decades, and significant employment and economic inequalities remain, opportunities in elite women's sport reveal a greater degree of gender equality than most sectors in society with increased sponsorship and the emergence of career opportunities in sports such as netball, football, rugby union, and a plethora of individual sports. In this setting, women are better able to assert their 'space' and challenge the prevailing male culture of sport.[30]

Having secured hosting rights for the women's World Cup in 2022, NZC now had an incentive to increase the number of females playing the game. Yet the ability to reverse the participation trend is not assisted by a dramatic decline in the presence of women in New Zealand's coaching and governance structure. An original reason for forming separate sporting organizations earlier in the twentieth century was that women were concerned they would lose control over their sport if they affiliated to men's organizations. But the argument in favour of amalgamating the men's and women's cricket administration in 1992 was that it confirmed an existing trend of amalgamations at club and provincial level, ensuring that funds from the wealthier men's organization would help to promote women's cricket and enable the game to be promoted as a family sport.[31] While some of these objectives have been met, the original concern is clearly justified. An independent and subsequently damning report commissioned by NZC in 2016 referred to female cricketers as 'a species on the verge of extinction' and noted that less than 10 per cent of coaches were female. The national team has very seldom had a female coach during this period. The percentage of women involved in the governance structure of cricket had declined from 38 per cent in 1993–1994 to 6.4 per cent in 2016 and only two of forty-three Board positions at regional level in 2016. Those interviewed for the report also believed that NZC regarded women's cricket as an obligation and a cost centre with no apparent return on investment. Women's development programmes were treated as an afterthought. In a subsequent press statement NZC conceded: 'We have allowed women's cricket to be run by men for women; we have neglected the women's game on the basis of cost, and a perceived lack of interest. We have sidelined women's cricket both structurally and philosophically. We were wrong, and we now need to address the areas we've allowed to slip.'[32] Efforts to close this gap, including the election of former international star Debbie Hockley as NZC's first female president in November 2016, were given further momentum in 2019 when Sport New Zealand and High Performance Sport New Zealand announced that as a formal condition for ongoing investment, all partner sports receiving government funding of over $50,000 a year would need to achieve a minimum of 40 per cent of women on their boards by December 2021.[33]

NZC also made significant, albeit relative, progress in the provision of professional contracts for elite female players. From 2015 ten women were awarded central contracts for the White Ferns national team ranging from $10,000 to $12,000 depending on the ranking of the player. Previously they had been paid only assembly and match fees when training and playing. Two years later fifteen players were contracted with a pay range from $20,000 to $34,000. In 2017 Northern Districts become the first major provincial association to offer retainers for women players—ranging from $500 to $4,000, depending on ranking.[34] By the 2019–2020 season a new master agreement for seventeen elite players as well as for development and domestic provincial players significantly increased the women's player payment pool to $4.136 million over the three-year term of the agreement. Seventy-nine players were now contracted and the White Ferns earned a base retainer of $44,000 to $64,000 per year plus match fees. Several of the best players also found opportunities in overseas T20 leagues, which enables them to be full-time professionals.[35]

But the pace of progress has its critics amid claims that female cricketers are playing in potentially illegal employment conditions. Retainers for the men's national team range from $100 to $236,000 with the full group of 116 male contracted players receiving a fixed revenue share of 26.5 per cent of all revenue generated from professional cricket. While male domestic provincial player contracts have a base retainer of $27,000 to $54,000 plus match fees for a season with a minimum of fifty-two playing days, female domestic players receive a $3,250 'compensation' contract, but no match fees, for a minimum of twenty playing days. For the provincial men's and women's T20 finals held on the same day in January 2020, and for which the men received an additional $575 match fee and the women nothing, an employment lawyer argued that under the New Zealand Human Rights Act introduced in 1993 people should not be offered different or less favourable terms and conditions for the same work based on gender. However, NZC argues that female domestic players are classed as 'amateur' rather than professional, with their participation in cricket considered secondary to other employment. The risk in increasing the volume of women's cricket and the payments for it too quickly was that players could get caught between careers and professional cricket demands and then leave the game. Heath Mills, who had negotiated the women's agreement on behalf of the CPA, added that aside from the number of playing days in respective seasons, men's cricket was more commercialized.[36] But a longer-term view suggests that New Zealand women's cricket has not kept pace with its international rivals. Whereas New Zealand was long regarded as being third behind Australia and England in the development of the game and the performance of the national team, the rapid transformation of the last decade, if judged by international results alone, has seen it slip behind India and South Africa and arguably the West Indies.

Māori and Pasifika Engagement

The final challenge at the core of NZC's One Cricket Project and the future of cricket more generally concerns actual and potential changes to the ethnic composition of the game. For much of the twentieth century, the largely urban base and relative expense of cricket placed it out of reach of a predominantly rural and economically vulnerable indigenous Māori population.[37] Subsequently, rapid Māori urbanization and relative economic improvement from the 1950s, followed by significant immigration by various Pasifika peoples to New Zealand from the 1960s, did not translate to noticeable participation in cricket. Such a lack of engagement is surprising on two counts. Firstly, Kilikiti, an indigenous variant of cricket, was Samoa's national sport and also played in other parts of the Pacific from the late nineteenth century. Therefore, Samoan immigrants in particular were familiar with the game and well equipped with the skills required to excel in cricket.[38] Secondly, Māori and Pasifika are involved in both community and elite sport at a level disproportionate to their percentage of the population. For example, a Sport and Recreation New Zealand survey in 2005 found that while those identifying as Māori made up about 15 per cent of the population, 33 per cent of Māori males and 16 per cent of Māori females played touch rugby, compared to figures for the total population of 14 per cent and 6 per cent, respectively. At junior and club level Māori were also statistically over-represented as coaches, parent helpers, and administrators. Similarly, since the mid-1980s, and especially once the number of Pasifika born in New Zealand outnumbered those who had migrated from the Pacific, there has been a disproportionate Pasifika presence at the elite level of most of New Zealand's major team sports. A 2005 analysis of 'carded athletes', those formally aligned to the New Zealand Academy of Sport, revealed that 43 per cent of rugby union players identified as Māori and 18 per cent as Pasifika while the figures for rugby league were 28 per cent and 58 per cent, with 21 per cent and 19 per cent for netball. Cricket was 85 per cent European, 8 per cent Māori, 3 per cent Pasifika, and 3 per cent 'other', with the surprisingly high figure for Māori perhaps pointing to a pattern whereby some players who identified their own identity as Māori were not publicly recognized as such by administrators and supporters of the game.[39]

In part, the explanation for the failure to embrace cricket is socio-economic in terms of sporting choices available to the majority of Māori and Pacific people with average incomes 20–25 per cent lower than the dominant European population.[40] Equally the explanation is cultural in that cricket was strongly perceived as an unwelcoming recreation of the White middle-class that consequently produced very few of the role models who may play a part in inspiring young players. There is also evidence, although not reinforced by systematic recent research, that the more communal structure and obligations of Māori and Pacific societies has produced a preference for collective team sports rather than individual activities or even a game such as cricket with its greater emphasis

on the performance of the individual within the team. During the twentieth century cricket claimed only a handful of Māori and Pasifika players
at first-class or men's and women's international level.[41] Although NZC
and its affiliated associations lent their support during the early 2000s to
various initiatives for Māori and Pacific cricket and Kilikiti tournaments,
these produced little momentum and cricket remained disproportion-
ately the domain of European New Zealanders.[42] Beyond reference
during the 1990s to the fact that players such as Adam Parore and Heath
Davis had Māori ancestry, there was no analysis as to why this was a rarity
in cricket.

Given the dominance of Māori and Pacific players in other sports,
it was surely inevitable that cricket would begin to ponder why it was
an exception and to explore ways to harness the potential player pool.
More concerted initiatives to promote Māori cricket began during the
2010–2011 season with the formation of the Northern Districts Māori
Cricket team for a series of regional fixtures. Initially the emphasis was
on T20 as a format more easily accommodated amid other commitments.
In 2013 the team was invited to play in an ICC indigenous tournament
in Brisbane, although nothing came of this invitation. In 2015 NZC in
conjunction with the Māori Sports Awards launched an annual Māori
Cricket Scholarship to support the most promising young male player.[43]
In early 2019 the first New Zealand Māori secondary school boys' team
was selected for a fixture against a governor-general's XI at which they
were capped by Trent Boult, one of the few current international players
of Māori ancestry. The New Zealand under-nineteen men's team selected
in 2019 contained four Māori players and another of Cook Islands heritage. A Māori girls' secondary school team was selected at the beginning
of 2020.[44]

As to Pasifika players, Ross Taylor, of Samoan ethnicity and one of
New Zealand's leading batsmen of all time, is clearly the exception to
the pattern along with another Samoan, Murphy Su'a, who played for
New Zealand during the early 1990s. But surprisingly, there has been no
meaningful analysis of Taylor's experience in the game as a Samoan New
Zealander. Indeed, although his heritage is widely acknowledged, there
is no reported evidence that it has ever prompted particular scrutiny or
anything in the realm of racist comment. Both Taylor and Su'a have urged
NZC to draw on Taylor's profile as a role model for young people who

undoubtedly have the athletic ability but have seldom been exposed to cricket at school.[45] As Samoan New Zealand academic Damon Salesa observed, 'If you have the potential to be a rugby or league player, male or female, they will find you. The pathways into the rugby system don't rest on self-navigation.' By contrast, the pathways into the cricket system were barely visible in schools with large Pasifika cohorts. Here there are undoubtedly stereotypes at play in that Pasifika athletes are widely regarded as ideally suited for physical and 'explosive' contact sports and, consciously or otherwise, have been channelled towards those rather than other sporting choices.[46] In conjunction with the CPA, former international bowler Kerry Walmsley ran the Hooked on Cricket programme from around 2010 to take the game into lower-decile schools with a high proportion of Pasifika children. As he explained the challenges, 'The most important thing in the Polynesian community is convincing parents it's worthwhile. The kids are often big and strong; they have great eyes to smash the ball and natural, uncoached bowling actions. However, we believed it was vital to sit down to explain the bigger picture and the pathways cricket offers because it is not a sport they're accustomed to and can be quite expensive. It's always a battle in low decile areas because $10 buys you a rugby ball which can entertain 30 kids, just like that.'[47] In the context of the ICC's expanding international structure, it was also emphasized that there are teams other than New Zealand for players to aspire to. Fiji, Samoa, and the Cook Islands are affiliate members of the ICC East Asia-Pacific region and cricket is active in Tonga, although its national body was suspended from the ICC in 2013 for membership breaches.[48]

Immigrants in New Zealand Cricket

The strongest contribution to ethnic diversity in New Zealand cricket since the turn of the century comes from a substantial increase in the migrant population, especially from South Asia. In 1986, there were 12,000 Indians in New Zealand and much smaller numbers from Bangladesh, Pakistan, and Sri Lanka. By 2006 there were 97,000 Indians and 233,000 by 2018. The number of Sri Lankans tripled to 17,000 between 1996 and 2018 and the number of Pakistani's increased sixfold to just over 6,000. Moreover, this was a young population—the group most likely to be active in sport. In 2006, 40 per cent of Indians were under twenty-five compared to 27 per cent of the European population.[49] From the early twenty-first century there were further changes in the ethnic landscape, with refugee resettlement and other initiatives bringing Afghanis and Zimbabweans, among others. By the early 2000s, New Zealand had the highest rate of immigration per head of population in the Organisation for Economic Co-operation and Development (OECD); by the 2006 census, the numbers of immigrants in the country, as a percentage, had exceeded those in Canada and were on a par with Australia. Auckland became the largest Polynesian city in the world during the 1990s; by 2013 nearly one quarter of its population was of Asian ancestry and at least 40 per cent were migrant—compared with 32 per cent for Sydney as the most migrant-rich Australian city.[50]

At the highest level, this growth resulted in four Indian-born players and two born in New Zealand of Indian parents being selected for the national men's team since 2006, including Ish Sodhi, Jeetan Patel, and Jeet Raval. Several others have appeared at provincial level in both the men's and women's game. A recreation participation survey covering 2013–2014 confirmed that although cricket was still numerically dominated by men of New Zealand European ethnicity, during the previous twelve months among adult males it had been played by 2.6 per cent of Māori, 4.2 per cent of Europeans, 7.3 per cent of Pasifika, and 12.9 per cent of Asians. By 2018, 43 per cent of registered club players in Auckland were Indian or from the wider subcontinent and this trend was spreading throughout the country.[51]

But the broadening of the ethnic player base is also deceptive in terms of NZC's objective to attract and retain players and channel the best of them to the upper echelons of the game. Although many players are participating as individuals or as part of ethnic teams in competitions under the auspices of NZC's provincial affiliates, many others are directing their cricket involvement to competitions organized within and between ethnic communities. From the mid-1930s teams from Indian Sports clubs were entering local competitions in cricket and hockey in particular and various interprovincial and representative fixtures were played under the control of the New Zealand Indian Sports Association formed in 1962.[52] Among other recent examples, a six-a-side T20 tournament was started in Palmerston North in October 2016 involving a Wellington Pakistan team, a Wellington Indian team, a Manawatu Indian team, and a Manawatu-Horowhenua Māori team. By the end of the season, the same organizers, working in conjunction with the City Council rather than the local cricket association, had established the Village Premier League consisting of Indian teams from throughout the North Island.[53] In Christchurch the NZC aligned Metro Cricket Association worked with the Christchurch Multicultural Council to establish a successful Ethnic Cricket Tournament from 2017.[54]

Finally, although they can scarcely be regarded as a challenge to the White middle-class tradition of New Zealand cricket, the influx of both South African migrants and professional players and coaches leaving South Africa in search of international opportunities represents another component to maintaining the New Zealand player base. By the end of the 2017–2018 season at least thirteen players born in South Africa, and mostly remaining there until their teenage years if not later, were regularly playing first-class cricket in New Zealand, with four of them, including Neil Wagner and B.J. Watling, regularly playing international cricket.[55] The population of South Africans, almost exclusively of European origin, increased from 15,000 in 2001 to 37,000 in 2018. It is evident, in Auckland especially, that this is translating to a disproportionate number of talented young players of South African origin.[56]

Conclusion

The ongoing changes to the player profile of New Zealand cricket can be seen at the elite level in a national men's squad that during 2019 included three players born in India, one in Zimbabwe, and four in South Africa, plus one of Samoan and one of Māori heritage. The women's team included one South African and two players of Māori heritage. Notwithstanding an annual cycle of political debate about the extent of immigration to New Zealand, the trend will only continue. The fragmentation of sport and leisure commitment, especially among the wealthier European population, shows no sign of abating and nor do the efforts of cricket and other sporting codes to develop an ethnically diverse player base. Predictions for the ethnic composition of the New Zealand population to 2038 indicate that 'European and Other' will be the only sector of the population to decrease its proportion, with significant growth continuing for Māori, Pasifika, and Asian broadly defined, but specifically rapid growth in people of Chinese and Indian origin. Auckland, as New Zealand's largest city, is likely to see its European population fall from around 75 per cent in 1996 to less than 50 per cent by 2038, while its Asian population will increase from 10 per cent to 30 per cent over the same period.[57]

In the absence of any systematic research into South Asian interaction with New Zealand cricket, conclusions must necessarily be tentative. Certainly there are parallels with Australia and especially the United Kingdom where distinct ethnic clubs and leagues have been formed, but the motivation for these in New Zealand appears rather different. The South Asian cricket fraternity in the United Kingdom is dominated by Muslims and especially Pakistanis. In turn there have been currents of Islamophobia and periodic displays of racism that have strained relations and retarded integration with the mainstream of English cricket.[58] In New Zealand the involvement with cricket is largely through players of Indian origin and the antagonistic anti-Islamic theme has not taken root in this context. While one minor political party has periodically sought to gain traction with claims of an Asian invasion, this has been directed more towards the Chinese and, relatively speaking, the mainstream media has not fanned the flames and has rather tended to a generally positive portrayal of multiculturalism.[59] Consequently, the motive for Indian teams and tournaments appears to be a desire to maintain community and cultural ties rather than any sense of exclusion or hostility from the dominant cricket culture. Indeed, the only instance of on-field racism reported in the New Zealand media during the last decade resulted in the abused player's team walking off the field in solidarity and the abuser being stood down for six weeks. A spectator who directed racial abuse towards England's Jofra Archer in late 2019 was banned from all grounds for two years.[60] Shortly afterwards, Ish Sodhi was reported as expressing his desire to do more for the global anti-racism campaign within international cricket, but made no reference to issues within the New Zealand game.[61] Perhaps mindful of the infamous 'Tebbit Test' from 1990 in which Lord Tebbit suggested that Asians could only be classed as British if they supported England against their country of origin during cricket matches,[62] there has only ever been light-hearted discussion in the New Zealand media about the loyalties of Indian New Zealanders when the Indian team is touring. Likewise, comment on the selection of Indian-born players is very much in terms of providing inspiration for others to follow the same path to New Zealand teams.[63] All indications are that New Zealand cricket followers are at ease with the changing face of the game.

Given the transnationalism of cricket in the twenty-first century and especially the dependence on the Indian market, and the wider New Zealand sporting reliance over the last quarter-century on players of non-European background, one senses that the increasing diversity of New Zealand cricket, in terms of both gender and ethnicity, is seen as a major opportunity and only as a challenge insofar as NZC has not fully developed the resources and strategy to take full advantage of it. While the NZC strategic plan confidently outlines the need for 'Celebrating and growing the women's game, and women's role across the sport as players, administrators, fans and advocates' and the creation of 'An expanded cricket family that takes the game to under-represented and under-engaged groups',[64] the devil remains in the specific detail.

Notes

1. Greg Ryan, *The Making of New Zealand Cricket* (London: Frank Cass, 2004), 219–232.

2. James Belich, *Paradise Reforged: A History of the New Zealanders from the 1880s to the Year 2000* (Auckland: Allan Lane, 2001), 440–443, 525–526; Bryan Roper, *Prosperity for All? Economic, Social and Political Change in New Zealand since 1935* (Southbank, Vic.: Thomson, 2005), 56–68.

3. G. Shroff, 'New Zealand's immigration policy', *New Zealand Official Yearbook, 1988–89*, 202–203.

4. Philippa Mein Smith, *A Concise History of New Zealand* (Melbourne: Cambridge University Press, 2005), 228–236.

5. Ibid., 242–245; G. Whimp, 'Representing the people: Pacific politicians in New Zealand', in *Tangta O Le Moana: New Zealand and the People of the Pacific*, eds. S. Mallon, K. Māhina-Tuai, and D. Salesa (Wellington: Te Papa Press, 2012), 265–284.

6. Figures derived from http://stats.espncricinfo.com/ci/engine/stats/index.html, accessed 15 January 2020.

7. Figures derived from http://worldpopulationreview.com as in October 2019, accessed 15 January 2020.

8. Canterbury Cricket Association, *Report of the Taskforce on Club Cricket* (Christchurch: Canterbury Cricket Association, 1997), B2. See also Greg Ryan and Geoff Watson, *Sport and the New Zealanders: A History* (Auckland: Auckland University Press, 2018), 254–256.

9. Ryan and Watson, *Sport and the New Zealanders*, 305.

10. Dylan Cleaver, 'New Zealand Cricket on junior rep teams: "We don't believe it's the right thing to do"', *New Zealand Herald*, 1 March 2019.

11. See, for example, Hillary Commission for Recreation and Sport, *Survey on Sport and Physical Activity in New Zealand* (Wellington: Hillary Commission, 1996); Sport New Zealand, *Sport and Active Recreation in the Lives of New Zealand Adults: 2013/14 Active New Zealand Survey Results* (Wellington: Sport New Zealand, 2015).

12. 'Revealed: The sports on the rise in New Zealand', *New Zealand Herald*, 14 January 2018.

13. Ibid.; *The Press*, 15 April 1998.

14. See in particular Steven J. Jackson, ed., *The Other Sport Mega-Event: Rugby World Cup 2011* (London: Routledge, 2014).

15. With New Zealand requiring six runs to win off the last ball during a one-day international at the Melbourne Cricket Ground on 1 February 1981, the Australian captain Greg Chappell instructed the bowler, his brother Trevor, to deliver the last ball underarm to prevent the runs being scored. The resulting controversy, including the New Zealand prime minister accusing the Australian team of cowardice, continues to infuse the sporting rivalry between the two countries. See J. Neville Turner, 'Underarm bowling incident', in *The Oxford Companion to Australian Sport*, eds. Wray Vamplew et al., 2nd rev. ed. (Melbourne: Oxford University Press, 1997), 362.

16. Alec Astle, 'Sport development: Plan, programme and practice—A case study of the planned intervention by New Zealand Cricket into cricket in New Zealand', PhD diss., Massey University, 2014, 93–94, 100.

17. Francis Payne and Ian Smith, *1995 Shell Cricket Almanack of New Zealand* (Auckland: Moa Publications, 1999), 9–10; Martin Crowe, *Out on a Limb* (Auckland: Reed Publishing, 1995), 241–248.

18. Astle, 'Sport Development', 1.

19. Ibid., 98; Francis Payne and Ian Smith, *2002 New Zealand Cricket Almanack* (Auckland: Moa Publications, 2002), 129, 172.

20. Greg Ryan, 'Amateurs in a professional game: Player payments in New Zealand cricket c1977–2002', *Sport in History* 25, no. 1 (2005): 114–135.

21. Andrew Alderson, Dylan Cleaver, and David Leggat, 'The shame game: Plenty of opportunities at game's grassroots level', *New Zealand Herald*, 5 December 2012.

22. Andrew Alderson, Dylan Cleaver, and David Leggat, 'The shame game: Sport that lost its way from boardroom table to the fans', *New Zealand Herald*, 3 December 2012.

23. 'Paltry crowd a worrying factor', *Otago Daily Times*, 4 December 2018; Ben Strang, 'Why New Zealand Cricket need to get in on the booming Big Bash', *Stuff*, 7 January 2018.

24. 'Cricket: "Financial crisis" sees sparks fly at meeting between New Zealand Cricket, association bosses', *New Zealand Herald*, 22 May 2019.

25. 'Cricket: New Zealand Cricket project leader Martin Snedden supports Harbour move', *New Zealand Herald*, 1 May 2019; 'Cricket must adapt to the times', *Otago Daily Times*, 28 October 2019; 'Decline in NZ school kids playing cricket calls for different approach', *Sunday News*, 21 March 2015. See also New Zealand Cricket, 'Community cricket', www.nzc.nz/community, accessed 28 January 2020.

26. 'New Zealand Cricket on junior rep teams: "We don't believe it's the right thing to do"', *New Zealand Herald*, 1 March 2019. See also Dana Johannsen, 'A sporting chance: The seismic shift happening in youth sports', *Stuff*, 4 January 2020; 'A sporting chance: How the professionalisation of junior sport spawned an entire industry', *Stuff*, 5 January 2020.

27. New Zealand Cricket, *Women and Cricket: Cricket and Women* (Christchurch: New Zealand Cricket, 2016).

28. 'Cricket must adapt to the times', *Otago Daily Times*, 28 October 2019; Suzanne McFadden, 'Women in cricket: Back from the brink', *LockerRoom*, 21 November 2017.

29. Human Rights Commission, *New Zealand Census of Women's Participation, 2012* (Wellington: Human Rights Commission, 2012), 13.

30. Ryan and Watson, *Sport and the New Zealanders*, 294–301; Holly Thorpe and Rebecca Olive, eds., *Women in Action Sport Cultures: Identity, Politics and Experience* (London: Palgrave Macmillan, 2016), 4–7; Holly Thorpe, 'Jibbing the gender order: Females in the snowboarding culture', *Sport in Society* 8, no. 1 (2005): 76–100.

31. Adrienne Simpson, 'New Zealand's wicket women', in *Sport, Society and Culture in New Zealand*, ed. Brad Patterson (Wellington: Stout Research Centre, 1998), 71.

32. New Zealand Cricket, *Women and Cricket*, 12, 14; 'Female cricketers "on verge of extinction"', *New Zealand Herald*, 9 November 2016. See also Human Rights Commission, *New Zealand Census of Women's Participation, 2012* (Wellington: Human Rights Commission, 2012), 2, 114.

33. Rachel Froggatt, 'The strategic case for gender equity on sports boards', *Stuff*, 19 June 2019.

34. Francis Payne and Ian Smith, *2015 New Zealand Cricket Almanack* (Auckland: Upstart Press, 2015), 8; *2017*, 8.

35. 'New master agreement ushers in big changes for women's cricket in New Zealand', *Stuff*, 13 August 2019; Mark Geenty, 'NZ cricket, players' association agree to 26.5 per cent revenue share in Master Agreement', *Stuff*, 26 July 2018.

36. Zoe George, 'Cricket's gender gap: Female players miss out compared to their male counterparts', *Stuff*, 18 January 2020; Sport New Zealand, *Women and Girls in Sport and Active Recreation* (Wellington: Sport New Zealand, 2018).

37. Ryan, *Making of New Zealand Cricket*, 90–93.

38. See in particular Benjamin Sacks, *Cricket, Kirikiti and Imperialism in Samoa, 1879–1939* (London: Palgrave Macmillan, 2019).

39. Farah Palmer, 'State of Māori sport', in *State of the Māori Nation*, ed. Malcolm Mulholland (Auckland: Reed, 2006), 268–270; Paul Spoonley and Catherine Taiapa, 'Sport and cultural diversity: Responding to the sports and leisure needs of immigrants and ethnic minorities in Auckland' (Auckland: Massey University & Auckland Regional Physical Activity & Sport Strategy, 2009), 10.

40. New Zealand Treasury, *Statistical Analysis of Ethnic Wage Gaps in New Zealand* (Wellington: New Zealand Treasury, 2018).

41. Greg Ryan, 'Few and far between: Māori and Pacific contributions to New Zealand Cricket', *Sport in Society* 10, no. 1 (2007): 84–100; Hillary Commission for Sport, Fitness and Leisure, *Ko Te Wai Wahi O Te Iwi Māori Ki Nga Hakinakina: Māori Participation in Physical Activity and Leisure* (Wellington: Hillary Commission, 1992).

42. Francis Payne and Ian Smith, eds., *2001 New Zealand Cricket Almanack* (Auckland: Hodder Moa Beckett, 2001), 142–144.

43. Sarah McKenzie, 'Stewart wants to boost Maori cricket profile', *Stuff*, 14 May 2013; 'New cricket scholarship for Māori', *Sunlive*, 29 November 2015.

44. Mark Geenty, 'New caps and a Trent Boult hongi greet first Māori Schools cricket team', *Stuff*, 6 March 2019.

45. 'Taylor going into bat for Pacific cricket', *Radio New Zealand*, 2 March 2018.

46. Madeleine Chapman, 'Where are all our Pacific cricket players?', *The Spinoff*, 3 June 2018.

47. 'The shame game: Talented Polynesian players left behind', *New Zealand Herald*, 5 December 2012.

48. International Cricket Council, 'Our members', www.icc-cricket.com/about/members/east-asia-pacific, accessed 20 January 2020; 'Sport: Tonga Cricket Association suspended from ICC', *Radio New Zealand*, 21 September 2013.

49. Figures derived from *New Zealand Census*, 1986–2018, www.stats.govt.nz, accessed 19 January 2020.

50. Shroff, 'New Zealand's immigration policy', 202–203; Spoonley and Taiapa, 'Sport and cultural diversity', 11.

51. Sport New Zealand, *Sport and Active Recreation Profile: Cricket—Findings from the 2013/14 Active New Zealand Survey* (Wellington: Sport New Zealand, 2015); 'Revealed: The sports on the rise in New Zealand', *New Zealand Herald*, 14 January 2018.

52. Geoff Watson, *Sporting Foundations of New Zealand Indians: A Fifty Year History of the New Zealand Indian Sports Association* (Auckland: New Zealand Indian Sports Association, 2012).

53. *Manawatu Standard*, 29 September 2016, 30 March 2017.

54. *Indian Weekender*, 21 September 2017.

55. Francis Payne and Ian Smith, *2007 New Zealand Cricket Almanack* (Auckland: Upstart Press, 2007), 8; 'Could a NZ South Africans XI beat the rest of the Black

Caps?', *The Spinoff*, 27 June 2018; Mark Geenty, 'Central Districts' South African connection strengthens, Black Caps will soon notice', *Stuff*, 27 October 2017.

56. Figures derived from *New Zealand Census*, 1986–2018, accessed 19 January 2020.

57. Statistics New Zealand, *National Ethnic Population Projections: 2006(base)–2026 update* (Wellington: Statistics New Zealand, 2010); *National Ethnic Population Projections: 2013(base)–2038 (update)* (Wellington: Statistics New Zealand, 2017).

58. See, for example, Daniel Burdsey, 'British Muslim experiences in English first-class cricket', *International Review for the Sociology of Sport* 45, no. 3 (2010): 315–334; Thomas Fletcher, '"Who do 'they' cheer for?" Cricket, diaspora, hybridity and divided loyalties amongst British Asians', *International Review for the Sociology of Sport* 47, no. 5 (2012): 612–631.

59. Richard Bedford, 'Contested ground: The politicisation of immigration and belonging', *New Zealand Journal of Geography* 114, no. 1 (2002): 9–10; Paul Spoonley and Andrew Butcher, 'Reporting superdiversity: The mass media and immigration in New Zealand', *Journal of Intercultural Studies* 30, no. 4 (2009): 355–372.

60. Joel Maxwell, 'Player cops six-week suspension from cricket after mid-match racial taunt', *Stuff*, 22 November 2017; 'Two-year ban for spectator who racially abused England cricketer Jofra Archer', *Stuff*, 14 January 2020.

61. 'Sodhi wants to do more to eradicate racism', *Otago Daily Times*, 14 July 2020.

62. See, for example, Jyoti Saraswati and Indraneel Sircar, 'Throwing Tebbit a googly: British Hindus and integration', *OpenDemocracyUK*, 1 October 2012, www.opendemocracy.net/en/opendemocracyuk/68371.

63. Sandeep Singh, 'Opinion: Split loyalties for Indian-New Zealand cricket fans', *Radio New Zealand*, 9 July 2019; Ravinder Hunia, 'Cricket World Cup: Who to support when you're New Zealand-Indian', *Radio New Zealand*, 9 July 2019.

64. New Zealand Cricket, *NZC Strategic Plan 2017* (Auckland: New Zealand Cricket, 2017), 5.

2

There Are Hearings but Is Anyone Acting?

Re-Making South African Cricket, or Following On?

Goolam Vahed and Ashwin Desai

Covid-19 has revealed not only the viral pandemic but the viral fault lines in every society across the world, given rise to Black Lives Matter exposed racism and has given people the freedom to speak out. What do we do? The Truth and Reconciliation Commission (TRC) report makes no reference to sport. I wonder, how did Ali Bacher become the TV guru that he is today when in the same year that the Olympic kicked us formally out of the Olympic Games he was captaining a team against Australia? The same 1976, 1980s uprising, when injustice was seen, he became the one that brought rebel tours to South Africa, but he is the 'respectable' spokesman, commentator on our lives ... [White people] have not faced the truth of what happened in sport. What we need to think about is, how do we continue a TRC? . . . It is not too late for a TRC in sport in the sense that the truth must be told otherwise the hunters will always write their own story, they will look at their own stats, they will lionize their own heroes.[1]

The release of Nelson Mandela in February 1990 began a whirlwind of change in South African society. Negotiations with the apartheid government began and in sport there was a push for unity between White and Black organizations. But, as Ebrahim Rasool points out, there was

Goolam Vahed and Ashwin Desai, *There Are Hearings but Is Anyone Acting?* In: *Cricket and Nationhood in the Twenty-First Century*. Edited by: Souvik Naha, Oxford University Press. © Oxford University Press 2024.
DOI: 10.1093/9780191982576.003.0003

no attempt or will to interrogate the past and expose those who drove apartheid sport and had sought to undermine Black sport. Rather, the leading lights of apartheid sport, such as Ali Bacher in cricket, quickly assumed leadership of the newly unified sports bodies. Bacher was lauded for his transformation efforts. These transformation plaudits have rung hollow in recent times as Black cricketers have, in the context of the global Black Lives Matter (BLM) movement, bore witness to the racism they faced when representing the national team. These exposés, while heart-rendering and headline-making, occlude the deep issues that run through cricket and reflect in many ways the fissures that permeate South African society three decades after the release of Mandela.

Rasool was speaking on the South African Broadcasting Corporation (SABC) television news programme, 'The Full View', on 30 July 2020. He is a member of the African National Congress (ANC) and was a United Democratic Front activist in the 1980s; the premier of the Western Cape from 2004 to 2008; member of the National Assembly during 2009 and 2010; and South African ambassador to the United States from 2010 to 2015. Rasool has been an important cog of the ruling party nationally and at the provincial level. The views he expresses here are in the context of the global BLM movement of 2020, and the criticism of some White former national team cricketers of present-day Black cricketers' support for BLM.[2]

This exchange between Black and White cricketers provides a basis to examine how cricket is negotiating race and the challenge it poses for South Africa's political transformation. Developments in cricket are a microcosm of events in wider society, and our analysis focuses on whether there is space for the renewal of non-racialism or whether the politics of race would imprison South African society. Some of the key themes examined here are the relationship between race and class in the creation of a repressive regime; White social mobility and Black proletarianization historically; the racializing discourses of transformation; and the normalization of 'Whiteness'.

Rasool's call for a Truth and Reconciliation Commission (TRC) has little credibility since the much-heralded TRC held in the 1990s did not deal with the economic crimes of apartheid. This was because the ANC had made a deal with Big Capital to reach a political settlement. As Frank

Meintjies put it, while the TRC was a good idea, the problem was it was
seen as an 'end point'

> rather than the beginnings of far reaching changes. And the concern
> is that we are not openly discussing the flaws of these vehicles of tran-
> sition. The TRC explored reconciliation not through punishment, but
> through trying to build a story about gross crimes against humanity
> and political reform. As far as individuals went, the TRC sought to
> combat impunity and rebuild a culture of accountability. For victims
> of gross violence it aimed to uncover hidden truths of what happened
> and assist families in getting 'closure'. As part of the process, commit-
> ments were made to victims of gross violence about reparations and, at
> least in recommendations towards the end, regarding broader reforms
> and changes. Yet because it could not bring itself to examine wider ex-
> ploitation and systematic oppression, the TRC's work was inadequate.
> The government has also failed to follow up and prosecute the perpet-
> rators of violence who did not apply for amnesty. In addition, it has not
> fully implemented reparations for victims of gross violations . . . But the
> TRC's bigger failure is that it failed to address the more collective loss
> of dignity, opportunities, and systemic violence experienced by the op-
> pressed. No hearings were held on land issues, on the education system,
> on the migrant labour system and on the role of companies that col-
> laborated with and made money from, the apartheid security system.
> As Mahmood Mamdani puts it, 'the TRC held individual state officials
> criminally responsible, but for only those actions that would have been
> defined as crimes under apartheid law. It distinguished between the
> law-driven violence of the apartheid state—pass laws, forced removals,
> and so on—as legal if not legitimate, and the excess violence of its op-
> eratives, as illegal'.[3]

Given this, why should there be a TRC for sport and what would it really
achieve? While Rasool, rightly, questions Bacher's role in South African
cricket, the question is: what empowered Bacher? The reason is that
Rasool's party, the ANC, pushed aside the South African Council of
Sport, which had flown the flag of non-racial sport for many years, in
pursuit of 'unity'.[4] Supported by Mandela and the country's first sports
minister Steve Tshwete, Bacher paved the way for South Africa's speedy

re-entry into international cricket. Mandela even wrote the foreword to Bacher's biography in which he lauded him as 'Mister Cricket in South Africa'.[5] For Rasool, an ANC loyalist, to call for a TRC seems incompatible with the party's policy.

When Rasool was articulating these views in early 2021, the ANC was facing factional battles and made headlines for corruption nearly every day. Its general secretary, Ace Magashule, the most powerful man in the party, was suspended in May 2021 on corruption charges. The Zondo Commission, a public inquiry launched by the South African government in January 2018 to 'investigate allegations of state capture, corruption, fraud and other allegations in the public sector including organs of state', heard incredible stories of the looting of state resources. Former president Jacob Zuma faced an array of charges, including contempt of court for refusing to cooperate with the commission. Zuma, in turn, spoke of a judicial dictatorship.[6]

The sense that the 'Rainbow Nation' of Mandela would build something extraordinary, confounding the well-worn trajectory of post-liberation countries in Africa, has started to wear thin.[7] The cricket teams, once among the best in the world, have also entered an uncertain corridor as allegations of racism and corruption swirl in a context where many prefer playing in the Indian Premier League rather than for their country, while others, reacting to racial quotas, are opting for foreign fields in the United Kingdom and New Zealand. All through this, the country, which would be in the top three of global rankings in all formats of the game, has fallen into the lower levels.[8]

Race, Quotas, and Transformation

By the late 1960s South Africa's exclusively White national sports teams were making international headlines. Anti-apartheid activists hounded the national rugby team on the playing fields of the United Kingdom and New Zealand. Many countries committed to never touring South Africa until apartheid was ended. Within South Africa, Black sport (Africans, 'Coloureds', and Indians) was marked by the lack of resources. The critics of the government among the leaders of sports organizations were often banned and denied passports. In cricket, the subject of this chapter, White people and Black people played under starkly different conditions. Black cricketers rarely had green wickets and carefully maintained grounds. Provincial teams travelled between 10 and 20 hours by bus to fulfil fixtures. White cricketers, in contrast, had access to world-class facilities. Many White cricketers played county cricket and received lucrative jobs and/or sponsorship.

The history of White South African cricket is mainly a narrative of class privilege and racial exclusion. Less well known is the struggle of 'non-White' cricket that long reflected apartheid's divisions to build a non-racial ethos that united Africans, 'Coloureds', and Indians in a single cricketing union. In the 1970s, non-racial cricket became integral to the slogan 'no normal sport in an abnormal society' and called for an international boycott of South African sport. This stance and the destruction of historic Black areas by the apartheid state had a profound effect on the game as it struggled to survive through the 1970s and 1980s.[9] As part of the political negotiations between the White minority National Party government and the anti-apartheid ANC in the mid- to late 1980s, the ANC sanctioned South Africa's re-entry into international sport before a political settlement had been agreed upon. The United Cricket Board of South Africa (UCB), formed in 1991 to unite White and non-racial cricket bodies, was dominated by White players and administrators, as were the teams that represented the country as South Africa entered the international stage.

Haroon Lorgat, chief executive officer (CEO) of the renamed Cricket South Africa (CSA) from 2012 to 2017, recounted that most cricketers from the former non-racial board were unhappy with this settlement because White players with access to superior training and facilities over many decades would obviously dominate the team, while White administrators would hold key positions since their financially strong unions dictated the terms of unity.[10] While Lorgat could be accused of 'tidying up' history retrospectively, many others spoke at the time of 'unity'. Former president of the non-racial Natal Cricket Board Ahmed Kharwa voiced his criticism during a public meeting in the town of Ladysmith in northern Natal in November 1991:

As sportsmen and administrators we accept and recognise the importance of unity as South Africa moves towards democracy. However, we feel betrayed by the breach of faith by the ANC in lifting the sports moratorium prematurely. It is disturbing that while the objectives of the sports moratorium to normalise South African society was far from achieved, there has been indecent haste to participate internationally. Unity for the sake of unity is unacceptable.[11]

Given the rocky start, it is not surprising that there were several areas of tension. Team selection was contentious. The mainly White se-lectors and coaches insisted that political considerations should not be taken into account when selecting teams, which were dominated by White players.[12] Protests by Black cricketers and administrators forced the UCB to convene 'Vision Seminars' from July 1997 to discuss trans-formation. Delegates initially disagreed over whether 'Africanization' in-cluded Indians and 'Coloureds', but after several seminars decided that 'Black' would include Africans, Indians, and 'Coloureds', with the proviso that the inclusion of Africans would be given special attention. While these discussions were going on, there was a public outcry when an all-White team was chosen for the historic first home test against the West Indies in 1998. South Africa won the match but the selectors had to draft in a 'Coloured' player, Herschelle Gibbs, to mollify public anger and a Monitoring Committee was established to ensure that future teams would include at least one Black player. The UCB unveiled a Transformation Charter on 3 January 1999 'to ensure that cricket flourishes among the truly disadvantaged of our society, who come mainly from *black African* communities' and a Transformation Monitoring Committee was formed to ensure that the objectives of the Charter were met.[13]

Many White people, ironically, felt under siege by these modest goals. Patrick Compton, for example, who contributed a weekly column to the *Daily News*, the evening newspaper that serves KwaZulu-Natal, wrote with regard to quotas that 'It's tough being an Umlungu' (White): 'You don't need to be over-endowed in the brains department to realize that it is becoming increasingly tough to be a white cricketer in South Africa today.'[14] As Andre Odendaal pointed out, a

whole mentality lies behind the opposition to cricket and broader transformation and the inability to see that the negative impact of the past needs to be addressed actively rather than ignored, wished away or rubbished. This mentality enables whites somehow to still feel the aggrieved party, despite them having blatantly supported and benefited from apartheid in the past.[15]

Public pressure saw a 'Coloured' person, Omar Henry, become Convenor of Selectors in 2002, and Haroon Lorgat, an Indian who was on the organizing committee of the 2003 Cricket World Cup which was held in South Africa, replace him in 2004. Lorgat's former provincial teammate in non-racial cricket, Gerald Majola, an 'African', replaced the White Dr Ali Bacher as CEO of the UCB. But as Lorgat explained, selectors faced great pressure in providing opportunities for Black players since every decision was scrutinized by White supporters, players, and journalists who demanded 'merit', and sponsors who wanted a winning team. At one point Imtiaz Patel, from sports broadcaster DSTV, arranged a meeting between Lorgat and White journalists where Lorgat explained why Black players were being given an opportunity in the team and why they merited selection. This policy, he believes, saw Black players like Ashwell Prince and Hashim Amla given more opportunities in the national team. The unwarranted constant criticisms, Lorgat recounted, affected team morale and performance.[16]

Quotas saw mainly 'Coloureds' and Indians making representative teams. The issue of the absence of Africans in the highest echelons of the game had been raised since the 1990s. In August 2001, when Dr Mtutuzeli Nyoka, a surgeon by profession and head of the UCB's Medical Committee, failed to defeat a 'Coloured' person, Percy Sonn, a three-decade veteran of non-racial cricket, for the presidency of the UCB, he told reporters, 'I hope one day this organization will be led by a Black African. It is what millions of marginalized people are calling for and I hope that time will come sooner rather than later.'[17] Nyoka resigned after his defeat, asking:

> How do we tell this country's 35 million black Africans that transformation is working when only one player [Makhaya Ntini] represents them? . . . The UCB's transformation record is a betrayal of African aspirations. No man can belong to an organization in which his people's inferiority is assumed without building up powerful resentments.[18]

The demand for Africanization appeared to ease when Gerald Majola, an African, became CEO, but his tenure ended in controversy when he was charged with corruption and dismissed in 2012 and replaced by Haroon Lorgat, an experienced administrator, who had served as chairman of the International Cricket Council. Lorgat's tenure as CEO from 2012 to 2017 was marked by more intensified debates about racial transformation which, this time, focused on the absence specifically of Black African players, coaches, and administrators. African players challenged Lorgat's administration for its failure to Africanize cricket.[19]

The issue of Africanization reared its head once more. African players chided Lorgat and the CSA in 2014 for what they saw as a lack of opportunities for African players, coaches, and administrators. A group, constituting itself as Black Cricketers in Unity, wrote to the CSA in November 2014 to address the historical marginalization of African cricketers and complaining that African players selected in representative teams were mainly used as 'drinks carriers', thus eroding their dignity. This showed a distrust of 'Black African players' ability to perform and assume responsibility and be charged with leadership roles.'[20] This is a charge made by others over the years.

Ethy Mbhalati played for the South Africa 'A' side for eight years and became downcast, he recounted, when he realized that he would never be given an opportunity for the Proteas.

> I played for SA A from 2004 until around 2012 and on a number of occasions I asked why I was not being selected for the Proteas, but there was never a good answer. I remember in the build-up to the 2011 World Cup, I was doing very well and I was in the preliminary squad. Just before the squad was announced, I got a call from one of the selectors who told me that I was not picked because of experience. I asked the selector how was I going to get experience if I was not given an opportunity. He said I would get my opportunity when [African fast bowler] Makhaya Ntini retired but I told him that I want to play with Makhaya so that he could mentor me.[21]

Mfuneko Ngam, whose career was cut short by injury, has been responsible for bringing through African players like Mbulelo Budaza, Gregory

Mahlokwana, and Kabelo Sekhukhune as a coach at the Fort Hare University Cricket Academy. He believes that the cricket establishment does not trust African players:

> As soon as guys get to the franchise setup they feel they're there because they're black. Some coaches don't believe in them but the system wants them so they'll just be there. Sometimes they don't bat, sometimes they don't bowl. Trust is a big thing . . . As soon as you start undermining a person, that's when you lose that player. But when you show interest and give your time, that's when they start to trust you. Transformation for me is a change of mindset.[22]

Only seven of the eighty-seven players to play test cricket for South Africa in the period 1990–2014 were Black African.[23] The CSA established a task team under its former president advocate Norman Arendse to investigate why this was the case. An early issue that the task team had to deal with was the non-selection of batsman Khaya Zondo during a tour of India in October 2015. Zondo was included and then excluded from the Proteas One Day International (ODI) team for the fifth and deciding match. The task team concluded that both Zondo's 'initial inclusion, and subsequent exclusion, were motivated on what was described as "cricketing grounds". What is apparent however, is that his exclusion . . . was contrary to the CSA Selection policy'. The task team found, as Ngam attests, that there was 'a mistrust of Black African players particularly when it comes to the Proteas playing in high-profile matches or in so-called "series" deciders'.[24]

Under Lorgat's watch, the category 'Black', which had included Africans, 'Coloureds', and Indians, was disaggregated so that the transformation remit now mutated into a focus on upping the numbers of Black Africans, a strategy that occluded broader questions of class privilege.[25] The racial targets introduced by the CSA stipulated that each provincial team of eleven had to field six players of colour, including three Black Africans. It was hoped this would increase the pool of Black African players available for the national team. The 'target' for the national team was four players of colour, including at least one Black African.[26] While most White players abhor quotas, as Merrett, Tatz, and Adair have pointed out, 'South African identity has always been shaped by racial quotas; that is, divisions, assignments, allowances and allocations based on socially created ideas of race and difference'.[27]

Despite interventionist measures, the lack of African representativity continued to hog the headlines. In October 2019, the Cape Cobras fielded a team with seven Black players, one more than the six required, but including only two African players, as opposed to the required three. The Cobras informed the CSA prior to the match that they wanted to give Proteas' hopefuls an opportunity to play; that the required number of African players would be met over the course of the season; and that they took a 'target' to be 'a non-obligatory selection criteria, in contrast to the word quota'. Both 'discarding the black African subsection of the target' and calculating targets over the season would 'change the landscape of the South African domestic scene'.[28] Then-CSA-president Chris Nenzani insisted that meeting transformation targets on a game-by-game basis was 'an obligation to a very important bottom-up approach' and that his board was obliged to take 'corrective action where non-compliance occurs'.[29]

The situation is flexible at the national level where the Proteas are required to field a minimum of six players of colour, including two Black Africans, but this is averaged over the course of a season. Allegations persist that the team is usually loaded with Black players against weaker opposition to meet these targets. Selectors find it difficult to meet racial targets when any of the handful of international class African players like batsman Temba Bavuma or bowlers like Kagiso Rabada and Lungi Ngidi are injured or out of form, especially because Black players like Hassim Amla, Vernon Philander, and J.P. Duminy, who were regular members of the team, have retired.[30]

This debate affirmed the distinction between Black and Black African. Moonda captured the complexity of race when she wrote:

> The rainbow nation is not without shades of grey. There is a difference in this country between black and black African and it is both problematic and necessary. While all black people were affected by the evils of the Apartheid regime, the black African population were the most severely marginalised and mistreated. They are also, by far, the biggest majority. Redressing the wrongs committed against them is non-negotiable but where does that leave other black people, those who are coloured, mixed-race or of Indian descent?[31]

One could also ask: where does it leave talented White cricketers? Emigration to the United Kingdom, Australia, or New Zealand? Playing in one of the lucrative T20 leagues? This has been happening as young White players are being recruited by agents to settle overseas. It remains to be seen how the COVID-19 pandemic will affect this trend. Brexit has already closed one avenue: that of South Africans playing domestic cricket in the United Kingdom without being counted as 'foreigners'.[32]

Several studies have questioned the effectiveness of quotas. Dove, Gray, Taliep, and Draper, for example, state:

> Findings indicate that despite providing opportunities to an increasing number of Black African players at the representative levels, and in-spiring young players to play cricket, the quotas have had a limited effect on other barriers and enablers to talent development. Holistic player development was identified as a more effective process of achieving sus-tainable transformation. Furthermore, quotas have had a negative im-pact on individual players of all ethnicities and exacerbated the limited inclusivity in team environments.[33]

Swart and Maralack make the following key point about quotas:

> The imposition of sport quotas in an attempt to reverse the deeply en-trenched racial, cultural, social and economic inequalities is a narrow strategy to overcome the real lived experiences of marginalized black sportspersons as it addresses a sliver of an instrumental, numerical and technicist approach. The quota system in South African cricket has been reduced to a box-ticking exercise serving narrow political optics, paying scant attention to the need to expand and democratize the game through greater representation at all levels . . . True development may not be happening at a pace and effectiveness that would help the sport in South Africa. The evidence suggests that transformation, its ideals and quotas as its vehicle have become more divisive than enabling equality.[34]

Quotas have generated debate in the wider society around the race-based access to Medical School, academic posts, awarding of grants and bur-saries, awarding of tenders, and so on. One critique is that this has led to skewed development. According to Bill Freund:

While creating an elite may involve enriching a small number of black ANC supporters, it is probably a necessity given the propensities of what remains of the established 'embedded elites' of the past. It is questionable however, whether this new elite has the sense of direction in pursuit of an industrialising economic model or a broad social model to carry through envisioned changes. Nor are its instincts necessarily democratic. While under the direction of the ANC the South African social structure is shifting in important ways and different sectors of the black population clearly benefit, the majority are not actively involved in a process of transformation that would offer the possibility of radical improvements.[35]

This trend is so evident in cricket. While quotas are facilitating the emergence of African players, this development 'fails to address the workings of class and privilege in cricket achievement'.[36]

A Skewed 'Development' Model?

The failure to produce African cricketers, and in the absence of facilities in townships, cricket administrators opted in the late 1990s to adopt a policy that placed talented Black cricketers in elite former White Model C (government) or private (independent) schools. It is mostly Black players from these elite schools, with access to a privileged education, excellent diet, outstanding facilities, and high-level coaching, who are selected to meet 'race' quotas and exhibited as proof of cricket's transformation. Hassim Amla of Tongaat on the north coast of KwaZulu-Natal, an Indian South African who became the first, and to date only, South African to score a triple century (against England in 2012), attended Durban High School which produced the legendary South African batsman of the 1970s, Barry Richards.

Proteas fast bowler Lungi Ngidi, the Proteas T20 and ODI Player of the Year for the 2019/2020 season, was raised in Kloof, west of Durban, and received a scholarship to attend Kloof Junior Primary School where his mother Bongi and father Jerome worked in the school's housekeeping and maintenance staff teams. According to Bongi, as a youngster, Ngidi 'would always say "I want to be like Makhaya Ntini." They even called him

Ntini.[37] Ngidi was awarded a scholarship to the prestigious private school Hilton College in Pietermaritzburg where he received coaching from a professional.

The school has produced South African cricketers like Roy MacLean (1951–1965), Mike Procter (1966), Johnny Waite (1951–1965), and Derek Crookes (1994). Ngidi and current English player Tom Curren are the latest internationals. The school has outstanding cricket facilities:

> The school is fortunate to have 8 cricket ovals. There are 8 turf nets, 8 astro turf nets and 5 indoor cricket nets. The main cricket oval is the Jack Hart-Davis Oval, a picturesque ground overlooking the rolling hills of the Midlands. This oval is the second oldest in KwaZulu-Natal, after the Kingsmead Oval . . . The push on dome cover used on Hart Davis, LED's in the scoreboard and state of the art bowling machine that were also donated by an old boy of the school have allowed all to benefit by increasing the standard of practices and practice options.[38]

Ngidi was selected for the South African Under-19 side while in Grade 11, and in his final year showed his leadership qualities when he was head of Newnham House. He also represented the province in swimming, rugby, and athletics. Ngidi's coaches included Neil Johnson, former Zimbabwe international player. According to Lungi's mother Bongi, Hilton College ensured that she and Jerome were able to support Lungi: 'They would send a car to fetch us. Sometimes it would be a metro cab.'[39] Sadly for Ngidi, his father Jerome died shortly after his test debut in 2018.

Kagiso Rabada, who came to international attention when he helped power South Africa to victory in the Under-19 World Cup in 2014, is one of the best fast bowlers in the world. Rabada's father is a medical doctor and his mother Florence a lawyer. Rabada lists 'playing piano' among his hobbies. He attended the Methodist St Stithians Boys College, where he had access to first class facilities. According to the school's website,[40] it is through sports, quoting W.S. Pollack, that a 'boy experiences an intense sense of belonging, of community, even of love that he may never find elsewhere. Sport is a rite of passage'. The school is littered with sporting history: 'A visit to the Boys' College dining hall will allow a young Saint to experience the sporting history of the school. All boys who fill leadership roles are trained in the art of captaincy through workshops.' The school's other current international cricketers include New Zealand's Grant Elliot and England's Michael Lumb. Rabada is undoubtedly a gifted sportsman, but his parents' support and the nurturing St Stithians environment no doubt allowed that talent to blossom.

Andile Phehlukwayo, a teammate of Rabada and Ngidi in the Under-19 World Cup winning team, was brought up by his mother, who worked as a helper in Port Shepstone on the south coast of KwaZulu-Natal. As he recounted:

> I didn't grow up in a family that was financially supported. My mum worked hard for me, and she worked long hours, just to get me into school. I really didn't enjoy the environment in which she worked, and, apart from my love for cricket, growing up, I was also motivated to succeed so that some day I can try and support her.

Phehlukwayo learnt about cricket when he saw it on television at the home of his mother's employer, but it was through hockey that he was given a scholarship to attend Glenwood High School in Durban. Glenwood was a Model C school, meaning that while it was not a private school, as a former White school it had outstanding sporting facilities and an excellent reputation for producing sportsmen. Phehlukwayo recounted: 'Nobody at the school knew that I could play cricket—they only found out in the first week of grade eight, when there were trials.'[41] Phehlukwayo was chosen for KwaZulu-Natal in 2015, made his international debut in 2016, and is now a regular member of the one-day teams. It would be fair to say that Phehlukwayo's talent did not stand out as obviously as that of Rabada and Ngidi, and without the pressure to include Black African players in the national team, it is unlikely that he would have been given an opportunity at such a young age.

In these three snapshot biographies we immediately see the importance that schools and opportunities play in players' lives. The absence of CSA structures in the townships, despite tens of millions of rands spent on 'development', is stark. These players had to be taken into an 'alien' environment. Given the dearth of sport in township schools, this is the only road that could be travelled. But within this, we also see the workings of class; Rabada's parents are both professionals and his path was cleared by this economic advantage. Phehlukwayo and Ngidi had to rely on chance.

The fact that they made it to the highest level attests to their abilities, but the institution of racial targets meant that provincial franchises had to give Black cricketers an opportunity. The enormous pressure on African players should not be lost. As Themba Bavuma, the first African batsman to score a century for South Africa, put it, 'there is extra pressure for Black players to deliver big performances each time they take to the field', or they would be seen as being there because of the colour of their skin.[42]

What Bavuma did not go on to detail is what happens beyond the field of play which Makhaya Ntini was to expose. White teammates did not want to join him, and he would often run to the ground rather than take the team bus. He was left isolated. As Swart and Maralack point out, 'the revelations by Ntini shows that the rainbow racial project paid scant attention to the lived experiences of black cricketers, denying the depth and multiple dimensions of racism'.[43] In many ways the whole nature of the development project is to pluck Black cricketers out of the townships and 'isolate' them in areas far removed from their everyday life.

Democratizing Cricket

The downside of this model of transformation is that it removes the imperative to develop a culture of cricket in townships where the majority of Africans live. Class is privileged. Enver Mall, then-CEO of KZN Cricket, argued in a 2006 interview that

> throughout the world your best cricketers come from private cricketing schools, whether it is in England, West Indies, India, or even Pakistan. Existing cricketing schools in South Africa have the infrastructure (coaches, grounds, equipment, tradition), and for the moment, given our various other needs, we are exploiting this situation for our advantage. We hope that in time we can establish similar schools in townships but that is some time off . . . The use of elite cricketing schools is the only practical option for the moment.[44]

There was a token attempt to take the game to the masses through a Memorandum of Understanding (MoU) signed between government and sports codes on 17 August 2015 to fast-track transformation by developing sports facilities in township and rural schools. CSA agreed to provide technical support to learners and officials, establish Cricket Hubs, and provide coaching at existing Cricket Hubs, Regional Performance Centres, and Provincial Academies. As then-sports-minister Fikile Mbalula argued in 2016, transformation was necessary 'because of the reality that 84 per cent of the country's under 18-year-old population grouping is Black African and only 16 per cent is White, 'Coloured', and Indian. To ignore this strategic reality from a sustainability perspective alone would be suicidal'. Mbalula warned that the Sports Ministry would take punitive measures if transformation targets were not met, including 'revoking the privilege of a federation to host and bid for international tournaments'.[45]

Fifteen years after Mall's comments, little has changed. Two former Black South African cricketers, Geoffrey Toyana and Mfuneko Ngam, expressed their frustration to journalist Ongama Gcwabe that the playing fields were still not level for African cricketers in townships. According to Toyana, a highly successful provincial coach:

The main challenge that we have in every township in South Africa is something that breaks me. I come from Soweto. It's quite sad as we speak that the Soweto Cricket Oval has not improved since I last played. I mean, I was involved in Soweto Cricket in late 90s and early 2000s. For me to see that there's no change and there's no improvement in that facility and other facilities as well all over South Africa. I know CSA has Hubs at the moment to try to close gaps but I don't think that's how you need to close gaps. It will be a shock for me to see a black African kid coming from the township, without any private education, go play franchise cricket . . . Do all coaches understand this? Are they taught about this? Or are they just given a piece of paper telling them they need to put in three black Africans per game without any explanation?[46]

According to Ngam, who was touted as one of the best fast bowlers in the world but who succumbed to a series of injuries, because of a poor diet, it is said, due to his family's dire circumstances:

If you go to Dan Qeqe [Stadium], in Port Elizabeth, those fields have not improved. That's a huge challenge that we always talk about but there's no action. Has cricket become inclusive? I'm from Motherwell and I can assure you that apart from the new nets the Motherwell Cricket Club was sponsored with, there's no improvement whatsoever. The stands are in bad shape, the club still struggles to this day.[47]

During his time as CEO, Lorgat was determined to change the racial complexion of cricket but explained that producing international standard African cricketers was complex:

> I'd think the lack of facilities, development and coaching, is the root cause of them not coming through. And particularly with batsmen, you know, bowling is a more physical thing, you can practice on your own whereas on the batting side you really need skilled coaches to work almost every day with you.[48] That may be a deficiency. And there could be social reasons for the lack of African players. There could be greater social demands on Black [African] people, including the need to work in order to bring essentials home. You go to school and then you've got to have time to practice and earn money by working. One of the three things will fall away. A White kid can go to school and play cricket at the same time. So there's a better synergy between those two demands and that kid has got little or no demands at home whereas it is expected from a Black [African] kid to do some work, to bring money to put food on the table or pay for some bare necessities. So out of those three demands in that kid's life, something fails.[49]

Lorgat's point that transformation is multifaceted and that class is critical is well taken. His argument that African children do not have adequate facilities at school, while also having to confront poverty, was poignantly captured by Toyana:

> I still remember as a young coach when I was still playing for Gauteng, where I was coaching at a school—there was this kid who was always late. And he was very talented, he was my best player but was always late. I was asking myself—'why is this kid always late?' Then one day I decided to follow this kid after school. He didn't see me obviously. So I kept following him up until I got to his place to see his house only to

realize that before he comes to training he basically has to cook for his mom first and his mom was HIV-positive. So, he has to do all those things before he comes to training. We don't understand our own people. Some white coach won't understand that for a black kid to go to the Wanderers for example, he has to take three taxis to get there. Some white coaches would go—'this kid has an attitude, he's always late.' Until we address those issues, that's when we're going to head in the right direction. But we've been talking about this for the last 20 plus years and it seems like there are no answers.[50]

Sports organizations like the CSA, Lorgat argued, lack the resources to 'truly transform the game. It is convenient for the ANC government to pass the blame on to sports bodies, when it has failed to fulfil its own role in transformation . . . There isn't a strategy . . . it's about facilities, it's about schools. We [CSA] simply do not have the capacity to address all of that'. Notwithstanding the hubs in townships, the bulk of the country's cricketers (and rugby players) will be produced in elite sports schools for the foreseeable future.

These paradoxes and conundrums reflect the broader challenges of the transition. The policies adopted by the ANC government have nurtured a small Black bourgeoisie and a middle class that is linked to state jobs. These policies, though, have exacerbated inequality and unemployment has spiralled to nearly 40 per cent. Cricket in this sense is like King Canute batting against the waves. One has one or two successes but cricket on its own cannot turn around township schooling. This project is made all the more challenging as international cricket dries up. Still the demand is for more Black players to play in provincial and national teams. Faced with this, cricket opts for the quick fix of snatching Black school players with potential and placing them in the old White schools and implementing the quota system.

Chaos—Government Steps In

Cricket is in turmoil as we are writing this chapter. Gerald Majola, the CSA's first African CEO when he replaced Ali Bacher, was ousted on grounds of corruption. The year 2017 saw the ousting of an 'Indian' South African, Lorgat, as CEO and his replacement by an African, Thabang Moroe. The rationale was that Lorgat was responsible for the failure of a domestic T20 tournament. Moroe with his ally, then-CSA-president Chris Nenzani, and the assistance of then-chief-financial-officer Naasei Appiah, laid several charges against Lorgat, including his being 'anti-transformational'. A committee failed to substantiate the charges but they put enough pressure on Lorgat to cause him to resign.[51] Journalist Craig Ray, for one, believes that Lorgat's ousting was part of an Africanization drive, reflecting trends in broader society.[52]

Under Moroe, the CSA undertook a number of steps without consulting with stakeholders. This included increasing the number of franchises from six to twelve without discussing this measure with the South African Cricketers' Association; they lost millions in pursuit of the T20 Mzansi Super League; they lost an arbitration dispute against the Western Province Cricket Association with costs after it tried to take control of the association; they tried to silence journalists critical of the CSA; and they suspended key employees without due process. With the CSA in turmoil, two of the five independent directors, Mohamed Iqbal Khan, who also acted as chairperson of the finance committee, and Professor Shirley Zinn, resigned and Standard Bank withdrew its R80 million per annum sponsorship of the CSA. The Board responded by suspending Moroe with full pay on 6 December 2019[53] and dismissing him in July 2020.

The CSA Board resisted releasing the 456-page Fundudzi Forensic Report, which was handed to it in July 2020, until November 2020 when it was compelled to do so by the Sports Ministry. The report confirmed, as Ray points out, 'what years of actions have shown—that Cricket South Africa's (CSA's) leadership was overwhelmingly self-serving and incompetent'. Among the allegations were that Moroe failed to follow procurement processes; failed to act in the best interests of the CSA in terms of the Companies Act; used the CSA credit card to spend R203 372.80 on alcohol alone; and failed to follow proper processes in making appointments.[54] In light of these detailed allegations of corruption, the Sports Ministry forced the entire board to resign and appointed an Interim Board under Chairperson Zak Yacoob, a retired justice of the Constitutional Court, to investigate the problems of the past three years that saw cricket lurch from one crisis to another, lose its major sponsors, and face bankruptcy.[55]

The Interim Board submitted its recommendations to Sports, Arts and Culture Minister Nathi Mthethwa in March 2021. Among its recommendations was a sleeker board comprising a majority of independent members in line with the Nicholson Commission of 2012, appointed when then-CEO Gerald Majola's administration had failed in its oversight duties, which had made two recommendations that were not implemented by the CSA: recommendation 357 called for 'a smaller board, with a majority of independent, professionally skilled, non-executive directors' and recommendation 359 stipulated that 'a board be constituted, consisting of nine non-executive directors, to be voted for by the affiliates, with each director being required to enjoy two thirds support from the total of affiliates. We would further advise that the other directors consist of the CEO, the treasurer and secretary'.[56]

The Members Council of the CSA, however, issued a statement that eight of its fourteen members had voted against a board comprising a majority of independent members. Sports Minister Nathi Mthethwa threatened that he would invoke his powers in terms of section 13 (5) of the Sports Act to withdraw government funding and recognition of the CSA, which would mean in effect that there could be no international cricket. After two such threats, the CSA eventually came to an agreement with the Interim Board and adopted a new Memorandum of Incorporation (MoI) on 30 April 2021, which was adopted at the organization's annual general meeting on 12 June 2021.[57]

A new Board is now in place but it arrived in the midst of a crisis around racism in the national men's teams, as Black players begin to reveal the kind of racism they faced in the dressing rooms around the world from White players. Startling testimony at what the CSA has called Social Justice and Nation Building (SJN) hearings, underway at the time of writing, has been given by Black players like Ashwell Prince, Aaron Phangiso, Paul Adams, Thami Tsolekile, Lungile Bosman, Makhaya Ntini, and Roger Telemachus. The common thread is the racism and ostracization that they faced, with Ntini testifying that he felt so alienated by White players that he ran to the ground rather than take the team bus, while Paul Adams was referred to as a 'brown shit'. Thirty years after cricket unity, the issue of race remains a burning issue as much as class divisions trespass the game.

Conclusion

The collapse of apartheid and the resumption of international sport saw a transformation of the provincial and national teams dominated by White players. In the euphoria of the 'Rainbow Nation' discourse, this was seen as a temporary measure as Black cricket would gradually benefit from increased resources which would change the complexion of the national team. The ANC government's Reconstruction and Development Programme (RDP) promised that the emphasis would be on allocating resources to those areas disadvantaged during apartheid. But the RDP was soon abandoned for a conservative macro-economic programme that Patrick Bond labelled an 'elite transition'.[58]

In cricket, instead of a mass approach that concentrated resources on township clubs and schools, the emphasis was on ensuring that international teams were competitive. The majority of the African players are either middle class or have been removed from townships into middle-class or private schools, to provide them with proper training, diet, and education. Cricket in apartheid-era African township schools remains non-existent. The same is the case in 'Coloured' and Indian schools in working-class areas. The aim, it appears, is to bring through a small number of African players who may not be disadvantaged economically.[59] Black cricket clubs that survived apartheid disappeared and school cricket in the townships never really took off. Part of the reason, as Haroon Lorgat so perceptively pointed out, is that cricket cannot provide facilities on its own, and the government, which cannot even provide toilets in schools, went instead for the numbers game in cricket. This model fits with the ANC government's notion of Black Economic Empowerment which has sought to foster a Black middle and upper class, often at the expense of the African poor.

The ANC government began to agitate at first for more Black players in the national team and gradually the language turned to more Black African players. Quotas were imposed that differentiated first between

White people and Black people, and eventually between 'Coloureds', Indians, and Africans as the whole ethos of non-racialism was jettisoned. The entering of the debate about BLM in July 2020 by Proteas fast bowler Lungi Ngidi brought race back into play as some former White Proteas players reacted critically to his call for support for the movement. What was occluded in this debate was the retreat from non-racialism, the neglect of township cricket, and the uncritical adoption of the racial categories of apartheid.

The CSA responded to the outcry of Black players by organizing hearings under the banner of their SJN project. While the need to publicly air the experiences of Black cricketers is important, there is a concern that these hearings become a kind of 'show-trial' and a cathartic venting of grievances, while the deep structural challenges are pushed lower and lower down the batting order.

Race and class remain at the forefront of discussions about cricket and society in South Africa. As long as the status quo remains, transformation will mainly be viewed as a race issue. Until facilities are extended into townships and the base of cricket expanded, the gap between the haves and have-nots will remain. Meanwhile, this class bias is over-ridden by an almost messianic drive that is enveloping some cricket administrators to Africanize the game, but in the absence of massive spending in school sports and townships more generally, the pool of African players will continue to come from an elite stratum of society and schools. To effect real change, macro-economic structural change that leads to a more equitable redistribution of resources is required. The coronavirus pandemic of 2020/1 has brought sport to a standstill and will make transformation more difficult due to the lack of funding. The CSA is bankrupt!

The government of Nelson Mandela adopted the RDP. In sport the RDP promised an emphasis on supporting sport in areas previously neglected by the apartheid regime. Rather than this happening, an elite model of change was adopted. How can the RDP be resurrected? In this context, would it have a positive impact on thinking about race and class if the CSA adopted a slogan that *All* Black Lives Matter? This would force the CSA and the Sports Ministry to not just racially bean-count but to account for who benefits from the resources they have accumulated and pressure them to pay more attention to township school sport.

Notes

1. Ebrahim Rasool, 2020. Interviewed on the South African Broadcasting Corporation (SABC) nightly prime time television news programme, 'The Full View', on 30 July 2020. The author heard the interview.

2. White ex-cricketers like Pat Symcox, Brian MacMillan, and Boeta Dippenaar were critical of Black fast bowler Lungi Ngidi who openly voiced support for the BLM movement. See Goolam Vahed and Ashwin Desai, 'Inside the cricket change room: Undressing whiteness in South Africa', *Journal of Contemporary African Studies* 39, no. 2 (2021): 199–213. DOI: 10.1080/02589001.2020.1863931.

3. Frank Meintjies, 'The TRC and CODESA failed South Africa: It's time we reflected on this', The South African Civil Society Information Service, 12 September 2013, www.apc.uct.ac.za/apc/projects/have-your-say/trc-and-codesa-failed-south-afr ica-its-time-we-reflected.

4. For a discussion of the politics of sport in the 1970s and 1980s, leading to cricket unity, see Goolam Vahed and Ashwin Desai, 'The coming of Nelson and the ending of Apartheid cricket: Gatting's rebels in South Africa', *The International Journal of the History of Sport* 33, no. 15 (2016): 1785–1803.

5. Rodney Hartman, *Ali: The Life of Ali Bacher* (Johannesburg: Viking, 2004).

6. Victoria O'Regan, 'Jacob Zuma fires back at Constitutional Court at Constitutional Court, claiming emergence of a "judicial dictatorship"', *Daily Maverick*, 26 March 2019.

7. For a discussion of these issues, see Patrick Bond, *Elite Transition: From Apartheid to Neo-Liberalism in South Africa* (Pietermaritzburg: University of KwaZulu-Natal Press, 2000); Hein Marais, *South Africa Pushed to the Limit: The Political Economy of Change* (London: Zed Books Ltd, 2013); Haroon Bhorat, 'Is South Africa the most unequal society in the world?', *Mail & Guardian*, 30 September 2015; Thuli Madonsela, 'State of capture', Report No. 6 of 2016/17. Public Protector of South Africa, www.da.org.za/wp-content/uploads/2016/11/State-of-Capture-14-October-2016.pdf; Vishnu Padayachee and Robert Van Niekerk, *In the Shadow of Liberation: Contestation and Compromise in the Economic and Social Policy of the African National Congress, 1943–1996* (Johannesburg: Wits University Press, 2019).

8. Haroon Lorgat discusses these issues in detail in Goolam Vahed, 'Negotiating the (uncertain) corridors of power in post-apartheid South African cricket', *South African Historical Journal* 72, no. 3 (2020): 495–519; see pp. 505–509.

9. See Ashwin Desai, Goolam Vahed, and Vishnu Padayachee, 'Beyond apartheid: Race, transformation and governance in KwaZulu-Natal cricket', *Transformation* 61 (2006): 63–88.

10. Interview by Goolam Vahed, 26 March 2019. See Vahed, 'Negotiating the (uncertain) corridors of power in post-apartheid South African cricket'.

11. Ahmed Kharwa, 'Public meeting criticises cricket unity', *Ladysmith Gazette*, 6 December 1991. Author was shown a copy of the article by Mr Kharwa.

12. Ashwin Desai, 'The race chase: The colour of cricket transformation in South Africa', *Africa Review* 11, no. 2 (2019): 122.

13. See Desai, Vahed, and Padayachee, 'Beyond apartheid'.

14. *Daily News*, 1 February 2001.

15. Andre Odendaal, *The Story of an African Game: Black Cricketers and the Unmasking of One of Cricket's Greatest Myths, 1850–2003* (Cape Town: David Phillip, 2003), 338.

16. See the chapter titled 'Hassim Amla: Beyond boundaries', in *A History of the Present: A Biography of Indian South Africans 1990–2019*, Ashwin Desai and Goolam Vahed, 99–128 (New Delhi: Oxford University Press, 2019).

17. *Sunday Tribune*, 5 August 2001.

18. *Johannesburg Star*, 10 April 2002.

19. Vahed, 'Negotiating the (uncertain) corridors of power in post-apartheid South African cricket', 501–502.

20. Mogamed Allie, 'Black South African cricket comes of age', BBC News, 2 February 2016, www.bbc.com/news/world-africa-35459185.

21. Mahlatse Mphahlele, 'Ex-South Africa "A" fast bowler Ethy Mbhalati lifts the lid on allegations of racism in cricket', *Times Live*, 14 July 2020, www.timeslive.co.za/sport/cricket/2020-07-14-ex-south-africa-a-fast-bowler-ethy-mbhalati-lifts-the-lid-on-allegations-of-racism-in-cricket.

22. Ongama Gcwabe, 'Being Black in South African cricket', *Cricket Fanatics Magazine*, 4 June 2020, https://cricketfanaticsmag.com/being-black-in-sa-cricket.

23. Ashwin Desai, Reverse Sweep. *A Story of South African Cricket Since Apartheid* (Johannesburg: Jacana, 2019), 128.

24. Cricket South Africa (CSA), 'Report of the Task Team constituted by the CSA Board on the recommendation of the Chairman of the Board to investigate the grievances of Black African cricket players', contained in a letter to the CSA, 9 November 2015.

25. Desai, 'The race chase', 132.

26. Firdose Moonda, 'CSA confirms guideline on selection quota', *ESPN Cricinfo*, 18 April 2016, www.espncricinfo.com/story/_/id/21176431/csa-confirms-guideline-selection-quota.

27. Christopher Merrett, Colin Tatz, and Daryl Adair, 'History and its racial legacies: Quotas in South African rugby and cricket', *Sport in Society* 14, no. 6 (2011): 754.

28. Firdse Moonda, 'South Africa transformation targets could change after Cape Cobras case', ESPNcricinfo, 13 November 2019, www.espncricinfo.com/story/_/id/28070258/south-africa-transformation-targets-change-cape-cobras-case.

29. Firdose Moonda, 'Black Lives Matter: South African cricketers mull fresh expression for 3TC game', Cricinfo, 8 July 2020, www.espncricinfo.com/story/_/id/29429297/south-african-cricketers-mull-fresh-expression-3tc-game.

30. Ibid.

31. Ibid.

32. This arrangement was known as 'Kolpak' after a 2003 European Court of Justice ruling that citizens of countries (like South Africa) that signed European Union Association Agreements (free trade agreement with any European Union country) had the same right of freedom of movement within the European Union as European Union citizens. South African cricketers were thus entitled to play in Britain. This ended when the British exited the European Union on 31 January 2021. The rule was named after Maroš Kolpak who had gone to court for this right. See Steve Greenfield, Guy Osborn, and J.P. Rossouw, 'Beyond Kolpak: European Union law's unforeseen contribution to the movement of African cricketers', *The International Journal of the History of Sport* 33, no. 15 (2016): 1748–1766. DOI: 10.1080/09523367.2017.1320987.

33. Mary-Ann Dove, Janine Gray, Mogammad S. Taliep, and Catherine E. Draper, 'Quotas in South African cricket—What the players say', *Sport in Society* 1 (2021): 1–20. DOI: 10.1080/17430437.2021.1922388.

34. Kamilla Swart and David Maralack, 'Black Lives Matter: Perspectives from South African cricket', *Sport in Society* 24, no. 5 (2021): 715–730, 726. DOI: 10.1080/17430437.2020.1819693.

35. Bill Freund, 'South Africa: The end of apartheid and the emergence of the "BEE Elite"', *Review of African Political Economy* 34, no. 114 (2007): 661–678, 661. DOI: 10.1080/03056240701819533.

36. Desai, 'The race chase', 132. On the broader debate about race-based quotas and their role in perpetuating racial identities, see Neville Alexander, 'Affirmative action and the perpetuation of racial identities in post-apartheid South Africa', *Transformation: Critical Perspectives on Southern Africa* 63 (2007): 92–105; Gerhard Maré, ' "Broken down by race . . .": Questioning social categories in redress policies', *Transformation: Critical Perspectives on Southern Africa* 77 (2011): 52–69.

37. Duncan Guy, 'Cricket sensation's path to glory', IOl, 23 January 2018, www.iol. co.za/saturday-star/cricket-sensations-path-to-glory-12870084.

38. Cricket South Africa (CSA), 2019, National Cricket Week. Khaya Majola Boys U-19. KwaZulu-Natal Inland, 16–20 December 2019, 23. chrome-extension://efaid nbmnnnibpcajpcglclefindmkaj/https://cricket.co.za/wp-content/uploads/2021/06/2019-Khaya-Majola-Tournament.pdf.

39. Guy, 'Cricket sensation's path to glory'.

40. https://www.stithian.com/content/page/bc-educational-philosophy-sport.

41. Staff reporter, 'The kids who should bloom into Proteas', *Mail & Guardian*, 14 September 2014, https://mg.co.za/article/2014-09-11-the-kids-who-could-bloom-into-proteas.

42. Mphahlele, 'Ex-South Africa "A" fast bowler Ethy Mbhalati lifts the lid on allegations of racism in cricket'.

43. See Swart and Maralack, 'Black Lives Matter: Perspectives from South African cricket', 721.

44. Interview by Goolam Vahed, 20 March 2006.

45. Fikila Mbalula, 'Sports Minister Mbalula's acceptance speech of Eminent Persons Group Report on sport transformation', *Eyewitness News*, 25 April 2016, https://ewn.co.za/2016/04/25/Sport-Minister-Mbalulas-acceptance-speech-of-EPG-report.

46. Gcwabe, 'Being Black in South African cricket'.

47. Ibid.

48. Lorgat's point about the difficulty in producing high-calibre batsmen is illustrated in the first-class cricket averages for the 2019/20 season. The highest-ranking African batsman (Wendile Makwetu) placed twenty-fourth on the list (eight of the top ten were White), while three African bowlers (Malusi Siboto, Lutho SIpamla, and Tshepa Moreki) placed in the top ten (Moonda, 'Black Lives Matter: South African cricketers mull fresh expression for 3TC game').

49. Interview by Goolam Vahed, 26 March 2019.

50. Gcwabe, 'Being Black in South African cricket'.

51. Craig Ray, 'The state of capture in SA cricket', *Daily Maverick*, 12 December 2019, www.dailymaverick.co.za/article/2019-12-12-the-state-of-capture-in-sa-cricket.

52. Ibid.

53. Ibid.

54. Craig Ray, 'Full Funduzi Report reveals CSA's catastrophic management failures', *Daily Maverick*, 25 November 2020, www.dailymaverick.co.za/article/2020-11-25-full-fundudzi-report-reveals-csas-catastrophic-management-failures.

55. The other board members were former CSA CEO Haroon Lorgat, Omphile Ramela, Stavros Nikalo, Andre Odendaal, Judith February, Andile Dawn Mbatha, Xolani Vonya, and Nkeko Caroline Mampuru. Yacoob stepped down as chairman in late January when he called a journalist 'idiotic' and 'dishonest' and was replaced by Nikalo, the Aspen Pharmacare Group's senior executive responsible for strategic trade development, as chairperson.

56. 'Nicholson Commission of Enquiry: Ministerial Committee of Enquiry to conduct investigation into affairs of Cricket South Africa', 2012, www.gov.za/documents/nicholson-commission-enquiry-ministerial-committee-enquiry-conduct-investigation-affairs.

57. The MoI can be accessed on CSA's website at https://cricket.co.za/cat/23/About-CSA/7543/csa-moi.

58. See Patrick Bond, *Elite Transition* (Pietermaritzburg: University of KwaZulu-Natal Press, 2005).

59. Desai, 'The race chase', 133.

3

What Do They Know of Cricket …?

English Cricket, Race, and Class in a Country 'Taken Back'

Stephen Wagg

Introduction

This chapter considers the politics of English cricket at the beginning of the 2020s. It was written during a period defined largely by two ongoing processes: the decision, reached via a referendum conducted in the UK in June 2016, that the United Kingdom cease membership of the European Union (EU)—universally referred to as 'Brexit'[1]—and the onset, in the spring of 2020, of the COVID-19 virus, which by early summer had caused severe curtailment of social activity, including sport events. The campaign to leave the EU was the context for much atavistic political rhetoric (including widespread recourse to the slogan 'Take our country back', first popularized by the American right-wing 'Tea Party' movement in 2009).[2] This in turn coincided, at state level and in the mainstream British media, with a growing hostility both to migrants and to 'multiculturalism'—usually, in practice, the same thing.[3] This can be understood as indicative of a long-drawn-out transition from one form of racism to another on the part of the British state. The chapter will argue that both the public ruminations about 'reclaiming' the country and the restrictions triggered by the virus (much of the 2020 cricket season was cancelled and what professional cricket took place did so in the absence of spectators) highlighted processes that had been in train for some decades. The chapter considers these processes and their present and likely repercussions on English cricket. In doing so, it takes up themes previously

Stephen Wagg, *What Do They Know of Cricket . . .?* In: *Cricket and Nationhood in the Twenty-First Century.*
Edited by: Souvik Naha, Oxford University Press. © Oxford University Press 2024.
DOI: 10.1093/9780191982576.003.0004

broached in an earlier article.[4] First, it considers the political context of the purported debate about 'multiculturalism'.

The Road to 'Multiculturalism': Cricket, the British State, and the End of Empire

Cricket is the definitive sport of the British Empire, an enterprise largely (and formally) concluded by the mid-1960s.[5] The game has naturally been contoured by the establishment, administration, and formal dismantlement of this empire. While the empire flourished, the attitude towards its subject peoples was in general brutally racist (as in the taking of territory and the violent suppression of dissent) but paternally racist in the belief that those peoples (largely those with black or brown skin) needed guidance and the benefits of an imposed Western culture.[6] In general, to the high-born English stewards of the game, cricket promoted the comity of nations within the imperial family.

For example, between 1894 and 1920 the Indian nobleman Ranjitsinhji Vibhaji Jadeja (known universally as 'Ranji') played cricket variously for Cambridge University, Sussex, and England. Indian princes such as Ranji were loyal to the British Empire and often sent their sons to British boarding schools. (Where it was deemed necessary, however, racism trumped class and previously favoured dark-skinned players were obliged to step aside: Ranji was not selected to tour South Africa with England in 1906, it is thought, at the request of the White South African authorities.[7]) And little, perhaps, better illustrates the narrative of the imperial-family-in-cricket than the reflections of *Daily Telegraph* cricket correspondent E.W. 'Jim' Swanton on the flourishing of West Indies cricket in 1976. Swanton wrote in *The Cricketer*, 'I suppose the biggest and happiest bonus that international cricket has had since the Second World War is the ascent of the West Indies into a great power in the game.' He recalled day one of the Lord's Test in 1950, which had resulted in West Indies' first victory over England: there had been 'a glorious day's cricket in lovely weather, with the King watching and the Royal Standard flying from the mast'. 'The last scenes', he recalled, 'were unforgettable to those present though they would pass with less notice in these less decorous days.' 'West Indian cricket', Swanton decided, 'had come of age.'[8] Swanton tempered this warm welcome to adulthood for a Black British colonial team with regret that: 'Alas', the West Indies' 'full emergence was followed by the departure, temporary at least, of South Africa'—a reference to the banishing of that country, which had practised state (specifically anti-Black) racism for nearly thirty years and fielded an all-White team, from Test cricket.[9]

Besides, any warm paternalist feeling towards the West Indies was soon abandoned by those who spoke for English cricket. The formidable West Indian teams of the 1980s were widely decried for their 'intimidatory' fast bowling and their British-based (usually or migrant-descended) supporters condemned as rowdies, who should keep quiet and leave their musical instruments at home.[10] This culminated in the so-called 'Tebbit test' of 1990, an ugly ascription by the Conservative cabinet minister Norman Tebbit of disloyalty on the part of Black British cricket supporters who might cheer for the West Indies.[11]

This change coincided with a new politics of migration and national identity which had been inaugurated in the early 1960s, designed to deal with the dissolution of the British Empire, the central figure of which was the Conservative politician and strategist Enoch Powell. Powell's infamous speech in the West Midlands town of Wolverhampton (for which he was Member of Parliament) in 1968 warned of a future of racial strife for the UK in which 'the black man will have the whip hand over the white man'.[12] By then, citizens of the old empire (now the British Commonwealth), while accorded a heavily qualified welcome as migrant workers during the period of post-war reconstruction, were being deemed surplus to requirements; legislation curtailing their entry to the UK had begun to be introduced, starting with the Commonwealth Immigration Act of 1962. Further restrictions followed in 1968 and 1971 and in 1981 the first Thatcher administration saw the British Nationality Act, which diminished the prospect of UK citizenship for people of the former colonies—as distinct from the (largely White) dominions.

From the early 1990s, with free movement guaranteed to people of the member countries of the EU, legislative attention turned to those seeking asylum in the UK from outside those countries. These were frequently citizens of nations which the United States (with British support, either political or military or both) had invaded: in 2020 Brown University in the United States reported that over 37 million people had been displaced by the United States' 'War on Terror'.[13] The countries that these displaced persons came from—Afghanistan, Iraq, Pakistan, Yemen, Somalia, Libya, and Syria—were predominantly Muslim. The prospect of migrants seeking asylum in Britain has been met with a dizzying succession of further prohibitive enactments—in 1993, 1996, 1999, 2002, 2004, 2006, 2007, 2009, and 2016. The recurrent emphasis of this legislation has been that, in order to be granted permission to stay in the UK, migrants must have skills deemed to be needed in the British economy.[14]

This, then, is the context for debating 'multiculturalism', a term in play in British public conversation since the early 1980s, and the effective cancellation of largescale Commonwealth migration to the UK. Multiculturalism, as a concept, is deployed at different levels. At the demographic level multiculturalism is a straightforward fact of life in a society of any complexity.[15] At a level of scholarship, in the UK 'multiculturalism' has for more than two decades been a major topic of debate among public policy intellectuals, notably Tariq Modood, professor of sociology, politics and public policy at the University of Bristol,[16] and the political philosopher and Labour peer Bhikhu Parekh, the latter chairing the Commission on the Future of Multi-Ethnic Britain set up by the Runnymede Trust in 1997.[17] These debates have variously weighed the effects of discrimination against minorities, the need for 'social inclusion', and the dangers of self-segregation (usually referring to the purported dangers of Muslim communities setting up sharia law and restricting the personal freedoms of females).

At a level of public commentary, the idea was at first treated with some scepticism among progressives. The influential writer Salman Rushdie, for example, wrote in 1982 that multiculturalism was simply 'the latest token gesture toward Britain's blacks'.[18] Nearly a quarter of a century later, however, he had realized the importance of defending it: 'In the age of mass migration and the Internet', he said in 2005, 'cultural plurality is an irreversible fact, like globalization. Like it or dislike it, it's where we live, and the dream of a pure monoculture is at best an unattainable, nostalgic fantasy, and at worst a life-threatening menace.'[19] Rushdie's change of heart can surely be explained by the growing hostility to 'multiculturalism': during the opening years of the twenty-first century, it became routine for elite politicians of the two main political parties to assert that multiculturalism, whatever it might be, had 'failed'. These assertions have gone hand in hand with two other rhetorical trends: the positing of Muslims as suspect and the rehabilitation of the British Empire. This in turn can be characterized as Powellism-redux: Powell, who died in 1998, had seen this coming, claiming in his last interview, 'I have lived into an age in which my ideas are now part of common intuition, part of a common fashion.'[20]

There are some key signposts in this regard. In 2005 four Muslim suicide bombers launched an attack on London, killing over fifty people. Perhaps to counter the notion that this attack had been in retaliation for the invasion of Iraq by US and British forces in 2003, UK state actors began to express disquiet about Britain's Muslims and their culture. In 2006, senior Labour minister Jack Straw publicly deplored the wearing of veils by Muslim women as a 'visible statement of separation and of difference.'[21] A few days later Secretary of State for Communities Ruth Kelly argued that it was 'dangerous to see Britain's foreign policy as evidence that the country was anti-Muslim' and warned Muslim groups that any state funding they received would be conditional on their 'tackling extremism.'[22] By this time the British government's 'counter-terrorism strategy', previously focussed on Northern Ireland, had been re-orientated on the specific premise that now: 'The principal current terrorist threat is from radicalised individuals who are using a distorted and unrepresentative version of the Islamic faith to justify violence.'[23] A central element in this reconstituted strategy has been the Prevent programme, designed to identify and forestall radical tendencies among Muslim young people in schools and universities. This programme was reaffirmed by Coalition Prime Minister David Cameron in 2011. In a speech in Munich, Cameron, while employing the vocabulary of social inclusion,[24] explicitly attacked thirty years of 'state multiculturalism' and once again Muslims were accused of incubating extremism, practising 'forced marriage', and inhabiting 'segregated communities behaving in ways that run counter to our values'. 'All this', he said, 'leaves some young Muslims feeling rootless. And the search for something to belong to and believe in can lead them to extremist ideology . . . Instead of ignoring this extremist ideology, we—as governments and societies—have got to confront it. Instead of encouraging people to live apart, we need a clear sense of shared national identity, open to everyone.'[25] In 2016, Trevor Phillips, the child of migrants from British Guiana and a former chair of the UK's

Equality and Human Rights Commission, declared that British Muslims were 'becoming a nation within a nation'.[26]

There had been a concurrent trend for senior political figures to celebrate the British Empire, along with 'British values'. In a speech in Tanzania in 2005, Labour Chancellor of the Exchequer Gordon Brown had informed his audience that 'the days of Britain having to apologise for its colonial history are over. We should move forward. We should celebrate much of our past rather than apologise for it. And we should talk, and rightly so, about British values that are enduring, because they stand for some of the greatest ideas in history: tolerance, liberty, civic duty, that grew in Britain and influenced the rest of the world. Our strong traditions of fair play, of openness, of internationalism, these are great British values'.[27] Three years earlier, Boris Johnson, editor of the Conservative journal *The Spectator*, had written of Africa: 'The continent may be a blot, but it is not a blot upon our conscience. The problem is not that we were once in charge, but that we are not in charge anymore . . . If left to their own devices, the natives would rely on nothing but the instant carbohydrate gratification of the plantain'.[28] The same year Johnson had referred to African children as 'piccaninnies', a term which Powell had used similarly in his Wolverhampton speech in 1968.[29] Johnson would become UK foreign secretary in 2016 and prime minister in 2019. According to press reports early in 2020, one 'third of people in the UK believe Britain's colonies were better off for being part of an empire, a higher proportion than in any of the other major colonial powers . . . Britons are also more likely to say they would like their country to still have an empire than people in France, Italy, Spain, the Netherlands, Belgium, Germany or Japan'.[30]

In 2012, Conservative Home Secretary Theresa May told the right-wing *Daily Telegraph* that for illegal migrants she planned a 'really hostile environment' entailing 'measures to limit access to work, housing, health care, bank accounts and more. It is characterised by a system of citizen-on-citizen immigration checks. The majority of these proposals became law via the Immigration Act of 2014 and have since been tightened or expanded under the Immigration Act 2016'.[31] Lest it be thought that this series of assertions and enactments might constitute an undeclared state racism, the government recruited a number of advisors from migrant families to assure the public that they were not. One key example here was Munira Mirza, the daughter of a Pakistani factory worker in the Lancashire former cotton town of Oldham. Mirza wrote for *Spiked*, a right-wing 'libertarian' website, on which she had claimed that institutionalized racism was a myth, that diversity was 'divisive', and that multiculturalism promoted political victimhood.[32] She was appointed head of the prime minister's Policy Unit in 2019.

English Cricket, Black Lives, and the Re-Eruption of 'Race'

These longstanding twin narratives of reasserted imperial virtue and the migrant enemy within have, of course, been contested and convincing analyses offered.[33] For instance, in response to Brown's Tanzania speech, journalist Seumas Milne had pointed out that while there was little evidence that British governments had ever 'apologized' for the empire, it was clear that English policy-makers and commentators had begun exploring new rationales for intervening in the affairs of other countries, based on notions of 'humanitarian intervention' and 'human rights'.[34] Sociologist Nandita Sharma has written powerfully of the longer process, in train since the Second World War, whereby Western countries have reaffirmed their national sovereignty and ruthlessly discriminated between 'natives' and 'migrants', the latter, welcome in the 1950s, now redefined as trespassers and the former (once imperial trespassers) recast as natives.[35] Nevertheless, the political narrative of 'multiculturalism' has inevitably become a yardstick against which English cricket—its national team and its wider culture—has been measured in recent times.

Many of the comments and interventions here have been couched in terms of social inclusion—that multiculturalism was flourishing in English cricket (and this was a good thing) or that there were obstacles to it (major or minor) and these needed to be addressed. And, while this debate was predominantly about ethnicity (and, by implication, race), the argument has necessarily often wound up being about social class and the widely acknowledged shrinking of cricket's social base in England. Some of the most optimistic commentary was triggered by England's victory in the World Cup of 2019, one of the best examples being by sportswriter Jonathan Liew, who suggested:

The climax to the greatest cricket game of all time began when England's Jofra Archer ran in to bowl the final ball of the men's World Cup final at Lord's. Born in Barbados to an English father, Archer grew up in a bungalow in Bridgetown, and learnt his bowling with battered tennis balls on a strip of grass adjoining a nearby graveyard. The ball was hit out into the leg-side, where it was fielded by Jason Roy. Born in Durban, South Africa, Roy moved to the UK with his parents at the age of ten and was earmarked for stardom from an early age. He won a sporting scholarship to the prestigious Whitgift School in south London. Roy advanced on the ball and hurled it towards wicketkeeper Jos Buttler. If Archer and Roy were both urban cricketers, Buttler is very much a product of the provinces. He grew up in the Somerset village of Wedmore ...

The whole thing, argued Liew, had banished the baleful nationalism attendant in the campaign to leave the EU and instead bolstered:

a different narrative: a triumph of our unique diversity, a resounding endorsement of immigration and open borders, a multicultural side that epitomised the very best of these islands. As well as Morgan, Roy and Archer, spin bowlers Moeen Ali and Adil Rashid are devout Muslims and the sons of Pakistani immigrants. Man-of-the-match Ben Stokes was born in New Zealand. Fast bowlers Mark Wood and Liam Plunkett hail from the industrial north-east. In character and background, this is a team that genuinely reflects the nation it represents.[36]

Similar sentiments, undoubtedly approved by the England and Wales Cricket Board (ECB), were expressed by England captain Eoin Morgan who assured the (normally anti-immigrant) *Daily Mail* of his 'pride at leading the multi-cultural World Cup winners'. Morgan (born in Dublin in 1986) likewise lamented the 'divisiveness' of the EU Referendum and reflected: 'In that final, Jason Roy (born in South Africa), Ben Stokes (New Zealand), Jofra Archer (Barbados) and I all started life somewhere else. Rash [Adil Rashid] is Muslim, and so is Moeen Ali, who didn't play at Lord's but was an important part of the squad. Let's be honest: the England team have never really been made up of 11 white Christians, anyway; these days more people seem comfortable about that.'[37] Cricket correspondent and doctoral student Firdose Moonda blogged similarly of England's 'multi-ethnic team [who] will take the field at a time when the country is still negotiating its exit from the European Union and anti-migrant rhetoric is high and may be able to show that there is unity in diversity in the UK'.[38] The mercurial Conservative writer Peter Oborne had earlier written a sympathetic profile of the cricketer Moeen Ali (who had made his England debut in 2014) for the news outlet *Middle East Eye*. Ali, his article said, was 'British, Muslim and proud' and 'does not apologise for his Muslim identity. He prays five times a day. He fasts during Ramadan. He does not drink. And he has the most magnificent beard since the Victorian sporting hero WG Grace more than a hundred years ago'. Admittedly, noted Oborne, Ali had worn wristbands bearing the slogans 'Free Palestine' and 'Save Gaza', but only out of 'humanitarian concern' for the victims 'on both sides' of the Israel–Palestine conflict. It was a pity, added the writer, that '[a]ny British Muslim who enters public life is subject to an unwritten law. This law states that if they want to get on then they must suppress their Muslim identity'.[39] Here Oborne depicts Ali's faith as no more than a personal observance, unpolluted by 'politics' or what the British state now defines as 'extremism'; Ali is rendered as Muslim, but loyal to the established order.

A similar, cautiously sanguine, view was offered in the *New York Times* by British literary journalist and novelist Sameer Rahim. Anti-Muslim hostility in the ruling Conservative Party, a 26 per cent rise in attacks on Muslims since the previous year, and largely negative views of Muslims expressed in a recent survey made for grim picture, wrote Rahim: 'Except, that is, on the cricket field. Perhaps surprisingly, the England cricket team, that most traditional of national institutions, has been leading the way in creating a more inclusive environment for its Muslim players'.[40] Thus, another voice was added to the chorus proclaiming English cricket as a happily multicultural affair.

These observations have not been seriously undermined by academic analysis, although a number of sociologists have pointed to difficulties faced by English Muslim cricketers. Thomas Fletcher, for instance, wrote of the residual problems faced by Yorkshire-born Asian cricketers in gaining acceptance at the highest levels of the county's cricket, and in being regarded as 'Yorkshire'. Myths of the county[41] persisted, he argued, and some White Yorkshire people might never accept locally born Asians.[42] Fletcher and Karl Spracklen found drink to be a stumbling block for British-Pakistani Muslim cricketers: either they risked marginalization by sticking to soft drinks or they elected to forgo their faith and take alcohol.[43] There were corresponding calls for greater sensitivity on the part of the White cricket authorities to the 'subjective realities' of British-Pakistani Muslim cricketers, a more welcoming environment, and an easing back on traditional bar culture.[44] Similarly, Fletcher, along with Kevin Hylton, Jonathan Long, and Neil Ormerod, counselled greater engagement by Yorkshire Cricket in the form of community events and partnerships, organized around the known commitments of Yorkshire Muslim families.[45]

To this research and recommendation, plainly supportive of multicultural cricket, should be added the work of Dominic Malcolm, which constitutes probably the most sustained and thoughtful assessment of social inclusiveness in the English cricket scene. Malcolm acknowledges the village green 'myths of whiteness' against which all English BAME (Black, Asian, and Minority Ethnic) cricketers are measured, but notes the growth of Muslim teams in England (amid an overall decline in the number of cricket clubs); the hybridity and fluidity of British Muslim identities (contrary to state/popular media notions of self-segregation); and the apparent lack of conflict between playing cricket and Muslim religious observance.[46] He also, importantly, distinguishes between *malign* and *benign* Englishness in taking stock of contemporary English national identity, malign Englishness being reflexively hostile to multiculturalism.[47] Of the prevalence of malign Englishness in English cricket culture there can be little doubt—witness, for example, the sour injunction by veteran sport journalist Michael Henderson to Moeen Ali that 'You're playing for England, not your religion' in the pages of the *Daily Telegraph* in 2014[48]—but Malcolm cites as evidence of a growing counter-current the travelling England supporters constituted as the 'Barmy Army'. Disparaged by the older guard of cricket commentators, the Barmy Army, first assembled for England's Ashes tour of Australia in the winter of 1994–1995, practised none of the reticence traditionally expected of a cricket crowd. They were expressive, liked a drink and a laugh, and relished their cricket in a way most associated with (and previously condemned in) West Indian supporters. They typified what some saw as a 'new cricket culture', itself an idea canvassed since the mid-1990s.[49] They sometimes hung out or partied with the England players and had a kindred spirit in Lancashire cricketer Andrew Flintoff, a plumber's son and *bon viveur* who represented England between 1998 and 2009. Flintoff was hailed as the archetypal, honest-to-goodness English bloke who had salvaged the English game and, according to the writer Richard Williams, provided a link to 'the founding myths of English cricket'.[50] Press commentary suggested that the English game was no longer a game for toffs.[51]

It is fair to say that much of this broad optimism has not stood the test of (a comparatively short) time. It's noticeable, for example, that since his retirement in 2009, Flintoff's career (notwithstanding a brief comeback in 2014) has been almost entirely unrelated to cricket—possibly because other (largely media) work offers better commercial opportunities. Moreover, the Barmy Army are merely consumers of cricket and, while televised cricket may incorporate crowd members as part of the spectacle, the constituency of English cricket is shrinking, a point made by Conservative writer/researcher David Skelton in 2019. Of the World Cup being staged at the time, he wrote:

> Outside of the grounds, few people in England are watching and plenty are barely aware that this tournament is taking place. Not a single game is being shown live on terrestrial television. This represents a catastrophic failure on behalf of England's cricketing authorities . . . It was only 14 years ago that cricket genuinely did play a role in the national imagination. The 2005 Ashes was perhaps the best test series in living memory and its pivotal moments—culminating in the sight of a drunken Freddie Flintoff stumbling into Downing Street—dominated conversation in schools, workplaces and pubs. Regent's Park and other outside spaces around the country were packed out to watch the decisive test match. The peak TV audience during that golden summer was over nine million. The top audience for England during this World Cup has rarely exceeded one million and has slumped as low as 500,000. Contrast this with the growing national mood of excitement around the Lionesses [England women's football team]: England's quarter-final against Norway attracted almost eight million viewers.[52]

Skelton's comment is typical of many in the emphasis it places on terrestrial television coverage, the doubtful but all-pervading assumption being that people will be drawn to engage in a certain activity simply by watching other (highly skilled) people doing it on-screen. Skelton was probably nearer the mark when he added that: 'Whereas the 2005 Ashes-winning team was dominated by state school players, the Commission for Social Mobility recently identified the England cricket team as one of the worst examples of "elitist Britain", with 43 per cent of the team privately educated (compared to 7 per cent of the population).'[53] Whether Skelton intended it or not, this pointed the argument back towards the elephant that has inhabited the room of English cricket for thirty years: privatization and the spectre not of culture or ethnicity but of social class. Since the British state began to reduce its funding of state schools in the 1990s, fewer and fewer of the nation's children have been taught the game of cricket as part of their curriculum and the maintenance of the English game (as elsewhere) has depended increasingly on private initiative, of one kind or another. The chapter returns to this issue shortly. Meanwhile, in the spring of 2020, the matter of race and multiculturalism returned to centre stage.

In late May 2020 a forty-six-year-old African American called George Floyd was stopped by police in Minneapolis, USA, on suspicion of passing a counterfeit cheque. A police officer pinned Floyd to the ground with his knee while onlookers filmed the incident on their phones and pleaded with the officer to relent; the officer calmly maintained his position for several minutes and Floyd died. Floyd's death, the latest in a long line of Black fatalities at the hands of US law enforcement officers, resulted in huge protests, many of which were organized by Black Lives Matter, a movement originating in the United States in 2013. In the British city of Bristol, a statue of seventeenth-/eighteenth-century slave trader Edward Colston was torn from its plinth and thrown into the nearby harbour. In Britain, according to the British Labour MP Zarah Sultana, protests took place at over 150 locations in the UK, a scale of public disquiet that compelled a response from politicians and public bodies—including the English cricket authorities.[54]

While it had in any event been questionable to posit either English society or the England cricket team as a haven of multicultural amity simply because leading English cricketers had been born in different parts of the old British Empire, the political issue of racism, in some form, now became inescapable for people involved in the English game. Quick-witted officials at Lord's announced in the *Daily Telegraph* that a portrait of

Benjamin Aislabie (1774–1842), the first honorary secretary of MCC,[55] had been removed from public display, since he was known to have owned slaves in Dominica and Antigua.[56] The following day a headline in the same paper announced, with less than complete conviction, that 'MCC have opportunity to confront Benjamin Aislabie's slave-trade link and use as a tool to educate'.[57]

The ECB announced that England players would wear the Black Lives Matter logo on their shirts in the forthcoming Test series against West Indies and they would kneel on one knee before each game in the manner already adopted by many Black sportspeople in the USA. County cricketers would do likewise. 'The England and Wales Cricket Board fully support the message that Black Lives Matter', stated Chief Executive Tom Harrison in an ECB press release. 'It has become a message of solidarity and a drive for progress and societal change. There can be no place for racism in society or our sport, and we must do more to tackle it.' He added a caveat: 'Our support of that message is not an endorsement, tacit or otherwise, of any political organisation, nor the backing of any group that calls for violence or condones illegal activity'.[58] This maintained the ECB response at the level of gesture and formal affirmation and (as in the days of South African apartheid) implied that those wishing actually to challenge racism could be assumed to be dealers in 'violence and illegal activity'.[59]

However serious Harrison might have been in his endorsement of 'progress and societal change', the realities of racism faced by Black English cricketers were soon spelled out. Ebony Rainford-Brent, an England international born into a working-class Jamaican family in the south London borough of Lambeth in 1983, spoke on a BBC radio programme about her experiences of racism. She did not hold back. She had, she said, been in tears for two days following Floyd's death and had been out on the street protesting (possibly a first for the BBC Test Match Special commentary team, of which she was a member). In her cricket career, she recalled being asked, 'Do you wash your skin?', having people run their fingers through her hair, and fielding comments such as 'I bet your Mum doesn't know who your Dad is.' 'When Obama was elected [in 2008] the paper was slapped down in front of me and I was told "I bet your lot are happy".[60] Ex-England player Michael Carberry, also of Caribbean descent, told the BBC that he didn't expect anything from the ECB on racism: 'They have put out pictures to say "we're not racist, look at

Jofra Archer and Adil Rashid hugging after winning the World Cup". The figures tell me otherwise.'[61] A week later (White) *Guardian* sportswriter Barney Ronay backed this up, pointing out how men such as Middlesex and England cricketer Mike Gatting, who had captained a 'rebel' cricket team touring apartheid South Africa in 1990, and David Graveney, who had organized the tour, both without apparent regret, were still prominent figures at the ECB. 'I'm not suggesting these men are actively racist', reflected Ronay, 'or that they don't have lots of great non-white cricketing mates. I'm also not suggesting the ECB is responsible for the wider forces driving cricket's retreat from the cities and from many state schools, a sport increasingly walled up in its own pristine green squares. But does anyone have a clue how this looks, in a system largely free of black administrators and coaches, and in a sport whose structures, geography and basic existence is still unavoidably bound in the spread of empire?'[62] By contrast, the West Indian players who had participated in the same 'rebel' tour had been banned for life, shunned in their communities, and become known as 'The Unforgiven'.[63]

Briefly, racism in English cricket flourished as a theme in sections of the mainstream media. Ronay sought out Lonsdale Skinner, born on the Caribbean island of Demerara in 1950, who had come to England as a child and played cricket for Surrey in the mid-1970s. Skinner recalled being called a 'black bastard' by his coach during that time and being regarded as expendable. However: 'Most of the racism came from outside the dressing room. It was from the committee room, the decision-makers. They had something to protect. If you had one bad year, you're gone. They didn't want you there.'[64] Skinner's friend Jamaica-born Richard 'Wes' Stewart, a fellow county cricketer of the 'Windrush generation' who had come to the UK in 1955, played for Middlesex between 1966 and 1968, and paid UK taxes for over five decades, was one of many who in their retirement had fallen foul of the 'hostile environment' policy operated at the UK Home Office.[65] Stewart had been told that his nationality had lapsed with Jamaican independence in 1962. A seven-year dispute was unresolved when Stewart died in 2019.[66]

Skinner, Rainford-Brent, and the ex-West Indian fast bowler Michael Holding were among a number of Black cricketers now calling for an end to institutionalized racism and it was not just outlets such as the left-wing *Morning Star*[67] who gave them a hearing—Sky TV, the BBC, the

Guardian, and right-wing papers such as the *Daily Mail* and the *Daily Telegraph* had all poked microphones in their direction. Towards the end of July Black England fast bowler Jofra Archer reported that he'd been racially abused after withdrawing from an England squad for breaching anti-virus restrictions.[68] But, by late summer, as a news story the issue of racism and multiculturalism in cricket had lost its impetus and it soon disappeared. However, a number of things may tentatively be said.

Few individuals or organizations actually endorse racism, any more than they did in the heyday of South African apartheid. Then, as now, many people and public bodies were wont to condemn racism and, at the same time, to distance themselves from opponents of racism on the ground that those opponents were making the matter 'political'. There has been a parallel tendency to see racism as a matter solely of personal attitude and not of the culture and practice of institutions. This pretty much defines the (largely unchanging) position of the English cricket authorities, who preside over a system within which Black cricketers have been racially abused, discarded when judged to be no longer of value, and almost never deemed suitable for coaching or administrative positions. And while, on the face of it, a cricket team including a couple of South Africans, a Bajan, a Muslim, and two men from the North of England may pass as a multicultural flagship, it could equally be argued that it simply disguises a growing postcolonial discrimination. Given the public comments of key state actors over the last twenty years and the directions of government policy—in August 2020, for example, a court decision held that the British Home Office had been using a racist algorithm in its immigration policy—this postcolonial discrimination is being sanctioned, effectively, by the state.[69] There can be no truly multicultural cricket in what—considering its surveillance of Muslims, its desire to expel long-resident migrants, its renewed defence of a lost empire, and its invocation of 'British values'—is an avowedly monocultural state.

What Do They Know of Cricket? The Bitter Fruit of Privatization

The (clearly) vital debate over racism and ethnicity must, as noted, properly be viewed as part of an even wider discussion of the shrinking social base of the game in England (and elsewhere). This section considers apparent causes and consequences for English cricket of dwindling public interest in the game—a situation exacerbated in 2020 by the restrictions compelled by COVID-19.

English cricket seems to have been in crisis since the late 1950s and during this century epitaphs have begun to proliferate. In 2001, for example, cultural theorist Paul Gilroy wrote that men's cricket in England seemed to be 'in almost terminal decline as a national spectator sport'.[70] There is broad agreement that men's cricket is in decline in the UK[71] while, by comparison, women's cricket flourishes.[72] Attendance at county grounds is low and features comparatively few young people. In his recent memoir Michael Henderson, a former staff sportswriter on *The Times*, the *Daily Telegraph*, and the *Daily Mail*, wryly observes of a day recently spent at the Nottinghamshire ground, Trent Bridge: 'In they wander, men and women glad to have survived another winter, in some cases recalling those who have not.'[73] Explanations for the loss of subsequent generations vary, although most of them are rooted in contemporary Conservative orthodoxy—the right-wing *Daily Telegraph* is, after all, according to the late BBC cricket correspondent Christopher Martin-Jenkins, the newspaper of choice among cricket lovers.[74] Michael Henderson's book of 2020 offers a good selection of reasons: the 'ruminative pleasures' of watching a cricket match over several days 'run counter to the spirit of our triumphantly demotic age' wherein people seek not sport but 'light entertainment';[75] the young would 'prefer to play games on electronic gadgets';[76] immigration—inner-city English-Caribbean boys are attracted to the 'higher profile' and 'untold riches' promised by football;[77] while 'the Muslim dimension to the recent wave of immigration has introduced a cultural difference that bland platitudes about "multi-culturalism" cannot disguise. Most Muslims live decent lives in harmony with their neighbours. A significant minority, it cannot be denied, have made little effort to integrate within British society'.[78] The greatest blame, however, seems to be attributed, by Henderson and others, to state schools and, more specifically, to the culture of these schools and to the agency of the people who teach in them.

State schools, it's said, show a culpable indifference to the nation's historic summer game. Henderson writes of their 'lack of interest'[79] and laments that only one in five state schools 'bothers' to play cricket.[80]

Elsewhere, right-wing critics have claimed that socialist teachers in state schools were undermining not only cricket but the competitive ethos itself. Commenting after the Schofield Review of English cricket prompted by the 5–0 Ashes defeat by Australia in the winter of 2006–2007, Nick Gandon, director of the Cricket Foundation, claimed that 'a generation of potential England cricketers have been lost', partly because of the ' "sanctimonious dogma" of some local authorities that competition can be harmful to children'.[81] Similarly, Douglas Henderson, for three decades in charge of cricket at Clifton College, a private boarding school in Bristol, assessing the problem in 2019 wrote that 'the 1960s zeitgeist was very much anti-competition and anti-elitism'[82] and quoted with approval Melanie Phillips' book *All Must Have Prizes* which had claimed an epidemic of anti-competitive teaching in state schools.[83]

However, putting it at its most generous, there are problems with this analysis. It may, for example, be that there has been a culture of rejection of competitive sports in English state schools but: (a) little evidence of it has ever been produced and Phillips' book was dismissed by educationists—eminent Professor of Education Ted Wragg, for example, described it as a confection of prejudices, anecdotes, and 'quotes from like-minded mates'[84] and (b) a survey by the MCC and Nick Gandon's own charity Chance to Shine found that around two thirds of children aged eight to sixteen would be 'relieved' if winning/losing were not a factor in school games.[85] The anxieties of the children expressed here should be respected and not written off as due to the malign manipulations of progressive teachers.

There have, in any event, been other factors at work here, as Conservative critics reluctantly accept. (It is often the way that the strongest evidence for the defence is quietly acknowledged by the prosecution.) Chief of these is the lack of facilities. Both Gandon[86] and Michael Henderson,[87] for example, cite the loss of state school playing fields, 10,000 of which were sold between 1979 and 1997, a period of uninterrupted Conservative government. This, and the fact that, since cricket is expensive to stage, in time, space, teacher-hours, and money, it is less likely to be adopted as a school sport, has inevitably meant that fewer and fewer state school pupils have had access to cricket and, thus, to know what it is. Another factor here will have been the Education Act of

1988, which inaugurated the National Curriculum and league tables for state schools: this meant that state schools would give increasing priority in the summer term to examinations. The Labour Party manifesto for the General Election of 1997 promised: 'We will bring the government's policy of forcing schools to sell off playing fields to an end' but the sales continued when Labour were in office.[88]

All this constituted a *de facto* privatization of English cricket, with responsibility for propagating the game passing to private schools, to local cricket clubs, and to outreach/talent identification initiatives such as Chance to Shine, which provided schemes via which state school children could sample cricket. In 2008 a YouGov survey, reported in the *Daily Telegraph*, suggested that only one child in ten was playing cricket in state schools.[89] Of the remaining 90 per cent we might very well ask, adapting C.L.R. James' famous phrase, 'What do they know of cricket?'

For many observers, all this put a different complexion on the debate about racial exclusion in English cricket. BAME youngsters could be seen as part of a much broader swathe of children who had simply had no experience of cricket. Most of them attended state schools where there were no facilities for cricket; very few of them attended expensive, fee-paying schools where often luxurious cricket facilities or even sport scholarships were available. Thus, the issue of race was part of a wider issue of social class. As Ebony Rainford-Brent pointed out, 42 per cent of children in inner-city Lambeth, embracing Surrey County Cricket Club, were BAME and there were very few British-born BAME players in the English system; many of those that were had learned their trade elsewhere.[90] This would explain why the number of Black British cricketers has declined[91] and why, by 2013, only half of county cricketers had attended state schools.[92] Therefore, some commentators have called for more diversity in English cricket. For example, in 2017, Labour peer Lord Patel called for more attention to be paid to Britain's cricket-playing Asians: 'Britain's South Asians represent only five per cent of the population, yet they account for 18% of the £685m spent on cricket every year . . . In the UK 30 per cent of recreational cricket is played by South Asians. If you add backstreets, tape-ball and so on, it's nearer 40%. Despite living in urban areas, in poverty and deprivation, they will still spend money on cricket—equipment, pitch hire and so on.'[93]

Conclusion: England Gone?

Michael Henderson's book is not only a purported requiem for the county cricket that was played in the 1950s and 1960s. In his (glowing) review of the book, Chris Waters of the *Yorkshire Post* noted: 'Henderson starts his journey in the spirit of A.E. Houseman, in the Worcestershire spa town of Malvern, in search of a representative view of England from high up on the "blue remembered hills". He gazes north to Shropshire and east to Birmingham, his eye moving towards Lichfield, Warwick, Worcester, Stratford-upon-Avon, Oxford, Tewkesbury, Hereford, and so on. All are centres of Englishness or English history; it is impossible to think of Worcestershire, for example, without hearing the music of Sir Edward Elgar.'[94] These are the same rhetorical country lanes trodden by Enoch Powell in his search for England's ancestors—ancestors whom he invoked in calling for the expulsion from Britain of 'the black man' who would otherwise have the 'whip hand over the white man'. One of the book's heroes is Fred Trueman, Yorkshire and England's greatest fast bowler who off the field was known for his fund of jokes, dispensed before the onset of 'political correctness'. 'The jokes', reflected Trueman's biographer, with saloon bar unctuousness, 'were mostly of the variety known in polite company as risqué, liberally sprinkled with racial overtones. It is doubtful, for instance, if Fred would ever be invited to read the lesson (or whatever the equivalent is) in one of the mosques of Bradford.'[95] Henderson, as he himself says, speaks for: 'The sort of people who find "diversity" an unjustified imposition.' If county cricket goes, says Henderson, 'that will be England gone',[96] quoting the misanthropic English poet Philip Larkin.[97]

There are considerable political ironies here. The chief one is that Powellite sentiments such as those expressed by Conservative cricket writers like Henderson have served to dignify a process through which the thing they cherished most—county cricket—was brought to the edge of extinction. At the centre of this process, as has recently been made clear by a group of progressive British BAME academics, lie the relinquishing of empire, the erosion of the welfare state, and the redefinition of the nation.[98] The notion of 'multiculturalism' has been abandoned at state level in order to mobilize the idea of a single, inherently White, national way of life, menaced by an array of groups/cultures/folk devils who neither deserve nor belong: asylum seekers crossing the English Channel in dinghies, long-term migrants without the proper documentation, knife-wielding Black youths, Pakistani sex-traffickers, self-secluding Muslim worshippers, and so on. These groups constitute the undeserving in relation to citizenship and thus to welfare; moreover, whatever benefits these Black/Brown groups enjoy have been rendered as part of a zero-sum game, so that any gain they made is seen as at the expense of White people.[99]

Here, for cricket, race and class converged. As the nation was re-defined, so was the national summer game: it became an acceptable casualty in the steady, managed decline of the welfare state. A progressive denial of resources to state schooling, hitherto a key part of the welfare state, meant a lack of access to cricket for the great majority of the nation's teens and pre-teens, encompassing, of course, most of those belonging to ethnic minorities. The English game today thrives only in historically and predominantly White spaces: the private boarding schools, the university academies, and, to a lesser degree, the villages. The young, English-Caribbean males cited by Henderson may have been attracted to football for its big pay packets, but few of them got the chance to play cricket and it was successive British governments—not the left-wing teachers of Conservative mythology—who took that chance away: indeed, many school playing fields were sold during the Conservative administration of the cricket-loving John Major between 1990 and 1997.[100] In another irony, evidence suggests that it is the England Muslim community—enemies within in the official narrative—who are helping to keep the game alive at the local level.

At the national level the nation's Test team maintains England as a brand and is sustained by the aforementioned private schools and university academies. It is routinely composed of players, mostly White, occasionally Black or Brown, born in various parts of the country and abroad and into various families and faiths. But that doesn't make it 'multicultural': it represents an increasingly narrow segment of the population and it does not reflect a society of happily coexisting cultures. The four-day county cricket circuit—another largely White enclave, so beloved of Conservative writers—is increasingly marginal to this enterprise since England cricketers play rarely for their counties. The *Daily Telegraph* readers and the 'old timers . . . nodding off in deckchairs at Hove or lolling under the limes at Chesterfield' have, as they half-acknowledge, been be-trayed by their own politicians.[101] But, while they grumble about 'diver-sity', diversity, in the form of England's migrant and migrant-descended players and entrepreneurs, may be the best hope for the survival of local and even county cricket in England. This 'England' may or may not soon be 'gone', but it will certainly not be saved by summoning the ghost of Enoch Powell.

Notes

1. For a penetrating analysis of Brexit, see Fintan O'Toole, *Heroic Failure: Brexit and the Politics of Pain* (London: Head of Zeus, 2018).

2. See Sean Illing, 'Racists love Trump: This is what they mean by "taking the country back"—yet another poll confirms racial and cultural resentment is driving Donald Trump's rise', 5 April 2016, www.salon.com/2016/04/05/racists_love_trump_this_is_what_they_mean_by_taking_the_country_back_yet_another_poll_confirms_racial_and_cultural_resentment_is_driving_donald_trumps_rise, accessed 26 April 2021.

3. See, for example, Pnina Werbner, 'Revisiting the UK Muslim diasporic public sphere at a time of terror: From local (benign) invisible spaces to seditious con-spiratorial spaces and the "failure of multiculturalism" discourse', *South Asian Diaspora* 1, no. 1 (2009): 19–45; Mike Berry, Inaki Garcia-Blanco, and Kerry Moore Kerry, 'UK press is the most aggressive in reporting on Europe's "migrant" crisis', 14 March 2016, https://theconversation.com/uk-press-is-the-most-aggress ive-in-reporting-on-europes-migrant-crisis-56083, accessed 26 April 2021; Rob McNeil, 'Migrants and the media: What shapes the narratives on immigration in different countries', 26 April 2019, https://theconversation.com/migrants-and-the-media-what-shapes-the-narratives-on-immigration-in-different-countries-116081, accessed 21 September 2020).

4. Stephen Wagg, 'Towards a safer past: Thoughts on the invocation of English cricket's soul', 10 September 2020, www.tandfonline.com/doi/full/10.1080/17430437.2020.1815709, accessed 15 September 2020.

5. See Dominic Malcolm, *Globalizing Cricket: Englishness, Empire and Identity* (London: Bloomsbury, 2013) and Stephen Wagg, *Cricket: A Political History of the Global Game 1945–2017* (London: Routledge, 2018).

6. See, for examples, John Newsinger, *The Blood Never Dried: A People's History of the British Empire* (London: Bookmarks, 2013); Caroline Elkins, *Britain's Gulag: The Brutal End of Empire in Kenya* (London: Bodley Head, 2014); Shashi Tharoor, *Inglorious Empire: What the British Did to India* (London: Penguin, 2018).

7. Mike Marqusee, *Anyone but England: An Outsider Looks at English Cricket* (London: Aurum Press, 2005), 206.

8. E.W. Swanton (George Plumptre, ed.), *As I Said at the Time: A Lifetime in Cricket* (London: Unwin Paperbacks, 1986), 164–166.

9. Swanton, *As I Said*, 164. For a fuller discussion of this issue, see Jack Williams, *Cricket and Race* (Oxford: Berg, 2001) and Stephen Wagg, ' "Calypso kings, dark destroyers": Representations of Caribbean cricket in the English sports press 1950–1984', in *Cricket and National Identity in the Post-Colonial Era: Following On*, ed. Stephen Wagg (London: Routledge, 2007), 181–203.

10. See Wagg, ' "Calypso kings" '; Marqusee, *Anyone but England*, 164–171.

11. See John Carvel, 'Tebbit's cricket loyalty test hit for six', 8 January 2004, www.theg uardian.com/uk/2004/jan/08/britishidentity.race, accessed 22 September 2020.

12. The speech can be read here: https://anth1001.files.wordpress.com/2014/04/enoch-powell_speech.pdf, accessed 22 September 2020.

13. See Watson Institute for International and Public Affairs, Brown University, 'New costs of war study: 37 million displaced by U.S. post-9/11 wars', 8 September 2020, https://watson.brown.edu/research/2020/Post-9/11DisplacementStudy, accessed 23 September 2020.

14. For a helpful summary of British immigration legislation between 1905 and 2016, see Alyssa Girvan, 'The history of British immigration policy (1905–2016) timeline resource', June 2018, https://static1.squarespace.com/static/5748678dc f80a1ffcaf26975/t/5b27e23d8a922dfca10ddeb1/1529340490557/Immigration+ Timeline.pdf, accessed 23 September 2020.

15. See Irene Bloemraad, 'The debate over multiculturalism: Philosophy, politics, and policy', 22 September 2011, www.migrationpolicy.org/article/debate-over-multiculturalism-philosophy-politics-and-policy, accessed 23 September 2020.

16. See, for example, Tariq Modood, *Multiculturalism* (Cambridge: Polity Press, 2007).

17. See Bhikhu Parekh, *Report of the Commission on the Future of Multi-Ethnic Britain* (London: Profile Books, 2000).

18. Salman Rushdie, 'The new empire within Britain', *New Society*, 9 December 1982, https://public.wsu.edu/~hegglund/courses/389/rushdie_new_empire.htm, accessed 23 September 2020.

19. Salman Rushdie, 'In defence of multiculturalism', 15 December 2005, https://uk.politics.misc.narkive.com/XY29FVxA/in-defence-of-multiculturalism-sal man-rushdie, accessed 23 September 2020.

20. Matthew d'Ancona, 'Matthew d'Ancona: This referendum is about what sort of nation we want to be', *Evening Standard*, 22 June 2016, www.standard.co.uk/comment/comment/matthew-dancona-this-referendum-is-about-what-sort-of-nation-we-want-to-be-a3278126.html, accessed 23 September 2020.

21. 'Straw's veil comments spark anger', BBC News, 5 October 2006, http://news.bbc.co.uk/1/hi/uk_politics/5410472.stm, accessed 24 September 2020.

22. Taia Branigan, 'Muslim groups must tackle extremism to gain funding, says Kelly', 11 October 2006, www.theguardian.com/politics/2006/oct/11/immigratio npolicy.religion, accessed 24 September 2020.

23. HMSO, 'Countering international terrorism: The United Kingdom's strategy', 2006, 3, https://assets.publishing.service.gov.uk/government/uploads/system/uploads/attachment_data/file/272320/6888.pdf, accessed 24 September.

24. For an account of the political appropriation of this vocabulary, see Tom Sykes, Stephen Harper, and Matthew Alford 'How Britain's most powerful institutions are hijacking social justice rhetoric', *Morning Star*, 25 September 2020, 11.

25. Oliver Wright and Jerome Taylor, 'Cameron: My war on multiculturalism', *The Independent*, 5 February 2011, www.independent.co.uk/news/uk/politics/cameron-my-war-on-multiculturalism-2205074.html, accessed 25 September 2020.

26. Maha Akeel, 'Trevor Phillips' research on British Muslims is dangerous and wrong: No wonder Islamophobia is on the rise', *The Independent*, 12 April 2016, www.independent.co.uk/voices/trevor-phillips-research-british-muslims-dangerous-and-wrong-no-wonder-islamophobia-rise-a6980331.html, accessed 27 September 2020.

27. Benedict Brogan, 'It's time to celebrate the Empire, says Brown', *Daily Mail*, 15 January 2005, www.dailymail.co.uk/news/article-334208/Its-time-celebrate-Empire-says-Brown.html, accessed 26 September 2020.

28. Boris Johnson, 'Africa is a mess, but we can't blame colonialism', *The Spectator*, 2 February 2002. The article can be read at www.spectator.co.uk/article/the-boris-archive-africa-is-a-mess-but-we-can-t-blame-colonialism, accessed 26 September 2020.

29. Stephanie Busari, ' "Watermelon smiles" and "piccaninnies": What Boris Johnson has said previously about people in Africa', 24 July 2019, https://edition.cnn.com/2019/07/23/africa/boris-johnson-africa-intl/index.html, accessed 27 September 2020.

30. See, for example, Robert Booth, 'UK more nostalgic for empire than other ex-colonial powers', *The Guardian*, 11 March 2020, www.theguardian.com/world/2020/mar/11/uk-more-nostalgic-for-empire-than-other-ex-colonial-powers, accessed 27 September 2020.

31. See Colin Yeo, 'Briefing: What is the hostile environment, where does it come from, who does it affect?', 1 May 2018, www.freemovement.org.uk/briefing-what-is-the-hostile-environment-where-does-it-come-from-who-does-it-affect, accessed 27 September 2020. See also Maya Goodfellow, *Hostile Environment: How Immigrants Became Scapegoats* (London: Verso, 2019).

32. See Munira Mirza, 'Diversity is divisive', 23 November 2006, www.spiked-online.com/2006/11/23/diversity-is-divisive, accessed 27 September 2020; Munira Mirza, 'Lammy review: The myth of institutional racism', 11 September 2017, www.spiked-online.com/2017/09/11/lammy-review-the-myth-of-institutional-racism, accessed 27 September 2020.

33. See, for examples, Wright and Taylor, 'Cameron'; Rowena Mason, '300 allegations of Tory Islamophobia sent to equality watchdog', *The Guardian*, 5 March 2020, www.theguardian.com/politics/2020/mar/05/300-allegations-of-tory-islamophobia-sent-to-equality-watchdog, accessed 27 September 2020;

Bethany Rielly, 'Hostile environment is "driving up racism"', *Morning Star*, 4 September 2020, 5.

34. Seumas Milne, 'Britain: Imperial nostalgia', 2 May 2005, https://mondediplo. com/2005/05/02empire, accessed 27 September 2020.

35. Nadita Sharma, *Home Rule: National Sovereignty and the Separation of Natives and Migrants* (Durham, NC: Duke University Press, 2020).

36. Jonathan Liew, 'As England's multicultural team celebrated at Lord's, it felt as if we were getting somewhere at last', *New Statesman*, 17 July 2019, www.newst atesman.com/politics/sport/2019/07/england-s-multicultural-team-celebrated-lord-s-it-felt-if-we-were-getting, accessed 9 October 2020.

37. Eoin Morgan, 'My pride at leading these multi-cultural World Cup winners . . . we were a team that derived strength from diversity, and represented the best of England', *Daily Mail*, 2 April 2019, www.dailymail.co.uk/sport/cricket/article-8177549/EOIN-MORGAN-pride-leading-multi-cultural-World-Cup-winners. html, accessed 9 October 2020.

38. Firdose Moonda, 'England's Cricket World Cup squad shows us that there is unity in diversity', 26 June 2019, www.soas.ac.uk/blogs/study/england-cricket-unity-in-diversity, accessed 13 October 2020.

39. Peter Oborne, 'British, Muslim and proud: Cricketer Moeen Ali shows how faith is no barrier to batting for England', 2 October 2017, www.middleeasteye.net/ opinion/british-muslim-and-proud-cricketer-moeen-ali-shows-how-faith-no-barrier-batting-england, accessed 9 October 2020.

40. Sameer Rahim, 'It isn't an easy time to be a British Muslim: Cricket helps', *New York Times*, 14 November 2018 www.nytimes.com/2018/11/14/opinion/ moeen-ali-islamophobia-britain-cricket-.html, accessed 12 October 2020.

41. Stephen Wagg, 'Muck or nettles: Men, masculinity and myth in Yorkshire cricket', in *Sporting Heroes of the North*, eds. Stephen Wagg and Dave Russell (Newcastle-upon-Tyne: Northumbria Press, 2010), 1–29.

42. See Thomas Fletcher, 'Aye, but it were wasted on thee: Cricket, British Asians, ethnic identities and the "magical recovery of community"', *Sociological Research Online*, 2 December 2011, https://journals.sagepub.com/doi/abs/10.5153/ sro.2468, accessed 12 October 2020; Thomas Fletcher, ' "All Yorkshiremen are from Yorkshire, but some are more 'Yorkshire' than others": British Asians and the myths of Yorkshire cricket', *Sport in Society* 15, no. 2 (2012): 227–245.

43. Thomas Fletcher and Karl Spracklen, 'Cricket, drinking and exclusion of British Pakistani Muslims?', *Ethnic and Racial Studies* 37, no. 8 (2014): 1310–1327.

44. Aarti Ratna, Stefan Lawrence, and Janine Partington, ' "Getting inside the wicket": Strategies for the social inclusion of British Pakistani Muslim cricketers', *Journal of Policy Research in Tourism, Leisure and Events* 8, no. 1 (2016): 1–17.

45. Kevin Hylton, Jonathan Long, Thomas Fletcher, and Neil Ormerod, 'South Asian communities and cricket (Bradford and Leeds)' (Leeds: Leeds Beckett University Institute for Sport, Physical Activity and Leisure, 2015).

46. Malcolm, *Globalizing Cricket*, 114–119.

47. Ibid., 123.

48. Michael Henderson, 'You're playing for England, not your religion', *Daily Telegraph*, 13 June 2014, www.telegraph.co.uk/news/religion/10897999/Youre-playing-for-England-Moeen-Ali-not-your-religion.html, accessed 27 April 2021.

49. Alastair McLellan (ed.), *Nothing Sacred: The New Cricket Culture* (London: Two Heads Publishing, 1996).

50. In *The Guardian*, 19 August 2009 and quoted in Malcolm, *Globalizing Cricket*, 139.

51. Malcolm, *Globalizing Cricket*, 133; for a full discussion, see ibid., 124–139.

52. David Skelton, 'English cricket only has itself to blame for the forgotten World Cup', *New Statesman*, 1 July 2019, www.newstatesman.com/politics/sport/2019/07/english-cricket-only-has-itself-blame-forgotten-world-cup, accessed 13 October 2020.

53. Skelton, 'English cricket'.

54. Zarah Sultana, 'You can't fight racism without fighting capitalism', *Tribune* (summer 2020): 47–49, 47.

55. Marylebone Cricket Club, owners of Lords cricket ground and cricket's governing body until 1997.

56. Nick Hoult, 'Exclusive: MCC removes Benjamin Aislabie artwork from public display due to slave-owning past', *Daily Telegraph*, 10 June 2020, www.telegraph.co.uk/cricket/2020/06/10/exclusive-mcc-removesbenjamin-aislabie-artwork-public-display, accessed 13 October 2020.

57. Nick Hoult, 'MCC have opportunity to confront Benjamin Aislabie's slave-trade link and use as a tool to educate', *Daily Telegraph*, 11 June 2020, www.telegraph.co.uk/cricket/2020/06/11/mcc-have-opportunity-confront-benjamin-aislabies-slave-trade, accessed 13 October 2020.

58. See https://wisden.com/stories/ecb-chief-support-of-black-lives-matter-message-not-political, 2 July 2020, accessed 13 October 2020.

59. See Wagg, 'Towards a safer past'.

60. 'Stumped—Racism in cricket', *BBC Sounds*, 13 June 2020.

61. Stephan Shemilt, 'Michael Carberry: "I don't expect anything from the ECB on racism"', 12 June 2020, www.bbc.co.uk/sport/cricket/53027054, accessed 13 October 2020.

62. Barney Ronay, 'Jobs for the boys attitude highlights English cricket's failings on race', *The Guardian*, 20 June 2020, www.theguardian.com/sport/blog/2020/jun/20/jobs-for-the-boys-attitude-highlights-english-crickets-failings-on-race, accessed 13 October 2020.

63. Ashley Gray, *The Unforgiven: Mercenaries or Missionaries?* (Worthing: Pitch Publishing, 2020).

64. Barney Ronay, 'Lonsdale Skinner: "Most of the racism came from the committee room"', *The Observer*, 26 July 2020, www.theguardian.com/sport/2020/jul/26/lonsdale-skinner-most-racism-committee-room-cricket-interview, accessed 14 October 2020.

65. The passenger ship the *Empire Windrush* docked at Tilbury in 1948 carrying over 400 migrants to the UK from Jamaica. The term 'Windrush generation' is a catch-all term referring to Caribbean migrants to Britain between 1948 and 1971.

66. See Ronay, 'Lonsdale Skinner'; Amelia Gentleman, 'Former Middlesex fast bowler in immigration limbo for seven years', *The Guardian*, 16 April 2018, www.theguardian.com/uk-news/2018/apr/16/former-middlesex-fast-bowler-in-immigration-limbo-for-seven-years, accessed 14 October 2020; Amelia Gentleman, 'Windrush victim dies with no apology or compensation', *The Guardian*, 22 June 2019, www.theguardian.com/uk-news/2019/jun/22/windrush-victim-richard-stewart-dies-with-no-apology-or-compensation, accessed 14 October 2020.

67. *Morning Star*, 'We want black lives to matter now', 9 July 2020, 16.

68. *Morning Star*, 23 July 2020, 16.

69. May Bulman, 'Home Office agrees to scrap "racist" visa application algorithm', *The Independent*, 4 August 2020, www.independent.co.uk/news/uk/home-news/home-office-visa-application-algorithm-racist-a9654016.html, accessed 14 October 2020.

70. Paul Gilroy, Foreword to Ben Carrington and Ian McDonald (eds.), *Race, Sport and British Society* (London: Routledge, 2001), xi–xvii, xv.

71. Matthew Engel, 'Matthew Engel on the decline of English cricket', *Financial Times*, 5 July 2013, www.ft.com/content/e63197a0-e441-11e2-91a3-00144feabdc0, accessed 15 October 2020.

72. Alexandra Topping, ' "I've a new lease of life": Why women are turning to cricket in droves', *The Guardian*, 26 December 2017, www.theguardian.com/sport/2017/dec/26/women-cricket-droves-new-lease-life-england-women-team, accessed 15 October 2020.

73. Michael Henderson, *That Will Be England Gone: The Last Summer of Cricket* (London: Constable, 2020), 62.

74. Christopher Martin-Jenkins, *CMJ: A Cricketing Life* (London: Simon and Schuster, 2013), 198.

75. Henderson, *That Will Be England Gone*, 5–6.

76. Ibid., 97.

77. Ibid., 132.

78. Ibid., 134–135.

79. Ibid., 6.

80. Ibid., 97.

81. Den Dirs, 'English cricket's real problem', 23 May 2007, http://news.bbc.co.uk/sport1/hi/cricket/england/6398835.stm, accessed 19 October 2020.

82. Douglas Henderson, 'State of play: Cricket is in crisis in all schools', *The Cricketer*, 26 November 2019, www.thecricketer.com/Topics/news/state_of_play_cricket_is_in_crisis_in_all_schools.html, accessed 27 April 2021.

83. Melanie Phillips, *All Must Have Prizes* (London: Little, Brown, 1996).

84. Ted Wragg, 'All Must Have Prizes by Melanie Phillips Little, Brown pounds 17.50', *The Independent*, 13 September 1996, www.independent.co.uk/voices/all-must-have-prizes-by-melanie-phillips-little-brown-pounds-1750-1363087.html, accessed 19 October 2020.

85. Matthew Jenkin, 'Does competitive sport in school do more harm than good?', *The Guardian*, 29 January 2015, www.theguardian.com/teacher-network/2015/jan/29/competitive-school-sport-harm, accessed 19 October 2020.

86. See Dirs, 'English cricket's real problem'.

87. Henderson, *That Will Be England Gone*, 97.

88. Jo Revill and Anushka Asthana, 'Ministers attacked over school fields sale', *The Observer*, 30 March 2008, www.theguardian.com/education/2008/mar/30/schools.uk, accessed 19 October 2020.

89. Darren Talbot, 'Cricket in state schools in the UK', 5 June 2008, https://bleacherreport.com/articles/27505-cricket-in-state-schools-in-the-uk, accessed 19 October 2020.

90. 'Stumped—Racism in Cricket', *BBC Sounds*, 13 June 2020.

91. See Malcolm, *Globalizing Cricket*, 117.

92. See Richard Garner, 'Exclusive: Only half of county cricketers come from UK state schools', *The Independent*, 8 July 201,3 www.independent.co.uk/news/education/education-news/exclusive-only-half-county-cricketers-come-uk-state-schools-8695905.html, accessed 19 October 2020.

93. Huw Turberville, 'It's now or never for Asian involvement in UK cricket, says Lord Patel', *The Cricketer*, December 2017, www.thecricketer.com/Topics/domestic/it%27s_now_or_never_for_asian_involvement_in_uk_cricket,_says_lord_patel.html, accessed 19 October 2020.

94. Chris Waters, 'Lament for the English game that is now gone forever', *Yorkshire Post*, 18 May 2020, www.yorkshirepost.co.uk/sport/cricket/lament-english-game-now-gone-forever-2856121, accessed 20 October 2020.

95. Don Mosey, *Fred: Then and Now* (London: Kingswood Press, 1991), 135–136.

96. Henderson, *That Will Be England Gone*, 10, 44.

97. Jonathan Raban, 'Books: Mr Miseryguts—Philip Larkin's letters show all the grim humour that was a hallmark of his great poems, but, as the years pass, they also chart the true depths of his misanthropy and despair', *The Independent*, 18 October 1992, www.independent.co.uk/arts-entertainment/books-mr-miseryguts-philip-larkins-letters-show-all-the-grim-humour-that-was-a-hallmark-of-his-great-1558190.html, accessed 20 October 2020.

98. Gargi Bhattacharyya et al., *Empire's Endgame: Racism and the British State* (London: Pluto Press, 2021).

99. Bhattacharyya et al., *Empire's Endgame*, 161–170.

100. Major was president of Surrey County Cricket Club during 2000–2001 and the author of *More Than a Game: The Story of Cricket's Early Years* (London: HarperCollins, 2008). In an interview in 2019 he described cricket as a 'universal

healer'—a palliative, however, denied to many state school children during his premiership; see Rich Evans, 'Exclusive: "Cricket is a universal healer"—Sir John Major', 7 May 2021, https://wisden.com/stories/interviews/exclusive-cricket-is-a-universal-healer-sir-john-major, accessed 29 April 2021.

101. Henderson, *That Will Be England Gone*, 110.

4

Indo-Pak Cricketing Relations in the Shadow of the Rise of Hindutva

Ali Khan

Introduction

After the Partition of British India in 1947, a remarkably complex, undulating, and often unpredictable relationship developed between the two newly formed nations of India and Pakistan. The support at the cricketing level in the face of wider political hostility started with the Board of Control for Cricket in India (BCCI) supporting Pakistan's application for entry to the Imperial Cricket Council, the ruling body for cricket at the time. This resulted in Pakistan playing its first Test match against India in 1952. Throughout this first tour, the Pakistan team were warmly received wherever they played in India. In subsequent tours, India to Pakistan and Pakistan to India, the general atmosphere remained positive. Crowds were welcoming and the relations between the players were good. The aggressive rhetoric of the nation-states had not yet filtered down to the common people who remained largely willing to embrace a process of reconciliation after the horrors of Partition.

This remained the case even after a sevente-year break in relations which followed a second war over Kashmir in 1965 and the 1971 war which saw the secession of East Pakistan. In fact, immediately after the resumption in relations in 1979 and throughout the 1980s, the BCCI and the Board of Control for Cricket in Pakistan (BCCP) developed a strong working relationship, forming the Asian Cricket Conference in 1983, winning the joint bid to host the 1987 World Cup in the subcontinent,[1] and then cooperating closely again to win the rights to hold the 1996

Ali Khan, *Indo-Pak Cricketing Relations in the Shadow of the Rise of Hindutva* In: *Cricket and Nationhood in the Twenty-First Century*. Edited by: Souvik Naha, Oxford University Press. © Oxford University Press 2024. DOI: 10.1093/9780191982576.003.0005 and 2011 World Cups. In 1996, they were joined by Sri Lanka in what turned out to be an illustration of the close partnership forged by South Asia's cricket administrators. But by 1989, significant and wide-ranging regional and global changes were occurring which changed the India–Pakistan relationship. It is to this crucial period in the 1990s to which I turn.

This chapter looks at how the overarching relationship between the nations impacted their cricketing interactions from the 1990s onwards. I argue that while in the past cricketing relations between the two countries have been warm, supportive, and amicable, contrasting markedly with the narrative of Indo-Pak hostility, this appears to have become less the case, particularly in the shadow of the rise of Hindutva in India.

Rising Nationalism

The Indian historian Ramachandra Guha argues that up until the late 1970s, 'win or lose sporting exchanges could be understood in a spirit of brotherliness, bhai bhai-ism'.[2] Many Pakistanis supported India in their 1983 World Cup win and in 1992 Indians reciprocated for Pakistan's win.[3] The scenario began to change in the 1990s. In India, the transition was all the more challenging because it came at a time when the country was going through its own social, economic, and political revolutions. The 1990s was the decade when the 'so-called Nehruvian consensus, based on secularism, socialism, and nonalignment', was finally put to rest.[4] In its place, along with liberalization, came the rise of Hindutva—the idea that the essence of Indianness is Hinduism, and therefore to be a true Indian is to be a Hindu.[5] Liberalization and economic change fed extremism as the emergence of a newly affluent middle class—which had earlier felt stymied, resentful, and disconnected by the Nehruvian 'third path' between communism and capitalism[6]—aligned perfectly with the pent-up desire of this class to express its wealth and power in extreme Hindu politics. McDonald further argues that Hindutva arose out of a sense of deprivation among Hindus—that the country was suffering because of a supposed favouring by the state of minority groups in particular.[7] Reinforcing this point, Hansen writes that Hindutva portrayed the Hindu community as the silent majority whose patience had finally run out.[8] There is therefore a simmering anti-Muslim hostility within the Hindutva ideology which is deepened by the fact that Muslims ruled over parts of the subcontinent for centuries. In addition, it has been argued that Hindutva, in its attempt to protect upper-caste privilege and prevent class solidarity, pits the mass of lower-caste Hindus against the Muslim population, many of whom are drawn from the lower castes themselves.[9] The 1990s also saw the start of the Kashmir insurgency, the destruction of the Babri Mosque in Ayodhya in 1992, the Mumbai riots (described by Metcalf[10] as an anti-Muslim pogrom), and the retaliatory bombings that followed. These communal incidents exacerbated tensions between Muslims and Hindus in India and further strained India–Pakistan relations.

The ideology of Hindutva grew in strength alongside the spectacular rise of the Bharatiya Janata Party (BJP), the two feeding off each other's success. By the 1990s, the Hindu nationalist movement started to monopolize the front pages of Indian newspapers when the BJP rose to power. From two seats in the Lok Sabha, the lower house of the Indian parliament, in 1984, the BJP increased its tally to 161 in 1996 when it became the largest party in that assembly. Two years later, they formed a coalition government, an achievement that was repeated after the 1999 mid-term elections. In Maharashtra in 1995, the Congress lost power for the first time ever to the BJP and its ally, the Shiv Sena. For the first time in Indian history, Hindu nationalism had managed to assume power.[11] Nationalism and national identity were remoulded from identity based on the Nehruvian Consensus—a political project contoured by the values of socialism, democracy, secularism, and inclusiveness of all ethno-religious and language groups—to a right-wing, chauvinistic, and anti-Pakistan/ Muslim ideology. The collapse of the Congress and the concomitant rise of the BJP meant that there was a significant ideological shift in the battle for the soul of Indian nationalism.[12]

The year 2002 saw more communal riots in Godhra, Gujarat. The rising communal tensions also put increasing pressure on Indian Muslims, calling into question their loyalty to India; in the 1990s, Bal Thackeray, leader of the Hindu nationalist political party the Shiv Sena, argued that Indian Muslims must prove that they were not Pakistani sympathizers and not anti-national by supporting India rather than Pakistan in cricket: 'I want them with tears in their eyes every time India loses to

Pakistan.'[13] Sengupta argues that the one aspect of politics that has been singularly affected by sport is nationalism (and national identities)—and that sports have the ability above all to tell us about who we are, and even who we want to be.[14] International cricket, because of its central position in civil society and as a significant element of popular culture, became one of the most effective forums for articulating Hindu chauvinist and communal ideologies.[15] An emerging and altered nationalism and cricket would thus increasingly influence one another, as well as the relations between India and Pakistan. India–Pakistan matches progressively became occasions to show nationalistic sentiment.[16]

A glimpse of changing relations could be seen in the quarter final of the 1996 World Cup between India and Pakistan in Bangalore. The encounter would be their first meeting in India or in Pakistan in seven years. Public support for the rivalry to resume led to the Shiv Sena 'allowing' the match to proceed.[17] Mike Marqusee, the American writer, journalist, and political activist, who wrote extensively on cricket in the subcontinent, observed that despite political tensions the Indian media took a positive approach to the renewal of Indo-Pak cricketing ties and urged fans to welcome the visitors. On the morning of the match, the newspapers were full of stories about players from the two countries mixing freely and of Hindustani–Pakistani *bhai bhai* (brotherhood). Cricket and the fans were still somewhat insulated from the wider political environment—so that, while many of the same papers in their news coverage and editorial comments struck anti-Pakistani poses, backed nuclear weapons and high defence spending, and took a tough line on 'Pakistani terrorism' and Kashmir, on this cricketing occasion they urged readers to celebrate the India–Pakistan contest in a friendly, if decidedly partisan, spirit. They did not, however, challenge the underpinning logic of Indo-Pakistan hostility.[18] There was also the positive impact of the South Asian rivals jointly holding the World Cup and of the solidarity they showed in their support of Sri Lanka when a joint Indo-Pak team played in Colombo following the suicide bombing that had threatened Sri Lanka as a venue for the tournament.

But by the time the match was underway, the crowd had grown increasingly hostile. McDonald speaks of the Hindu nationalist influence in cricket being increasingly evident through the partisan nature of crowds.[19] Marqusee adds weight to this finding when he refers to the atmosphere during the match as being characterized by 'hate-filled chauvinism with communal overtones'.[20] India's 'victory precipitated an orgy of national celebrations, which seemed less about progressing to the semi-final, and more about victory over a nation considered a political, military, social, and economic inferior'.[21] McDonald goes on to refer to an incident that the historian Ramchandra Guha witnessed when he stood to applaud the exit from international cricket of one of Pakistan's great batsmen, Javed Miandad, after his dismissal, which effectively secured the match for India:

> 'What are you clapping him for' yelled a man behind me. Through a long evening I had stood the crowd's shameful partisanship, now I responded. 'You should clap him too. He is truly a great player, and we shall never see him again'. The short definitive reply—'Thank God I'll never see the bastard again'.[22]

The Indian team also began to develop a more aggressive posture, reflecting the changes occurring in the wider society. This was in stark contrast to earlier encounters, particularly with Pakistan and especially in the 1980s. Not only had Imran Khan's fast-bowling prowess shattered the famed Indian batting in 1982–1983, but Javed Miandad inflicted a near fatal blow when, in 1986, he won the Austral–Asia cup final against India by hitting the last ball of the match for six. The winning hit became legend on both sides of the border and gave Pakistan a massive psychological advantage which was to last for more than a decade—Pakistan won twenty-one of their next twenty-six encounters against India.

In keeping with the stereotypes promoted by the advocates of Hindutva, Indian fans perceived the Pakistanis as belligerent, aggressive, and unashamedly nationalistic in contrast to the docile and apologetic Indians who repeatedly buckled under pressure. Some even claimed that Pakistan's religious identity gave them an advantage on the cricket field. Pakistan were helped by a series of contributing factors. Firstly, several Pakistani players played in the extremely competitive World Series Cricket rebel league, where they locked horns with some of the best cricketers in the world. Along with regular stints in the English county system, this provided these cricketers with a new-found competitiveness and self-belief as well as a hunger to win against any opposition. They also, in Mushtaq Mohammad and later Imran Khan, had two leaders with an attacking mindset that moulded teams in their own image. Pakistan's more aggressive approach was reinforced by the press, particularly the English press, labelling them as a team that would do anything to win, including cheat.[23] Finally, particularly in comparison to India, Pakistan boasted a series of hostile fast bowlers more suited to aggression than India's guileful slow bowlers. At the time, Pakistan was more suited to an aggressive mindset.

The narrative in India became one where in order to match the enemy, India would have to emulate them; it would have to rediscover itself as a Hindu nation. One of the major themes of Hindutva has been the need for Hindu aggression to compensate for centuries of deprivation, insult, and injury at the hands of Muslims.[24] Christophe Jaffrelot in fact argues that there was a noticeable 'inferiority complex' among the Hindi majority of India vis-a-vis not only India's Muslim 'other' but also other players in the international arena.[25] The economic and political rise of India and its association with a strong Hindutva-inspired identity began to address and reduce the 'inferiority complex' issue. It was also assisted significantly by the emergence of a number of outstanding players and an intelligent and ambitious leader in Sourav Ganguly in the year 2000. One could argue that India have always produced outstanding cricketers. However, all of the aforementioned factors combined gave rise to a new self-belief in the psyche of the Indian cricket team. In fact, from the middle of the first decade of the 2000s, the roles have reversed—with India now holding a significant psychological advantage over Pakistan. Since 2012 the two teams have met in nineteen one-day and T20 internationals. India has won thirteen of these. Overall, Pakistan still leads the rivalry seventy-five to sixty-one, highlighting their earlier dominance.

Guha and Sengupta both suggest that the rise of cricket nationalism in India during the 1990s can be linked to the rise of Hindu chauvinism seen at the same time.[26] The Indian 'self' was increasingly equated with the Hindu 'self' which contrasted with Pakistan as India's 'Islamic other'. The hardening of identities and their distinctive opposition coupled with the political tensions between the neighbours strengthened the view that the Islamic nation of Pakistan was an inveterate enemy of Hindu India and no longer merely an arch-rival. We had reached a point where India–Pakistan matches were 'war minus the shooting', a phrase used by the Indian media to describe the Bangalore match.[27] In time, this narrative would begin to filter down to the larger population with the more damaging impression that the Pakistani nation or the people as a whole were inimically disposed towards India, and that India too should resort to similar comprehensive hostility in order to bring Pakistani hostility to heel. Accordingly, any triumph over Pakistan in any sphere of life is taken as a cause of celebration; any setback is seen as a national humiliation.[28] This in fact makes the Pakistan tour of India in 1999 and the tours to Pakistan and India between 2004 and 2006 particularly striking in how they defied expectations.

A False Spring: 1999 Pakistan Tour to India

By 1998, deteriorating Indo-Pak relations would be pushed to the brink. In May 1998, India and Pakistan conducted tit-for-tat nuclear tests, all the while exchanging fire across the border. Nawaz Sharif, then Pakistan's prime minister, accused the Indian government of 'taking South Asia to the brink of war'.[29] In response, then Indian prime minister Atal Bihari Vajpayee warned Pakistan that 'India would use a firm hand to respond to any attack on its border' and that the Indian army would 'repulse the nefarious designs of Pakistan'.[30] The turnaround in relations occurred in September 1998 when the two prime ministers bonded over lunch in New York.[31] A raft of confidence-building measures followed. It was decided that foreign secretary-level talks would be held between India and Pakistan, and a direct bus service between Lahore and Delhi was proposed.[32] When Sharif returned to Pakistan, he pushed for the Pakistan cricket team to tour India in January and February of 1999—ten years after the last Test series that they had played.[33] The diplomatic importance that Sharif attached to the tour can be gauged by the fact that he requested former foreign secretary (later Pakistan Cricket Board (PCB) chairman) Shaharyar Khan to be the manager for the tour.

In India, the Shiv Sena announced a hostile boycott of the tour—as they had throughout the 1990s. As part of a ruling coalition, they also threatened to withdraw parliamentary support if the series were not cancelled.[34] Prime Minister Vajpayee's BJP, the leading party in the governing coalition, refused to give in to the threats even after the Shiv Sena damaged the Delhi pitch, attacked the BCCI offices in Mumbai, mounted a noisy demonstration outside the Pakistan Embassy in New Delhi, and threatened to release venomous snakes in the grounds where Pakistan played.[35] However, just as the Pakistan team landed in Delhi, they found the threats had been withdrawn. From that point onwards the tour proceeded to become an enormous cricketing and public relations success.

The groundswell of public acclaim as the tour progressed provided the ideal stage in both countries for Vajpayee's historic bus journey to Lahore in February 1999. It also brings up the contrary nature of India and Pakistan's relationship. The rise of extremist ideologies had escalated in both nations and the states had more often than not continued to trade bellicose statements. And yet, whenever given even a small opportunity, the people on both sides of the border appeared desperate to live in peace and amity. The 1999 tour

> provided a unique opportunity to humanize, if not normalize the strained relations between the two nations. The cricketing skills on display, the emotions on the field, all draw people on one side towards the other side—and the appreciation can sometimes go beyond national pride.[36]

Unfortunately, in spring 1999, Pakistan's army instigated a limited war in Kargil[37] and Pakistan and India endured yet another break in cricketing relations between 1999 and 2004.

The Last Opportunity?

As a result of the Kargil episode in 1999, the Government of India reverted to the position that until Pakistan refrained from engaging in military adventures in Kashmir and promoting cross-border terrorism, India should stop playing Pakistan in one-to-one encounters. There were a few bilateral matches in international tournaments on 'neutral' venues. Sengupta, Chatterjee, and Bandyopadhyay all refer to the 2003 India–Pakistan encounter in the 2003 World Cup played in South Africa as indicative of a changed relationship.[38] By 2003, the nuclear rivalry, the Kargil war, and the skirmishes that nearly led to a war in 2002 had increased antagonisms between the two countries. The partisanship of the crowds made for an uglier, more confrontational atmosphere in the ground—and when India defeated Pakistan it was followed by a

> deluge of nationalistic triumphalism as top BJP leaders such as Prime Minister Atul Bihari Vajpayee, Deputy Prime Minister Lal Krishna Advani promptly sent their congratulations. The defeat sent Pakistan crashing out of the World Cup which appeared to make it all the sweeter.[39]

Chatterjee quotes a middle-aged Indian waving a tricolour following India's win: 'That's it. I don't care if India loses every single match from here on. The World Cup is over for me. We have won. We have thrashed the Pakis.'[40] Whatever South Asian solidarity had existed up until the 1990s seemed to have been destroyed by Kargil and the continued bad blood that followed. And then in the kind of turnaround that had been seen in the past, relations unexpectedly took a turn for the better.

Vajpayee, encouraged by Musharraf's commitment to clamp down on cross-border infiltration, again offered a raft of confidence-building measures which Pakistan responded to in kind. In this dramatically improved atmosphere, the resumption of cricketing relations was announced with the India tour of Pakistan scheduled for March 2004. Famously, Vajpayee would urge the Indian team: 'Khel hi nahin, dil bhi jitiye' ('Not only the game, win hearts as well'). The placards being waved around while Vajpayee met the team featured messages such as 'Best of Luck' and 'Atal ne diya cricket ka uphaar, India–Pakistan sadbhavana ka prachar' ('Atal's cricket gift spreads harmony in India and Pakistan').[41]

In fact, the tour was an unprecedented success in terms of bilateral relations, the consequences of which would be felt for years. The cricket was exciting and the players exemplary in their behaviour and sportsmanship. Moreover, the tour allowed the first real people-to-people contact for fifteen years. The time that had elapsed meant a generation of Indians and Pakistanis had not interacted directly. Instead, state narratives on both sides had fed sensationalized accounts, leading to a polarizing of their images as Hindu and Muslim opposites. As walls went up, a new generation had grown up knowing each other only through media stereotypes and the propaganda that was spewed out by politicians. The previous generation of Indians and Pakistanis at least had the experience and interaction of having lived together. People traffic between the countries had also been more frequent in the past. Those linkages were now loosening, and this had led to Pakistan and India viewing themselves as enemies that were ill-disposed towards each another rather than merely being arch-rivals.

Despite all this, the efforts of the BCCP (now re-christened the PCB), the media, and an improved political environment paid dividends. The spirit of bonhomie and bridge-building had been taken to heart and it was the response from the Pakistani public that set the optimistic tone for the tour. In the very first match in Karachi which India won narrowly, the crowd erupted in spontaneous applause for the Indian team. Rahul Bhattacharya wrote:

> The mind went back to the beautiful occasion in Chennai in 1999, when Wasim Akram led his team for a victory lap to a standing ovation after a startling win in a stunning test . . . Indeed, the applause at Karachi had been far more spontaneous than at Chennai.[42]

The outstanding success of the Karachi One Day International (ODI) set the tenor for the remaining series. Everywhere the Indian team went, they were welcomed with immense enthusiasm. This success also appeared to spur a rush of Indian fans to seek visas for the tour. It also settled the Indian players' nerves as security concerns eased to the extent that the teams were happy to socialize with one another. However, in an indication that the Indian psyche had changed since the 1980s and that years of 'inferiority' were being erased by a new, more confident India, Bhattacharya quotes a Pakistani cricketer saying that in the past:

> The Indians were polite compared to us. Who was there to abuse? There was one Jadeja. And there was one Prabhakar. Sidhu was also a little like us. He's Punjabi after all! But this Indian team is very different. They are aggressive.[43]

Contrast this with what the Pakistan captain Mushtaq Mohammad had stated about the Indian team when they toured Pakistan in 1978–1979:

> The Indians were very mild in comparison. When they appealed against us they almost appeared apologetic while asking the umpire

the question. Our appealing was hostile and aggressive and plenty of bad language was used in between. It definitely upset the more calmer-natured Indians, who were gentlemen and great cricketers but very, very soft.[44]

Again, the general public's attitude could not be ignored. An enabling environment had been provided by the governments, the boards, and the players—and the response from the general public was extraordinary. Decades of hostility, confrontations, and enmity had led only to suffering, poverty, and hardship for the populations of both countries.[45] As people from across the border interacted, they found a very different reality to what they had expected and a realization of commonalities rather than difference. Jaswant Singh, in his book on Jinnah, says of Pakistan, India, and Bangladesh: 'we have all been born of Partition: we were one, India, Pakistan and Bangladesh, up till the third quarter of 1947, now we are three separated entities, but are we truly all that different?'[46] For people who shared a common history, culture, and language, here was a vision of what peace could bring. The public grabbed it with both hands.

While the heights of the first tour were never achieved again, the subsequent series of 2004, 2005, 2006, and 2007 continued to stimulate goodwill between the countries. There was a definite change in the way that Indians and Pakistanis viewed each other, with cricket being used as an important vehicle for this change in perceptions. Marqusee, who watched the 1996 World Cup on the subcontinent and returned to watch Pakistan's tour of India in 2005, also remarked how the ambience had transformed. He had castigated the Bangalore crowd of 1996 for its jingoistic nationalism,[47] and he found in Bangalore in 2005 handwritten signs welcoming the tourists, praising Indo-Pak friendship and declaring that cricket is the path to peace.[48] On the same tour he states that at Mohali, the change in atmosphere was palpable, '[a]nd it cannot be credited to either politicians or the media—they have merely followed the lead from below, from the bases of both societies, where the desire for South Asian peace has overcome decades of fearful mythologies.'[49] For Marqusee, South Asian cricket remained 'a reliable barometer of the society in which it is played. In the Indo-Pak series, it has provided a vehicle for the expression of a hunger for south Asian harmony that has been gestating for years.'[50]

Cricket thus provided a multi-level tool for improving relations between India and Pakistan. It provided conversational space for Indian and Pakistani leaders to meet and have discussions on areas of political conflict. It also provided the largest opportunity for people-to-people contact between 2004 and 2007. The improvement in relations led to a raft of cultural exchanges. In 2005, the first passengers from either side of the border crossed divided Kashmir as the landmark bus service across the ceasefire line dividing the Indian- and Pakistani-controlled Kashmir got underway.[51] The ban on Indian films was lifted in 2008[52] in Pakistan after a period of over forty years and a number of Pakistani artists began working in Bollywood and some Indian actors appeared in Pakistani films.[53] Unfortunately, from the high of 2008, a series of setbacks would send India–Pakistan relations into a potentially irreversible tailspin.

The Point of No Return?

On 26 November 2008, ten Islamic militants carried out twelve coordinated shooting and bombing attacks lasting four days across Mumbai which took the lives of 165 people.[54] The incident caused Indo-Pak relations to plunge and India's proposed tour to Pakistan, which was already under threat due to security concerns, was immediately called off.[55] The Indian media and public demanded a strong response. Cultural and sporting links were significantly downgraded and the goodwill among the public for Pakistan dissipated rapidly. Yusuf argues that the potency of Mumbai in India dwarfed what Kargil managed in its aftermath.[56] He is also right in highlighting that a whole generation of young Indians had grown up who saw Pakistan primarily as a nuisance. Pakistan equalled Mumbai in their minds. This was not the Partition generation that had known the 'other' and had experienced a shared history, culture, and legacy. This was a generation that saw each other as enemies, ill-disposed towards each other, different from each other. There would be little if any support for reaching out to Pakistan. All this while the Hindutva project was contributing to new aggressive nationalism which found its ideal home under Modi's new regime.

Four months after Mumbai, twelve gunmen attacked a bus carrying the Sri Lankan cricket team to the Qaddafi stadium in Lahore. Seven cricketers and an assistant coach were injured. In another vehicle, a driver was killed and a Pakistani umpire was shot twice. Eight Pakistanis lost their lives.[57] If the attack was calamitous in itself, the response by the PCB and the government was nothing short of catastrophic even in a period when chaos reigned in Pakistan.[58] Ijaz Butt, the chairman of the PCB at this difficult time, then proceeded to dismantle whatever sympathy Pakistan may have had following the attack. Far from offering condolences to those who lost their lives or accepting the PCB's responsibility for not providing the foolproof security they had promised, he went ahead and proclaimed that there had been no security failure and that it was a 'big lie' that there were no police to protect the Sri Lankans and match officials.[59] In the weeks that followed, Pakistan was stripped of its hosting rights for the 2011 World Cup with the International Cricket Council (ICC) resolving that all matches would be played in India, Sri Lanka, and Bangladesh.

Pakistan's offer to host their share of matches in a neutral venue such as the United Arab Emirates was rejected by the co-hosts India, Sri Lanka, and Bangladesh, who all argued that a neutral country would dilute the concept of the event being held in the subcontinent.[60] More damaging was the PCB's attempt to move the entire tournament to 2015 through veiled allusions to poor security throughout South Asia. Ijaz Butt's statement included references to 'Sri Lanka's long running civil war, Bangladesh recently facing a mutiny by its armed forces and India's relocation of IPL [Indian Premier League] due to the law and order situation'.[61] For obvious reasons this further angered India, Bangladesh, and Sri Lanka.[62] The Asian boards withdrew support for Pakistan. According to Bose:

> [Butt felt that the Indians took] advantage of the terrorist strike in Lahore. He made public and private comments blaming the Indians for isolating Pakistan's cricket and forcing it [Pakistan] to play all its home matches overseas . . . I am told the Indian cricket officials are not on speaking terms with Butt.[63]

It is unsurprising, then, that a supportive relationship between the two boards was transformed into a hostile one. Months later, a spat with Lalit Modi, the Indian board official who was responsible for the IPL at the time, also led to Butt ordering Pakistani players to be withdrawn from the cash-rich IPL on security grounds. Thus, while many of the world's best cricketers played alongside one another in the IPL, Pakistan's cricketers have not played that tournament since 2009. Pakistan was on a quick path to isolation from world cricket—and while the overall security environment of the country was beyond the PCB's control, the board's policies hastened Pakistan's seclusion precisely at a time when they most needed the support of their Asian neighbours.

In 2014, the BJP (led by Narendra Modi, the hardliner Hindu leader) won the Indian national elections. Modi's new vision for India, the coming to fruition of the Hindutva project, the effect of the Mumbai attacks, a burgeoning and increasingly nationalistic media, and rampant commercialization—all these factors combined to produce an environment that was not only not conducive for better India–Pakistan cricketing relations but was also in fact progressively hostile to any improvements. Pakistan's own policies towards India during this period added to creating an antagonistic environment.

Modi's initial overtures to Pakistan—Prime Minister Nawaz Sharif was invited and attended Modi's swearing in[64] and Modi made a surprise visit to meet Sharif in Lahore in December 2015 on his way back from Afghanistan[65]—led to a warming in relations. But almost immediately after the Sharif–Modi meeting at the end of 2015, a suspected Pakistan-based terrorist group attacked an Indian airbase in Pathankot, Punjab, killing seven Indian soldiers. At this juncture, the better bilateral relations up until that point led to a decision by both countries to collaborate on a joint investigation of the attack.[66] The attack, though, was followed in July 2016 by the killing of the pro-separatist Kashmiri leader Burhan Wani[67] in a gunfight with the Indian army, leading to days of deadly violence in Kashmir[68] and a sharp deterioration in Indo-Pak relations.[69] In September 2016, militants crossed the Line of Control and attacked an army base in Indian-administered Kashmir, killing seventeen soldiers. This attack on the Indian army base in Kashmir signalled a watershed in India's policy towards Pakistan. Departing from India's past strategic restraint, Modi ordered strikes across the Line of Control in response to the attack.[70] There were other escalations as well, particularly along the Line of Control where a heavy Indian counter-bombardment policy was being implemented.

Soon after the attack on the army camp, it appears that Narendra Modi's government, building on the growing anti-Pakistan sentiment, put in place a policy to isolate Pakistan in every possible sphere—politically, economically, and culturally. In the immediate aftermath of the attack, Modi stated at a rally in India: 'Let the terrorists make no mistake, India will never forget ... We will leave no stone unturned to isolate Pakistan in the world.'[71] In fact, despite the initial warming of the relations between Sharif and Modi, the signs for better relations were already unfavourable. Modi had appointed traditional hardliners on Pakistan to important positions in his cabinet and in associated institutions in order to appease his right-wing constituency and his own ideological convictions. The historian Ramachandra Guha and Nobel Laureate Amartya Sen have both been critical of the BJP government for placing loyalists and Hindu hardliners at the head of major educational and cultural institutions.[72] Both have subsequently been pressured out of positions in Indian educational institutions.[73] Sen was scathing in his criticism of what he calls 'extraordinarily large' interference of the government in academia. 'Nothing in this scale of interference has happened before. Every institution where the government has a formal role is being converted into where the government has a substantive role', he alleged.[74] With hardliners dominating these institutions, there was therefore little chance of or interest in any compromise with Pakistan in political, economic, or cultural spheres. It was also the case that India did not need to compromise; such was the power disparity—economic, political, and with respect to the military—between the two countries.[75]

The BCCI was no exception. And, as McDonald writes, the Hindu nationalist influence was increasingly evident in cricket through, among other things, the occupying of key administrative posts by supporters of Hindutva ideology.[76] In 2016, Anurag Thakur was president of the board, having earlier been the secretary. Thakur was a BJP Member of Parliament and a serving member of the Indian territorial army[77] while heading the BCCI. An indication of the kind of views espoused by him can be gauged from his pronouncements at an election rally in early 2020. In a widely circulated video of the rally, Thakur is seen leading the cheer by saying 'desh ke gaddaron ko', after which the crowd adds a rejoinder, 'goli maro salon ko' ('shoot the traitors')—a slogan that has often been used in pro-BJP and anti-Citizenship Amendment Act (CAA) gatherings.[78]

Under new leadership, the Indian board fell in line with Modi's policy. The BCCI had already engineered, in 2014, a highly contentious and controversial change in the governance of the ICC by concentrating power and finances in the hands of the three richest boards—India, Australia, and England,[79] known as the 'Big 3'. The wildly profitable IPL had swelled the board's finances immeasurably.[80] Alongside being the largest market for cricket in the world, the BCCI's economic heft has distorted cricket's finances to such an extent that the health of other boards is increasingly determined by how often their team played India. Opposition to the 'Big 3' initially came from South Africa, Sri Lanka, and Pakistan. But financial incentives broke down the resistance. Pakistan was the only country left resisting, even turning down an offer of three series against India in eight years.[81] Eventually, a change in the PCB regime and a promise of six series against India between 2015 and 2023, four to be hosted by Pakistan, led to Pakistan dropping their opposition.[82]

However, Pakistan and India did not play even a single series, with India consistently arguing that bilateral series were dependent on governmental permission which was not forthcoming. Unlike in 2003, the Indian board, far from being fiscally less secure, was now the financial powerhouse of world cricket. Pakistan continued attempting to persuade the BCCI to honour its commitment but found the response to be lukewarm at best, with the board unwilling to push their government to resume bilateral series. The BCCI also asked the ICC not to group Indian and Pakistan cricket teams together in international tournaments, keeping in mind border tensions between the two countries. Despite these setbacks, the PCB continued to try for a resumption of bilateral cricketing relations. The inability to play at home because of security concerns and India's reluctance to play against Pakistan had placed immense financial strain on the PCB. A resumption in Indo-Pak matches would have reversed this. Ultimately, the Big 3 model itself was revoked[83] and Pakistan subsequently took the BCCI to court for not honouring the Memorandum of Understanding, though the case was later settled in favour of India.[84]

While the decision to form the Big 3 may have been commercially driven, it has allowed the BCCI to isolate Pakistan by demoting them from top-tier decision-making. The 'exclusion' of Pakistani players from the IPL was another way of ensuring Pakistan's continued separation.

While no ban was put in place officially, the IPL teams refrained themselves from buying any Pakistani cricket players during the 2009 auction. None of Pakistan's eleven players were picked up by any of the IPL teams, despite Pakistan being the T20 world champions at the time.[85] The Pakistani players felt this had been a deliberate and humiliating snub. There were strong rumours that the franchises were pressured by the BCCI and the Government of India not to pick Pakistani players. At the time a few IPL team owners, most prominently film-star Shahrukh Khan, raised concerns about the 'ban' on Pakistani players. However, with Khan being a Muslim, his comments in favour of Pakistani players led to a strong backlash by Hindu fanatics who subsequently launched a boycott of his latest film.[86]

Pakistan had already become the pariah of international cricket following the attack on the Sri Lankan cricket team in 2009. They also lost the rights to co-host the 2011 ODI World Cup. This hit their finances dramatically. An Indo-Pak series would have revived the PCB's sinking financial position immeasurably. Not playing—as India ensured—became another method by which to sanction, punish, and isolate Pakistan. Moreover, this was a time when India increasingly began to try and downgrade the traditional Indo-Pak rivalry, pushing instead the importance of their encounters with Australia and England.

Ehsan Mani, who had previously been the chairman of the ICC and is currently the PCB chairman, spoke to me of problems recently with the politicization of the BCCI. He said: 'In the past we were able to put aside our political differences. Now the BCCI is deeply influenced by the political situation.' He also mentioned that ideological issues had become increasingly ingrained in the BCCI and that on one occasion a senior English board official had confided to Mani about the deep hatred of Muslims that an Indian board official had displayed in a private conversation. Mani believes that these factors have led to the BCCI attempting to isolate Pakistan.

The Future of South Asian Relations

What would help most would be a normalization of Indo-Pak relations. Unfortunately, far from normalizing, the deterioration in relations with

India has not been stemmed. On 14 February 2019, a suicide bomber killed forty-six paramilitary police officers in Pulwama in Indian-administered Kashmir. The Pakistan-based militant group Jaish-e-Mohammad (JeM) claimed responsibility.[87] India undertook air strikes on an alleged JeM training camp in Balakot, the first time it has struck inside Pakistan since the 1971 war. Pakistan responded by downing an Indian fighter jet and capturing a pilot. Eventually, an unexpected chain of events that included the unconditional release of the Indian pilot by Pakistan, and the Pakistani prime minister Imran Khan's emotional peace overture, prevented an escalation and brought a quick-fix peace in the world's most militarized flashpoint.[88]

Despite the uneasy peace that followed, the skirmish caused more bad blood and a reinforcement of negative attitudes. The day after the Pulwama attack, India revoked Pakistan's Most Favoured Nation trading status, raised customs duties to 200 per cent, and reiterated its vow to isolate Pakistan in the international community.[89] There were more condemnations from Bollywood.[90] The Indian cricket team donned military caps in their match against Australia in solidarity with the armed forces and to pay homage to the 'martyrs of Pulwama'. The Indian cricketers would go on to donate their entire match fees to the National Defence Fund. The BCCI donated the entire budget of the IPL opening ceremony for the benefit of the families of those killed in the terrorist attack.[91] A media-inspired nationalistic frenzy took hold with anti-Pakistan sentiment being a focus.

In a continued push for Pakistan's isolation, the Indian cricket board called on the 'cricketing community to sever ties with countries from which terrorism emanates' and to have Pakistan banned from the 2019 World Cup altogether.[92] Several former Indian cricketers called for India to forfeit the match rather than play Pakistan and some current players also allegedly stated that they did not want to play Pakistan.[93] Eventually, the match would go ahead with no untoward animosity or incident between players or fans. Earlier, an Indian event management company—IMG Reliance—pulled out of its deal as official producer of the Pakistan T20 cricket league, putting the broadcasting of the tournament in doubt.[94] The official broadcaster of the Pakistan Super League (PSL) in India announced that it would not show the matches, and digital coverage of the tournament was also blocked in the country.[95] Pakistan responded by blocking the broadcast of the IPL in Pakistan[96]—as a result, the fans on either side of the border have even less chance of sharing experiences. The pettiness of the exchanges highlighted how far relations had fallen.

Nevertheless, the Pulwama attack and Modi's bellicose response helped him to a thumping electoral win in 2019. But the fanciful idea that this may moderate Modi's policies ended when, in August 2019, following a deployment of tens of thousands of additional troops and paramilitary forces to the region, the Indian government revoked Article 370[97] of the Indian constitution, removing the special status[98] of Indian-administered Kashmir. Since then, Kashmir remains under lockdown, with internet and phone services intermittently cut off and thousands of people detained.[99] This has further inflamed relations with Pakistan, leading them to downgrade diplomatic ties, expel the Indian ambassador, and suspend bilateral trade.[100] In his 2019 address to the United Nations, Prime Minister Khan expressed his fear of an uncontrolled escalation over Kashmir:

> I fear there will be a massacre and things will start to go out of control . . . My main reason for coming here was to meet world leaders at the UN and speak about this. We are heading for a potential disaster of proportions that no one here realises . . . It is the only time since the Cuban crisis that two nuclear-armed countries are coming face to face. We did come to face to face in February.[101]

In an environment of fear and intolerance, signs of dissent against the government's policies have become increasingly rare. The police have truncheoned, detained, and shot protesters dead. Many more are intimidated and threatened by BJP ministers and their extremist allies.[102] Ugra writes of the lack of opposition against the CAA among sporting celebrities in India but reminds the reader that while there is very little government influence in funding or operations of the BCCI, there is 'far too much of it in its centres of power'.[103] The BCCI recently appointed Jay Shah, the son of the home minister Amit Shah, the man at the centre of the controversial citizenship laws and in public opposition to the protesters, to the post of secretary of the BCCI. This makes it extremely unlikely that there will be any opposition from existing cricketers to the government's policies. In fact, in early December, BCCI president Sourav Ganguly's teenage daughter Sana excerpted a few lines from Khushwant Singh's writing on her Instagram post, including these words—'Every fascist regime needs communities and groups it can demonise in order to thrive.' The post was quickly deleted with Ganguly saying that his daughter's account had been hacked and asked the public to 'keep Sana out of it' as she was 'too young a girl to know about anything in politics'.[104]

The BJP's ideological march and growing hegemony increasingly means that dissent is not tolerated[105] and polarization between India and Pakistan continues unabated; unlike in the past, there can be little expectation of calls for a resumption in cricketing ties from the Indian society, including from cricketers themselves. This is unfortunate considering the influence of India's cricketing heroes on their public. Gone are the days when on the outbreak of the 1965 war Mansoor Ali Khan Pataudi, the Indian captain and Hanif Mohammad, the Pakistani captain, both playing for a Rest of the World side against England at Scarborough, sent a joint telegram to their respective governments:

> We wish to express deep regrets at the war between India and Pakistan. We find unity on the cricket field by reaching for a common objective. We fervently hope both countries can meet and find an amicable solution.

By a strange coincidence, when the 1971 war broke out, Sunil Gavaskar and Zaheer Abbas were playing again for a Rest of the World team in Australia and would share a room—'they shared the tension while consoling each other'.[106]

Now recently retired cricketers on both sides have traded barbs against one another and their respective countries. Pakistan's Shahid Afridi on a visit to Pakistan's side of Kashmir berated the Indian government for the troop presence in Indian-administered Kashmir, proceeding then to state: 'the world is currently infected by such a big disease [Covid-19]. But the bigger disease is in Modi's mind'.[107] There were strong responses from Indian cricketers including Yuvraj Singh, Harbhajan Singh, and Gautam Gambhir. Gambhir is a vocal critic of Pakistan and his animosity goes back to an incident on the field in 2007 with Afridi; this animosity has grown since his retirement and his entry into politics in 2019 when he joined the BJP. Despite all this, the inflammation of public opinion against Pakistan in India is not matched to the same extent in Pakistan. India's current struggle with Hindutva-inspired hypernationalism lends itself to anti-Muslim and anti-Pakistan bias which is deepened by a frenzied media.

Pakistan's lack of cricket at home has made crowds desperate for the return of international competition. The growth of coverage of cricket and the telecast of the IPL (until recently) have made Indian cricketers household names in Pakistan. Many current Pakistani cricketers profess their admiration of their Indian counterparts—some go further, barely disguising their awe of international cricket's superstars. Fans are equally effusive in their admiration of Indian cricketers. I recall an image of a young Pakistani fan of the Indian captain Virat Kohli; he was riding his motorbike along the roads of Lahore wearing Kohli's 18 number shirt[108] with the name Kohli emblazoned on it. Another fanatical Kohli fan was jailed after he jubilantly waved the Indian flag from his house in Pakistan after his idol's match-winning knock saw India defeat Australia. He was later granted bail.[109] During the PSL T20 competition held in March 2020, banners have been displayed asking the Indian team to visit. In 2020, when Sri Lanka made the first full tour to Pakistan in a decade, a Pakistan cricket fan in Lahore held up a sign, requesting Virat Kohli to come and play cricket in Pakistan.[110] There have been similar calls by former Pakistan cricketers as well.[111] While there were some positive responses on social media, it is unlikely that similar messages of support for the resumption of cricket would be possible in the current climate in India. In Pakistan, there is far less societal backlash against calls for a resumption in cricketing relations. It is true that Pakistan needs the resumption much more than India; that Pakistan-based militant groups through activities inside India—Kashmir, Mumbai, New Delhi—have caused more chaos in India than India has caused in Pakistan; and that public opinion has not been inflamed in Pakistan against India in the way it has against Pakistan in India.

India's unwillingness to play Pakistan stems from a host of reasons that have been discussed in this chapter and which include the currently parlous state of political relations, the polarization of society (particularly more recently in India), and the magnifying of these differences through the media. India has also used the refusal to play cricket with Pakistan as a political tool in their wider policy to isolate Pakistan. An agreement to resume ties could be construed as a compromise, an act of support for a beleaguered and isolated enemy. A rekindling of the cricketing relationship, if we look at it historically, opens up a potential path to better overall relations. It also creates opportunities for people-to-people contact and—as in the past—the possibility of breaking down stereotypes that have hardened over the years. Cricket allowed President Zia and Prime Minister Rajiv Gandhi the opportunity to meet at a time of high tension. Manmohan Singh and Yousaf Raza Gilani repeated cricket diplomacy. More importantly, Indo-Pak tours brought the peoples of the two countries together, allowing them to see that they are not as different as their state and media narratives have made them out to be. The heightened emotions surrounding cricketing encounters have even facilitated the softening of hardline views as in the case of L.K. Advani or when Indian fans in Lahore cheered the arrival of General Pervez Musharraf, the man responsible for the Kargil war. There is also enormous potential for better wider relations when, for example, fans on both sides see opposing players shaking hands before and sharing a light-hearted moment after, as was the case when Virat Kohli joked with a group of Pakistani players after the Champions Trophy which was held in England in 2017, or when Mahendra Singh Dhoni was photographed holding Pakistan captain Sarfaraz Ahmed's son in his arms before the same match. In the recent T20 World Cup, the India–Pakistan match was played in excellent sporting spirit. However, it appears unlikely that Modi's hardline government is in favour of a rapprochement with Pakistan and as a result cricketing ties are likely to remain in cold storage. Prime Minister Khan, having often spoken of the thrill of playing cricket against India during his career, has stated that until the political atmosphere improves between the two nations, cricketing ties will be difficult.

India–Pakistan relations and Pakistan's wider relations with other South Asian nations have been affected by the overarching political relations between the countries. Up until the last decade, even when political relations were fraught, cricketing relations between the boards, or the desire for cricketing relations between the fans and players, were strong—so that whenever the opportunity arose, cricket provided the ice-breaking moment. Unfortunately, the environment has lately turned more hostile and it has affected relations at all levels.

Recently, the Indian cricketer Yuvraj Singh announced his retirement from the game. Tributes poured in from India but also from across the border where he was one of the last generations of Indian cricketers who had played in the neighbouring country. An entire cohort of cricketers from India and Pakistan will complete their careers without playing each other in a Test series. The fissure has changed relations between the players. There is still a shared language, a shared cuisine, and a shared culture—but the bonhomie of the past has not been allowed to prosper. The players are cordial, but the old ties, the friendships that come with spending hours and days together during a tour, have gone. India and Pakistan now only play in the occasional international tournament. It has created a physical and emotional distance.

This is also influenced by the fact that the Indian cricketers have become the biggest stars of the cricketing world, earning more than their counterparts in Australia and England. The cash-rich, glitzy, Bollywood-style IPL has made bigger stars of them than the superstars of the Indian cinema. While the Indian cricketers have breached the stratosphere of stardom, their Pakistani counterparts have struggled over the last decade to even, until recently, play in front of their own crowds. Pakistani cricketers, famed in the 1970s, 1980s, and 1990s for their charisma and panache, are now itinerant travellers. This distance is compounded by the exclusion of the Pakistanis from the IPL. While cricketers from all over the world—Bangladesh, Sri Lanka, Afghanistan included—play alongside one another, building new friendships, no Pakistani players are allowed to participate. This has created a massive distance and has reduced the rapport with their now much richer, much more successful, and much more savvy cousins. Even among the junior teams there was a distinct lack of camaraderie in the 2020 World Cup. Two years earlier, the Pakistani team had spent a considerable amount of time speaking to the legendary Indian coach Rahul Dravid. In the latest edition the teams avoided each other studiously.[112]

What does the future hold for Indo-Pak relations? The history of relations would indicate that a turnaround in relations is possible and can occur with surprising speed, like the flowering of a desert. In the past, India and Pakistan's shared history and culture have made this possible. History is not easily forgotten, even though, unforgivably, both countries seek to redefine their past through changing their textbooks.[113] Unfortunately, recent history indicates that a resumption of ties is unlikely in the near future. This remains a tragedy for world cricket, and for Indian and Pakistani cricketers and fans all over the world.

Notes

1. Ramachandra Guha, *A Corner of a Foreign Field: The Indian History of a British Sport* (London: Picador, 2003), 330; Osman Samiuddin, *The Unquiet Ones: A History of Pakistan Cricket* (New York: HarperCollins, 2015), 301–302; Mike Marqusee, *War Minus the Shooting* (London: Heinemann, 1996), 79.

2. Guha, *Corner*, 396.

3. Ibid., 427; Jayanta Sengupta, 'Globalizing patriotism: Some lessons from the cricket World Cup of 2003', in *Sport in South Asian Society*, eds. Boria Majumdar and J.A. Mangan (London: Routledge, 2005), 270.

4. Devin T. Hagerty and Herbert G. Hagerty, 'India's foreign relations', in *South Asia in World Politics*, ed. D. Hagerty (New York: Rowman & Littlefield, 2005), 34. Rajni Kothari and Mushirul Hasan in fact both argue that the Nehruvian Consensus disappeared by the 1960s. But any remnants of the ideology appear to have been wiped out some decades later—Rajni Kothari, 'Political consensus in India: Decline and reconstruction', *Economic and Political Weekly* 4, no. 41 (11 October 1969): 1635, 1637, 1639, 1641–1644; Mushirul Hasan, *Legacy of a Divided Nation: India's Muslims from Independence to Ayodhya* (London: Routledge, 1997).

5. Shankar Gopalakrishnan, 'Defining, constructing and policing a "new India": Relationship between neoliberalism and Hindutva', *Economic and Political Weekly* 41, no. 26 (2006): 2803–2813; Iain McDonald, 'Between Saleem and Shiva: The politics of cricket nationalism in a "globalising" India', in *Sport in Divided Societies*, eds. John Sugden and Alan Bairner (Aachen: Meyer and Meyer Sport, 2000), 218.

6. Thomas Blom Hansen, 'Globalisation and nationalist imaginations: Hindutva's promise of equality through difference', *Political and Economic Weekly* 31, no. 10 (1996): 603–605, 607–616; P. Chacko, 'Marketizing Hindutva: The state, society, and markets in Hindu nationalism', *Modern Asian Studies* 53, no. 2 (2019): 377–410.

7. McDonald, 'Between Saleem and Shiva', 219–220.

8. Hansen, 'Globalisation and nationalist imaginations'.

9. G. Aloysius, 'Trajectory of Hindutva', *Economic and Political Weekly* 29, no. 24 (11 June 1994): 1450–1452. See also Badri Narayan's *Fascinating Hindutva* (London: Sage, 2019) for an examination of how the promise of democracy and equal opportunity has been used by Hindutva politics in order to mobilize the lower castes to their ideology.

10. Barbara Metcalf, 'Madrasas and minorities in secular India', in *Schooling Islam: The Culture and Politics of Modern Muslim Education*, eds. Robert Hefner and M. Qasim Zaman (Princeton, NJ: Princeton University Press, 2006), 87–106.

11. Christophe Jaffrelot, *Sangh Parivar* (Oxford: Oxford University Press, 2005); Christophe Jaffrelot, *Hindu Nationalism* (Princeton, NJ: Princeton University Press, 2007), 3; Ashutosh Varshney, *Ethnic Conflict and Civil Life: Hindus and Muslims in India* (New Haven, CT: Yale University Press, 2002), 72.

12. McDonald, 'Between Saleem and Shiva', 216.

13. Guha, *Corner*, 410.

14. Sengupta, 'Globalizing patriotism', 250.

15. Ibid., 265.

16. Jishnu Dasgupta, 'Manufacturing unison: Muslims, Hindus and Indians during the India-Pakistan match', *International Journal of the History of Sport* 21, nos. 3–4 (2004): 573–584; Souvik Naha, 'When politics ran riot in Eden Gardens', *IIC Quarterly* 44, nos. 3–4 (2018).

17. Marqusee, *War*, 209–212.

18. Ibid., 215.

19. McDonald, 'Between Saleem and Shiva', 221.

20. Mike Marqusee, 'From baying for blood to screaming for sixes', *ESPN CricInfo*, 1 May 2005, www.espncricinfo.com/story/_/id/23060813/from-baying-blood-screaming-sixes, also quoted in Emily Crick, 'Can cricket be used as multi-track diplomacy in the context of Indo-Pakistani relations? With particular reference to the period between 1999 and 2005', MSc thesis, 2006, 47.

21. McDonald, 'Between Saleem and Shiva', 229.

22. Guha, *Corner*, 402–403.

23. Jack Williams, 'Paki cheats!', in *Sport in Postcolonialism*, eds. J. Bale and M. Cronin (Oxford: Berg, 2003); Chris Searle, 'Cricket and the mirror of racism', *Race and Class* 34, no. 3 (1993): 45–54; Subhash Jaireth, 'Tracing orientalism in cricket', *Sporting Traditions* 12, no. 1 (1995): 103–120.

24. McDonald, 'Between Saleem and Shiva', 219; Marqusee, *War*, 209–212.

25. Jaffrelot in Kingshuk Chatterjee, 'To play or not to play: Fabricating consent over the Indo-Pak cricket series', in *Sport in South Asian Society*, eds. B. Majumdar and J.A. Mangan (London: Routledge, 2005), 288.

26. Guha, *Corner*, 2003; Sengupta, 'Globalizing patriotism', 265.

27. Marqusee, *War*.

28. Chatterjee, 'To play or not to play', 289.

29. Rifaat Hussain, 'Pakistan's relations with Azad Kashmir and the impact on Indo-Pakistani relations', in *Prospects for Peace in South Asia*, eds. Rafiq Dossani and Henry S. Rowen (Stanford, CA: Stanford University Press, 2005), 130.

30. Hussain, 'Pakistan's relations with Azad Kashmir', 130.

31. Nicholas J. Wheeler, *Trusting Enemies* (Oxford: Oxford University Press, 2018), 198–199; Jaswant Singh, *Jinnah: India, Partition, Independence* (Oxford: Oxford University Press, 2010), 161.

32. Nabiha Gul, 'Pakistan-India peace process 1990–2007: An appraisal', *Pakistan Horizon* 60, no. 2 (2007): 47–64.

33. Shaharyar M. Khan, *Cricket: A Bridge of Peace* (Oxford: Oxford University Press, 2005), 5.

34. Guha, *Corner*, 409.

35. Guha, *Corner*, 411; Shashi Tharoor and Shaharyar Khan, *Shadows across a Playing Field* (New Delhi: Roli Books, 2009), 122–125.

36. Kausik Bandyopadhya, 'Pakistani cricket at crossroads: An outsider's perspective in cricket', *Sport in Society* 10, no. 1 (2007): 101–119.

37. Hagerty and Hagerty, 'India's foreign relations'; Ian Talbot, *Pakistan: A Modern History* (London: Hurst and Company, 2005).

38. Sengupta, 'Globalizing patriotism'; Chatterjee, 'To play or not to play'; Bandyopadhya, 'Pakistani cricket'.

39. Sengupta, 'Globalizing patriotism', 270.

40. Chatterjee, 'To play or not to play', 290.

41. Kausik Bandhopadhya, 'Feel good, Godwill and India's friendship tour of Pakistan, 2004: Cricket, politics and diplomacy in twenty-first-century India', *International Journal of the History of Sport* 25, no. 12 (2008): 1654–1670, 1663.

42. Rahul Bhattacharya, *Pundits from Pakistan* (London: Picador, 2005), 71.

43. Ibid., 156.

44. Mushtaq Mohammad, *Inside Out* (Toronto: Uniprint, 2006), 193.

45. This is the line taken by Shaharyar Khan and Varun Sahni who both indicate that poverty, unemployment, education, and health were issues of concern to populations in both India and Pakistan rather than Indo-Pak hostility. Sahni carried out a review of opinion polls in India in the print and television media between 1996 and 2004 and concluded that poverty, unemployment, and education were consistently ranked as the highest issues of concern; Indo-Pak or Hindu–Muslim relations were rarely mentioned. See Varun Sahni, 'The protean polis and strategic surprises: Do changes within India affect South Asian strategic stability?', *Contemporary South Asia* 14, no. 2 (June 2005): 219–231.

46. Singh, *Jinnah*, 413.

47. Marqusee, *War*.

48. Marqusee, 'From baying for blood'.

49. Mike Marqusee, 'The lovable marquee', *Outlook India*, 21 March 2005, www.outlo okindia.com/magazine/story/this-lovable-marquee/226831.

50. Mike Marqusee, 'A committed neutral speaks', *Outlook India*, 17 March 2005.

51. 'Reunited Kashmiris' tears of joy', *BBC News*, 7 April 2005, http://news.bbc.co.uk/1/hi/world/south_asia/4419109.stm.

52. Aftab Borka, 'Indian films breathe life into Pakistani cinemas', *Reuters*, 25 April 2008, www.reuters.com/article/us-pakistan-bollywood/indian-films-breathe-life-into-pakistani-cinemas-idUSISL17078720080425.

53. Nandini Ramnath, 'A brief history of Pakistan-India cultural ties', *Dawn*, 27 September 2016, https://images.dawn.com/news/1176320.

54. Prem Mahadevan, *A Decade on from the 2008 Mumbai Attack: Reviewing the Question of State-Sponsorship* (The Hague: International Centre for Counter Terrorism Publications, 2019); Sengupta, 'Globalizing patriotism'.

55. 'India cancel 2009 cricket tour of Pakistan', *CNN*, 18 December 2008, http://edit ion.cnn.com/2008/SPORT/12/18/india.pakistan.cricket.tour/index.html.

56. Moeed Yusuf, 'Difficult ties', *Dawn*, 3 June 2014.

57. Peter Oborne, *Wounded Tiger: A History of Cricket in Pakistan* (New York: Simon and Schuster, 2014), 481.

58. Ibid., 482.

59. Ibid.

60. Osman Samiuddin, 'PCB keen on UAE venues despite ICC snub', *ESPN Cric Info*, 26 June 2009, www.espncricinfo.com/story/_/id/22789023/pcb-continue-push ing-uae-venues.

61. 'Full statement of PCB chairman Ijaz Butt', *ESPN Cric Info*, 9 May 2009, www. espncricinfo.com/story/_/id/22808350/full-statement-pcb-chairman-ijaz-butt.

62. 'All emotion, no logic', *ESPN Cric Info*, 10 May 2009, www.espncricinfo.com/ story/_/id/22807738/all-emotion-no-logic.

63. Mihir Bose, 'Conflicting loyalties: Nationalism and religion in India-Pakistan cricket relations', in *The Cambridge Companion to Cricket*, eds. A. Bateman and J. Hill (Cambridge: Cambridge University Press, 2011), 216.

64. Andrew Buncombe, 'Narendra Modi sworn in as India's new PM with Pakistani counterpart Nawaz Sharif looking on', *The Independent*, 27 May 2014, www.inde pendent.co.uk/news/world/asia/indias-new-pm-narendra-modi-to-meet-with-pakistani-premier-nawaz-sharif-after-being-sworn-in-9436226.html.

65. 'India PM Modi in surprise Pakistan visit', *BBC News*, 25 December 2015, www. bbc.co.uk/news/world-asia-35178594.

66. Sameer Lalwani and Hannah Haegeland, 'Anatomy of a crisis: Explaining crisis onset in India-Pakistan relations', *Stimson Centre*, 2018, www.stimson.org/wp-content/files/InvestigatingCrisesOnset.pdf.

67. Burhan Wani was a commander of the Pro-Pakistani militant group Hizbul Mujahideen. Wani was popular on social media for his advocacy against Indian rule in Kashmir and his calls suggesting violent insurrection against the Indian state and has been credited for reinvigorating the Kashmiri uprising. He was twenty-two when he was killed, with reports suggesting that his funeral was attended by so many supporters that there was no space for funeral prayers—'Why the death of militant Burhan Wani has Kashmiris up in arms', *BBC News*, 11 July 2016, www.bbc.co.uk/news/world-asia-india-36762043.

68. Ibid.

69. Vijayta Lalwani, 'Data check: Ceasefire violations along Line of Control this year are already more than all of 2017', *Scroll.In*, 27 September 2020, https://scroll. in/article/888719/data-check-already-more-ceasefire-violations-along-line-of-control-this-year-than-all-of-2017.

70. Vinay Kaura, 'India's Pakistan policy: From 2016 "surgical strike" to 2019 Balakot "airstrike"', *The Round Table* 109, no. 3 (2020): 277–287; Karthika Sasikumar,

'India-Pakistan crises under the nuclear shadow: The role of reassurance', *Journal for Peace and Nuclear Disarmament* 2, no. 1 (2019): 151–169.

71. 'India's Modi threatens to "isolate Pakistan" after Kashmir attack', *Financial Times*, www.ft.com/content/bb7592de-82e3-11e6-8897-2359a58ac7a5.

72. For example, BJP loyalist Gajendra Chauhan's nomination as chairman of FTII; the replacement of Gopalkrishna Gandhi at Simla's Indian Institute of Advanced Study by Chandrakala Padia; Lokesh Chandra who claims Modi is a greater leader than Gandhi as head of the Indian Council of Cultural Relations; and Sudershan 'Ramayana-is-history' Rao's designation as head of the Indian Council of Historical Research. Girish Chandra Tripathi, a state-level RSS functionary, was appointed as the vice-chancellor of Banaras Hindu University; Baldev Sharma, former editor of the extremist RSS mouthpiece *Panchjanya*, was appointed chairman of the National Book Trust. See Girish Shahane, 'Why the BJP is appointing C-listers to head top institutions', *Scroll.In*, 22 July 2015, https://scroll.in/article/743006/why-the-bjp-is-appointing-c-listers-to-head-top-instituti ons; Soumya Shankar, 'The takeover: How the Modi govt has filled key positions in 14 institutions', *Catch News*, 13 February 2017, www.catchnews.com/india-news/the-takeover-how-the-modi-govt-has-filled-key-positions-in-14-instituti ons-1436365046.html.

73. Soutik Biswas, 'Ramachandra Guha: How the right wing hounded out a Gandhi biographer', *BBC News*, 3 November 2018, www.bbc.co.uk/news/world-asia-india-46069120; 'Amartya Sen's 9-year-long association with Nalanda University ends', *The Economic Times*, 23 November 2016, https://economictimes.indiati mes.com/news/politics-and-nation/amartya-sens-9-year-long-association-with-nalanda-university-ends/articleshow/55586972.cms?from=mdr.

74. Shankar, 'The takeover'.

75. Yusuf, 'Difficult ties'.

76. McDonald, 'Between Saleem and Shiva', 221.

77. 'Anurag Thakur becomes first serving BJP MP to join Territorial Army', *Indian Express*, 29 July 2016, https://indianexpress.com/article/india/india-news-india/anurag-thakur-territorial-army-bjp-mp-2942887. Thakur was removed from the BCCI in 2017 by the Supreme Court: 'Anurag Thakur: India cricket board chief ordered to resign', *BBC News*, 2 January 2017, www.bbc.co.uk/news/world-asia-india-38487340.

78. 'Union minister Anurag Thakur leads "goli maaro saalon ko" slogans at rally', *Scroll.In*, 27 January 2020, https://scroll.in/video/951289/watch-anurag-thakur-minister-of-state-for-finance-lead-goli-maaro-saalon-ko-slogans-at-rally.

79. Gideon Haigh, 'Divide and rule at the ICC: the great carve up of world cricket', *ESPN Cric Info*, www.espncricinfo.com/wisdenalmanack/content/story/735865.html.

80. James Astill, *The Great Tamasha: Cricket, Corruption and the Turbulent Rise of Modern India* (London: Wisden, 2013); Amit Gupta, 'The IPL and the Indian domination of global cricket', *Sport in Society* 14, no. 10 (2011): 1316–1325. The IPL has recently been valued at $7 billion with per-game revenues close to

those of football's English Premier League—'Hit for six: India's IPL cricket league floored by coronavirus', *Financial Times*, www.ft.com/content/8c3e38b8-9dc3-43b7-9ef4-04e6792cd36b.

81. Haigh, 'Divide and rule at the ICC'.

82. Nabeel Hashmi, 'Pakistan receives major share of "Big Three" spoils', *The Express Tribune*, 26 June 2014, https://tribune.com.pk/story/727501/pakistan-receives-major-share-of-big-three-spoils?print=true.

83. Daniel Brettig, 'New ICC finance model breaks up Big Three', *ESPN Cric Info*, 27 April 2017, www.espncricinfo.com/story/_/id/19253630/new-icc-finance-model-breaks-big-three.

84. Nagraj Gollapudi, 'PCB's case against BCCI dismissed by ICC dispute panel', *ESPN Cric Info*, 20 November 2018, www.espncricinfo.com/story/_/id/25328 942/pcb-case-bcci-dismissed-icc-dispute-panel.

85. 'Pakistan players hurt and angered by snub', *ESPN Cric Info*, 19 January 2010, www.espncricinfo.com/story/_/id/22686959/pakistan-players-hurt-angered-snub-auction.

86. Bose, 'Conflicting loyalties', 215.

87. 'Kashmir attack: Tracing the path that led to Pulwama', *BBC News*, 30 April 2019, www.bbc.co.uk/news/world-asia-india-47302467.

88. Abhinav Pandya, 'The future of Indo-Pak relations after the Pulwama attack', *Perspectives on Terrorism* 13, no. 2 (2019): 65–68.

89. 'Pulwama attack: What are Modi's options?', *BBC News*, 19 February 2019, www. bbc.co.uk/news/world-asia-india-47278145.

90. 'Pulwama fallout: Bollywood films refuse to cross the border; cricketers mull against playing Pak in WC', *The Economic Times*, 18 February 2019, https:// economictimes.indiatimes.com/magazines/panache/pulwama-fallout-ban-on-pak-artistes-actors-sports-stars-get-generous/standing-with-our-soldiers/slides how/68046008.cms.

91. 'Team India wear special army caps in ODI against Australia', *Telegraph India*, 8 March 2019, www.telegraphindia.com/sport/team-india-wear-special-army-caps-in-odi-against-australia/cid/1686420.

92. Nagraj Gollapudi and Sidharth Monga, 'BCCI mulls asking for Pakistan World Cup ban', 21 February 2019, www.espncricinfo.com/story/_/id/26045366/bcci-mulls-asking-pakistan-world-cup-ban.

93. 'Pulwama attack: BCCI calls on ICC to act following Kashmir incident', *BBC Sport*, 22 February 2019, www.bbc.co.uk/sport/cricket/47333834; 'India vs Pakistan: Yuzvendra Chahal wants action against those guilty in Pulwama attack', *Hindustan Times*, 22 February 2019, www.hindustantimes.com/cricket/india-vs-pakistan-yuzvendra-chahal-wants-action-against-those-guilty-in-pulwama-att ack/story-7bBHV4Ihz3ovM2EoqtjuvI.html.

94. 'PCB files damages claim against IMG-Reliance for PSL pull-out', *ESPN Cric Info*, 19 November 2019, www.espncricinfo.com/story/_/id/28114967/pcb-files-dama ges-claim-img-reliance-psl-pull-out.

95. 'Indian broadcaster pulls out of Pakistan cricket league', *AlJazeera*, 18 February 2019, www.aljazeera.com/news/2019/02/indian-broadcaster-pulls-pakistan-cricket-league-190218082302541.html.

96. Omer Farooq Khan, 'Pakistan bans broadcast of IPL matches', *Times of India*, 2 April 2019, https://timesofindia.indiatimes.com/sports/cricket/ipl/top-stories/pakistan-bans-broadcast-of-ipl-matches/articleshow/68693272.cms.

97. 'Kashmir under lockdown', *AlJazeera*, 27 October 2019, www.aljazeera.com/news/2019/08/india-revokes-kashmir-special-status-latest-updates-190806134011673.html.

98. Lindsay Maizland, 'Kashmir: What to know about the disputed region', *Council of Foreign Relations*, 7 August 2019, www.cfr.org/in-brief/kashmir-what-know-about-disputed-region.

99. Hannah Ellis-Petersen, '"Many lives have been lost": Five month internet blackout plunges Kashmir into crisis', *The Guardian*, 5 January 2020, www.theguardian.com/world/2020/jan/05/the-personal-and-economic-cost-of-kashmirs-internet-ban.

100. 'Pakistan to downgrade ties with India over Kashmir move', *AlJazeera*, 7 August 2019, www.aljazeera.com/news/2019/08/pakistan-downgrade-ties-india-kashmir-move-190807134255247.html.

101. Julian Borger, 'Imran Khan warns UN of potential nuclear war in Kashmir', *The Guardian*, 26 September 2019, www.theguardian.com/world/2019/sep/26/imran-khan-warns-un-of-potential-nuclear-war-in-kashmir.

102. Supriya Sharma, 'We knew Adityanath was hostile to Muslims: But did we expect his regime to be so savage?', *Scroll.In*, 30 December 2019, https://scroll.in/article/948194/we-knew-adityanath-was-hostile-to-muslims-but-did-we-expect-his-regime-to-be-so-savage?fbclid=IwAR1-jHJ6sZHPuQnIrbvZpNnxql_agi9RtZO4eBRLLCAVNi5P_BJ_IfvAw_M.

103. Sharda Ugra, 'Why aren't our sports celebrities speaking out?', *The India Forum*, 6 March 2020, www.theindiaforum.in/article/why-aren-t-sports-celebrities-speaking-about-caanrc-protests.

104. 'Keep my daughter out of this, says Sourav after "Sana's CAA post"', *Times of India*, 19 December 2019, https://timesofindia.indiatimes.com/india/keep-my-daughter-out-of-this-says-sourav-after-sanas-caa-post/articleshow/72878319.cms?frmapp=yes&from=mdr.

105. Sanjay Ruparelia, 'Modi's Saffron democracy', *Dissent* 66, no. 2 (2019): 94–106.

106. Guha, *Corner*, 394.

107. 'We will never accept such words', *India Today*, 17 May 2020, www.indiatoday.in/sports/cricket/story/yuvraj-singh-slams-shahid-afridi-controversial-comments-against-india-pm-narendra-modi-1679022-2020-05-17.

108. '"Virat Kohli" spotted in Lahore donning Pakistan World Cup kit', *The News*, 9 June 2019, www.thenews.com.pk/latest/482201-virat-kohli-in-pakistani-kit-roaming-in-lahore.

109. 'Pakistani Kohli fan facing 10 years in jail for hoisting Indian flag', *The Express Tribune*, 28 January 2016, https://tribune.com.pk/story/1035634/pakist

ani-kohli-fan-facing-10-years-in-jail-for-hoisting-india-flag; 'Virat Kohli's Pakistani fan Umar Daraz who hoisted tricolour gets bail', *Business Standard*, 27 February 2016, www.business-standard.com/article/pti-stories/virat-kohli-s-pakistani-fan-who-hoisted-tricolour-gets-bail-116022700242_1.html.

110. 'Virat Kohli, come to Pakistan and play cricket: India captain's fan in Lahore wins hearts', *India Today*, 10 October 2019, www.indiatoday.in/sports/cricket/story/virat-kohli-pakistan-cricket-fan-lahore-gaddafi-stadium-banner-pak-vs-sl-1607889-2019-10-10.

111. '"Can trade onion, tomatoes then why not play cricket": Shoaib Akhtar on India-Pakistan bilateral series', *Hindustan Times*, 18 February 2020, www.hindustantimes.com/cricket/can-trade-onion-tomatoes-then-why-not-play-cricket-shoaib-akhtar-on-india-pakistan-bilateral-series/story-BQmMDWKAEKa8OZd5yw2QfL.html; 'Mushtaq Ahmed calls for resumption of India-Pakistan cricketing ties', *NDTV*, 17 November 2019, https://sports.ndtv.com/cricket/mushtaq-ahmed-calls-for-resumption-of-india-pakistan-cricketing-ties-2133978.

112. Sreshth Shah, 'Indian and Pakistani players go about their business, game faces on, blinkers in place', *ESPN Cric Info*, 3 February 2020, www.espncricinfo.com/story/_/id/28625641/indian-pakistani-players-go-their-business-game-faces-blinkers-place.

113. Marie Lall, 'Educate to hate: The use of education in the creation of antagonistic national identities in India and Pakistan', *Compare* 38, no. 1 (2008): 103–119.

5

'One Team, One Nation'

Cricket's Promise of a New National Identity in Sri Lanka?

Ben Hildred

Introduction

In 2009 Sri Lanka emerged scarred from a brutal civil war, which exacerbated rifts that continue to be felt across the country. The framing of the war as a secessionist dispute between a Tamil minority and a Sinhalese majority obscures the fact that Sri Lanka is an island of far greater ethnic, religious, and political diversity, and does not reflect the fact that such complexities have proved problematic for far longer. Having been ruled by colonial powers for 400 years, rocked by political instability post-independence, and after a twenty-six-year-long civil war, Sri Lanka is in anthropologist Sharika Thiranagama's words 'the nation that has never been one'.[1] As cricket has been Sri Lanka's most popular sport for decades, a common denominator across this diversity, various public figures in the last decade including international cricketers, politicians, and local non-governmental organizations (NGOs) have endorsed cricket as one method of creating a new national identity, of fostering unity and enabling reconciliation.[2] For Sri Lanka—like many of the countries covered in this volume—cricket appears integral to notions of national identity, something highlighted by the national team's slogan 'One Team, One Nation'. However, when the sport is recommended for something as important as post-war reconciliation, for addressing what Sri Lanka means *as a nation*, it provokes a series of pertinent questions: why has this association been made? What is implied by this association? And: will it work?

Ben Hildred, *'One Team, One Nation'* In: *Cricket and Nationhood in the Twenty-First Century*. Edited by: Souvik Naha, Oxford University Press. © Oxford University Press 2024. DOI: 10.1093/9780191982576.003.0006

Drawing from ethnographic fieldwork carried out in Sri Lanka from 2018 to 2020, I will show how the historical and cultural context of Sri Lanka underpins this assumption that cricket can logically be associated with reconciliation. However, as this association is framed in a broadly simplistic manner, implying a causal relationship where cricket merely entails reconciliation, the actions of important stakeholders are equally simplistic and often appear ineffective. Meanwhile, the cricketing rhetoric of 'One Team, One Nation' is portrayed as inclusive, yet with its distinctly middle-class underpinning it also elides difference. I therefore contend that this causal framing captures little of the complexity of the Sri Lankan context, and that cricket is not a panacea. Furthermore, I argue this reflects the inherent difficulty for scholars assessing sport in relation to reconciliation. If sports are both reflective and constitutive of society, drawing from and influencing other social phenomena outside of the sporting arena,[3] then we must assess sport for development and peace (SDP) contexts with greater awareness of sociocultural complexity, and understand the diverse forms of social *engagement* with cricket. Delving into the rhetorical and idiomatic dimensions of cricket in Sri Lanka, I foreground the positive effects experienced by my informants, team-mates I played with in a multi-ethnic amateur hardball team. I suggest that if these effects are broadly unintended consequences of engagement with cricket, this indicates one should perhaps not even really assess the relationship 'between' sport and reconciliation at all, but the employment of sport in navigating the social world, and the ramifications this might have on concepts *like* reconciliation. An anthropologically grounded reading may be that cricket has effects on a much deeper level. The answer to 'does it work?' probably lies in deeper—potentially imperceptible—social change.

Why Cricket for Reconciliation?
A New National Identity?

Since the end of the war, cricket has often been associated with reconciliation, never more explicitly than when former international cricketer Kumar Sangakkara gave the 'Spirit of Cricket' lecture at the Marylebone Cricket Club (MCC) annual dinner in 2011.[4] Sangakkara spoke passionately about the capacity of cricket to unite, and concluded by claiming that 'the conduct and performance of the [national cricket] team will have even greater importance as we enter a crucial period of reconciliation and recovery', further noting that 'the spirit of cricket can and should remain a guiding force for good within society'.[5] This perspective was established in mainstream cricket when the national team's official slogan became 'One Team, One Nation' in 2016, and remains a prominent part of their branding to this day.[6] Similar rhetoric has been employed by the Sri Lankan Cricket Board's (SLC's) charity arm 'Cricket Aid', who stated that in Sri Lanka, 'cricket is the one unifying force that transcends all boundaries of race, religion, cast [sic] or creed, in an extremely diverse culture'.[7] The recent association made between cricket and reconciliation must be understood within the local perception of cricket as a pan-Sri Lankan sport. Literature on both SDP and reconciliation frames my interpretation of this Sri Lankan context, clarifying the logic behind cricket being deemed a useful tool for reconciliation.

Cricket has been Sri Lanka's most popular sport for decades. Although the country is historically very diverse and multi-ethnic, with a majority Sinhalese population and several distinct minorities including Tamils and 'Moors', cricket is engaged in across these distinctions and has become something of a common denominator on the island.[8] Although initially a game reserved for the (post)colonial elites, cricket gained mass appeal when Sri Lanka first won the Cricket World Cup in 1996. It was a moment that shifted the Sri Lankan Cricket Board from a relatively amateurish set-up to a fully funded entity with political power.[9] By proxy of competing as 'Sri Lanka', cricket enables some sense of a unified nation, and indeed cricket is an obvious means to achieve and demonstrate ethnic and religious inclusion, as players from all backgrounds including Tamil, Burgher, and 'Moor' have played for Sri Lanka.[10] Muttiah Muralitharan has been a figurehead here due to being arguably Sri Lanka's best player, and his Tamil ethnicity.[11] This widespread participation underpins an assumption that cricket must be in some way unifying. Since the secessionist war ended, this inclusive rhetoric has only become stronger and cricket has been increasingly associated with reconciliation.

These claims that cricket is reconciliatory should be situated within the wider context of SDP, an emerging global movement where sport is idealistically portrayed as a panacea capable of curing any number of social ills.[12] Since the early 2000s, a loose coalition of various aid agencies including NGOs, governments, and sporting organizations have been increasingly promoting sport as a vehicle for development and peace,[13] predicated largely on the notion of sport as a space of neutrality and equality.[14] Such claims have been pushed by so-called 'sports evangelists', often sportspeople who have benefitted from sport and have a skewed concept of its power for change.[15] As an international sportsman, Sangakkara is an obvious example of a sport evangelist, and his MCC lecture neatly tied the existing inclusive cricketing rhetoric in Sri Lanka to the broader SDP movement. Sangakkara's words are therefore emblematic of a wider move within the international community to promote sport for reconciliation in post-conflict zones.[16]

Examining the merits of cricket for reconciliation in more detail suggests the association appears logical. The view of cricket as inclusive is enabled by the vague and generalized, largely idealistic images and metaphors of sport, or 'mythopoeic' discourses.[17] Such idioms as a 'level playing field' and 'it's not cricket' lead to the intrinsic value of sport rarely being questioned.[18] However, these idioms do little to hide the conflict and partisanship that sport often invokes. Football hooliganism is an obvious example, or the tense, politically inflected games of cricket between India and Pakistan.[19] Sport, like any collective human endeavour, is a malleable social construct that requires contextualizing and must not be essentialized.[20] Put simply: 'in and of itself, sport is of no intrinsic value: it is neither naturally good nor irrevocably bad'.[21] Yet if sport has 'no intrinsic value', this suggests it must be the *employment* of cricket as social enterprise that could effect reconciliation. One mode of employment derived from the literature on apology and forgiveness might be the notion of creating a 'space'. In the example of the apology by the Australian government to the 'stolen generations',[22] 'the apology, while not enough in itself, has offered a space where such a relation is possible'.[23] Similarly, for the Truth and Reconciliation Commission (TRC) of South Africa, while apologies did not necessarily foster reconciliation directly, they 'opened up new emotional spaces' where conversations about reconciliation could occur.[24] Although sport might be 'intrinsically value free', it may provide a realm within which reconciliatory dialogue can take place. As people from all ethnicities and religions participate in cricket, this is particularly pertinent.

In terms of such dialogue, the literature on reconciliation in Sri Lanka suggests that an acceptance of identities and accommodation of diverse localities is key to progress.[25] This is a task rendered difficult by the ethnic and religious complexity of Sri Lanka. On an individual level, Thiranagama suggests the civil war created new modes of knowing the self that now have to be 'negotiated anew'.[26] I believe this same negotiation may be extended to larger units like 'ethnicities' and 'the state'. Indeed, after a string of recent events including a constitutional crisis, terrorist attacks, and the ten-year anniversary of the war ending, multiple local commentators have framed ethnic tensions in terms of a need to resolve the 'national question', of defining what Sri Lanka is.[27] Reconciliation scholar Priscilla Hayner asserts there must be a reconciling of the past, achievable only through 'official recognition' of the 'facts' of conflict by the state.[28] This contends the state will play an integral role in any reconciliation processes in Sri Lanka. Similarly, anthropologist Richard Wilson states that reconciliation commissions often become part of a 'nation-building project',[29] and indeed the Lessons Learnt and Reconciliation Commission, the previous reconciliation commission of 2011, aimed to 'develop a Sri Lankan identity' as a potential way of addressing this national question.[30] Sangakkara's speech alluded to this Sri Lankan identity, suggesting it may find expression in the cricketing arena. Furthermore, if cricket is classed as a performance of the nation, like art, literature, or cultural property,[31] and indeed 'sport as spectacle is a means through which the state displays its legitimacy',[32] then cricket may be the playing out of a new pan-ethnic identity. Thus, cricket appears a logical unifier, something that may resolve some of the complexity in the Sri Lankan situation, and this helps explain the public proclamation of its power for reconciliation.

History, Structure, and Participation in Cricket

While cricket appears a logical unifier and reconciliatory aid, examining both the history of cricket on the island and the current structure reveals some of the issues with this assumption. Cricket has long-held associations with ideas of the nation in Sri Lanka, and the nature of cricket's establishment in the country calls attention to why cricket has been assumed to be unifying, further highlighting why this assumption is rarely questioned. Drawing from my ethnographic fieldwork, which centred around playing and training with amateur teams and coaches, I show that nonetheless participation in hardball cricket remains relatively limited, continuing to be played by a privileged few, and so the extent to which cricket can be said to be unifying remains equally limited.

The history of cricket in Sri Lanka is long and complex, and as such I draw out two key features: cricket's long-standing ties to Sri Lankan nationalism and the ethnic diversity of the initial middle-class participants.[33] Cricket has been associated in some small way with nationalism since the first European-Ceylonese game in 1882. By representing the island, the entirely Burgher[34] team were essentially 'Ceylonese by proxy'.[35] Yet despite their ethnic homogeneity, the team chose the name 'Young Ceylon' for themselves, following the name of a nationalist magazine set up in 1850, emulating Mazzini's 'Young Italy' movement.[36] Rather than merely being 'Ceylonese' as opposed to the Europeans, they framed themselves in overtly nationalist terms. Over the following century, Ceylon and then Sri Lanka played various visiting teams more often, helping crystallize the idea of cricket as a *national* sport. Strong showings against international opponents in the 1970s and 1980s, plus the efforts of Sri Lankan politician Gamini Dissanayake, persuaded the International Cricket Council to admit Sri Lanka to full Test status in 1981. Sri Lanka's first World Cup win fifteen years later cemented the island's love affair with cricket.[37] The game was suddenly a source of immense national pride, solidifying Sri Lanka's relevance on the international stage in the minds of its people. Cricket as a locus of nationalist fervour has dropped slightly since this peak in 1996, but remains strong to the present day.

Looking back to more humble beginnings and the development of the sport on the island, cricket was well established in Ceylonese colonial settings by the 1830s, spreading to colonial schools in the ensuing decades.[38] The soldiers played the first game between Europeans and Asians, as the British took on their Malay colleagues in 1872. The Malay Cricket Club followed, founded later that year, while a number of Burgher clubs combined to form the 'Colts' Cricket Club in 1873.[39] One could argue the Malays set the trend of establishing clubs along ethnic lines, with the Burgher Recreation Club, the Tamil Union, the Sinhalese Sports Club, and the antithetically named 'Nondescripts' Cricket Club all established by 1900. That the ethnic minorities of Ceylon were the first to take up cricket shows that participation in cricket has always been ethnically diverse, and might explain the underlying sense that cricket is unifying. However, these minorities were the urban elites: Burghers in particular held higher positions than other ethnicities vis-a-vis the British. With greater capacity for participation in recreational sports, the national Ceylonese teams remained dominated by these elite minorities, and it was only with increasing Sinhalese participation in the 1980s that the national team took on a more majoritarian character. The present make-up of the national squad (predominantly Sinhalese and Buddhist) reflects this trend.

Sri Lanka has long been geographically and economically orientated towards the capital: 'all roads, so to speak, led to Colombo',[40] and cricket in Sri Lanka is equally Colombo-centric. The ethnic plurality of the metropole somewhat explains cricket's uptake by the minorities, but it was really the schools that cemented it as a preserve of these elites. Cricket has been central to the school system since the first 'Big Match' between two of Sri Lanka's oldest and most prestigious schools, Royal College and St Thomas' College, in 1879. Here, the predominantly Burgher students, part of 'the top rungs of the social hierarchy below the British',[41] were the first to be taught cricket and how to be gentlemen, and to be inculcated in 'Muscular Christianity'[42] by their colonial schoolmasters. As Sri Lankan cricket historian Michael Roberts puts it, the nature of cricket in Ceylon was essentially 'anglophile'.[43] The centrality of cricket in these elite schools gave rise to this association of cricket and unity, and suggests why it continues to go unquestioned. These schools maintain a diverse intake, and even today those within the close-knit community fostered by schools' cricket claim that they mix with people of all ethnicities and religions, suggesting this is evidence of cricket's unifying power. As the majority of national players come from these colleges, most of the wider discourse promotes inclusivity too. That the top handful of these elite colleges supplied an overwhelming number of prime ministers and presidents in Sri Lanka's early independence years shows that cricket and its modernist sense of fairness and equality may well have been part of rhetoric in government, too. However, while many middle-class people may indeed mix in these elite schools, this does not reflect the extent to which their lower-class counterparts do not.[44] It elides the fact that cricket elsewhere remains far less hybrid. Until the World Cup win in 1996, far fewer people outside of these elite schools took up the game. Historically, while cricket has appeared diverse and unitary, it has rarely been so.

The way cricket is structured in Sri Lanka only reinforces that cricket is not necessarily unifying, being still largely the preserve of the privileged. Physically engaging with 'real' hardball cricket remains out of reach for many due to cost, and thus softball cricket is a huge part of recreational cricket,[45] with regular tournaments played in parks across the country, often for cash prizes, with huge fanfare, MCs, umpires, and trophies. However, softball cricket is somewhat looked down on, with hardball players advised not to play softball much by coaches, who claim it hinders proper technique. Furthermore, softball does not provide the international recognition the Sri Lankan hardball team can, or facilitate nationalism in the same way. Thus, hardball is certainly seen as the 'true' form, even if people can't play it. For many Sri Lankans, then, including the majority of women,[46] their primary engagement with 'real' cricket is watching the national team and the global game rather than through playing the sport itself.

Even among these privileged few who can partake, the system is difficult to navigate. Boys pursuing a career in the game must travel to the capital, and if we follow geographer Tariq Jazeel's argument that Colombo forms itself through an extractive relationship with its outside, then the city also harvests cricketers from the outstations.[47] The schools retain dominance here: recent national players hailed as being 'finds from the outstation' or 'from humble beginnings' often finished their schooling on scholarships at the elite colleges in Colombo.[48] The path is not this simple. Many boys attend academies and work hard on their skills from a young age, but there are increasingly varied demands put on a child's time by their parents, including numerous other extra-curricular activities and excessive levels of personal tutoring on top of regular schooling. Furthermore, with only an under-twenty-threes tournament below first team cricket, those aged nineteen to twenty-two who do join a professional club may struggle to gain selection. As former Sri Lankan cricketer Aravinda de Silva put it: 'with there being very little money in the game, many young men on the fringes . . . just couldn't sit and hope to be selected,'[49] something worse for those whose home is not Colombo.

Sri Lanka's corporate sector previously filled this gap, employing outstation cricketers and providing them with the capacity to train, but as my informants told me, this support has now reduced dramatically. All of these factors contribute to boys being dissuaded from pursuing cricket by their parents, and encouraged to focus on more traditionally lucrative careers.

Of those who played at their schools, fewer still keep playing into adulthood. Hardball cricket is an expensive hobby to have in a developing country, and participation seems something of a luxury. While some of my team-mates from the amateur club I played for during my fieldwork often complained about money, many could pay their fees without much issue. Even so, hardball is remarkably limited. The divisional system, built on a tournament rather than a league structure, means there is far less cricket played than one might expect. My team in Division 3 (the lowest) of the Sri Lankan system had five games around April to May. If we didn't progress to the next stage, then that was essentially it for their cricket for the year. The rest of the fixtures we played were friendlies, organized between teams of a similar standard, but very much on an ad hoc basis. The lack of grounds was also problematic. No amateur team has their own ground, instead renting a local ground for the day. This is expensive, and with the density of clubs situated in Colombo, it meant we often played outside the capital, with both teams travelling from the city. Even if we wanted to play each weekend, we rarely did so. Thus, this shows that few members of the population physically engage with hardball cricket. It cannot be said that cricket is a universal sport in Sri Lanka at the moment, certainly not the 'real', hardball version anyway.

One Team, One Nation

Jazeel argues that Colombo was central to an anti-colonial re-negotiation of Ceylonese nationhood post-independence. Such ideas were negotiated through middle-class architecture harking back to a rural state with 'precolonial purity', a concept that 'extend[s] imaginatively out and into the space of the independent nation-state'.[50] That Colombo still dictates to the margins can also be seen through the extractive relationship to cricketers outlined earlier, and in the way predominantly middle-class participants promote a cricketing rhetoric based on a unifying assumption. This is mobilized most clearly in the national team's slogan 'One Team, One Nation'. Such rhetoric about the nation makes a simplistic claim that cricket enables unity, but a closer look shows that through promoting inclusivity, this works towards an elision of difference.

The establishment of the 'One Team, One Nation' branding in 2016 shows the SLC took on board Sangakkara's claims cricket could cultivate a new 'Sri Lankan identity', and as a public body with reasonable political power, it legitimizes them. However, as cricket has been part of the political realm for some time,[51] and due to the dominance of Sinhala Buddhist nationalism in politics,[52] it is possible that claiming reconciliation for cricket is a politically motivated move in a tense post-war period. It may be that 'One Team, One Nation' is simply a neat, easy way for the now dominantly Sinhala Buddhist organization to package unity for wider consumption. Three elements support this interpretation. Firstly, the team often undergoes overtly Buddhist rituals, like the *Pirith* ceremonies before departing for foreign tours.[53] Some minority cricketers, including former national captain Angelo Mathews (a Tamil/Burgher catholic), have been admonished in popular and social media for not complying with such rituals appropriately.[54] Secondly, other minority players, especially more successful ones like Muralitharan, are widely celebrated but have in the process been 'co-opted into the defence' of the Sri Lankan state, paraded as evidence of 'Sinhalese benevolence'.[55] Making matters more difficult, some of Muralitharan's comments on the war have been unpalatable for Tamils in the north.[56] Thirdly, packaging the Sri Lankan national team as 'One Team, One Nation' is only unifying if one has the means to buy into this concept. It reinforces these middle-class and Sinhala Buddhist Nationalist views about unity—which are inclusive—while failing to alter the status quo. In other words, if you feel the team doesn't represent you already, this rhetoric does little to change that. While cricket ensures a unified 'Sri Lanka' is represented by proxy of totalizing the island, this branding breaks down once the cricketing event is done. Thus, the 'One Team, One Nation' rhetoric formulates unity and reconciliation in an overly simplistic manner by eliding the differences inherent in a country of great diversity. Such a simplistic framework has ramifications for how reconciliation is pursued through cricket.

Ramifications of This Framing: 'Doing' Reconciliation

The ramifications of this logical assumption that cricket is unifying, and the simplistic framing of inclusivity as reconciliatory, can be seen in the way various stakeholders including NGOs and government go about 'doing' SDP. My ethnographic work in Sri Lanka corroborates that efforts to use sport for reconciliation largely function on the basis of inclusivity; that is, spreading the game around the country. Again, this approach fails to capture the complexity of Sri Lanka and struggles against structural problems and the geographical issues of a disparate island focussed on the capital Colombo.

Sangakkara's words are important given that he, along with other former cricketers like Muralitharan, plays an active role in the Foundation of Goodness (FoG), arguably the foremost NGO using cricket for reconciliation. There are now a number of actors working with cricket in Sri Lanka, a small yet growing portion of the development sector. All have varying levels of engagement with cricket, and include local and international NGOs (e.g. Sri Lanka Unites, UNICEF), businesses carrying out corporate social responsibility (CSR) initiatives (e.g. Tokyo Cement, Coca-Cola), government departments (e.g. the Ministry of Sport, Ministry of Health, and Ministry of Education), and of course the SLC. The FoG brings in other global partners, including Marylebone Cricket Club and Surrey County Cricket Club. These actors primarily aim to increase participation in cricket, focussing on expansion of access to cricket in the 'outstations'.[57] Practically, this involves funding and developing cricket facilities, from founding new cricket grounds, to developing practice wickets, to providing equipment in rural areas. This addresses the structural issues of cricket in Sri Lanka, and is a noble goal in itself, but is much closer to 'sport development' than 'sport for development',[58] which reveals how understandings of cricket's role in reconciliation tend to be both simplistic and causal.

Stakeholders' motivations are similarly revealing. For many, cricket is an obvious venture: it retains island-wide appeal and often simply requires sourcing partners capable of facilitation and supplying funding. Several government ministries employ a low-risk strategy by undertaking cricket programmes, which will almost always be welcomed. Tokyo Cement ran a scheme laying concrete pads for practice wickets, an easy CSR win, one that is now prominent in their advertising. It seems the prestige of association outweighs many other considerations. Of course, profit and prestige also mean that corruption is often an issue. The SLC's charity arm 'Cricket Aid' was investigated for fraud in 2019,[59] having done much fundraising with little in the way of implementation. Conversely, funding partners have often dropped out of the FoG's projects at short notice; it appears many actors wish to fund and be associated with cricket, but are less inclined to actually get things done. Ironically, the enthusiasm with which people want to promote cricket can also be problematic. At one government workshop I attended, each of the Ministry of Sport, Ministry of Health, and Ministry of Education gave presentations on cricket projects they were currently running. It became apparent that all were undertaking very similar work, yet none of the ministries were aware of what the others were doing. Broadly speaking, most stakeholders have an overly simplistic, causal approach, which revolves more around implementation than social development.

Closer analysis of the FoG's work reveals that even actors truly engaged in SDP can come undone. Their primary cricket for reconciliation project has been the Murali Harmony Cup,[60] an annual schools tournament held from 2011 to 2016 for specifically reconciliatory purposes. From 2012 it was held at different locations in the north of Sri Lanka—a region that was one of the worst affected by the war—with the aim of bringing youth teams of various ethnicities and religions from around the country together and reconnecting northern cricket to the rest of the island. Most editions have seen a 'Jaffna combined XI' and a 'Northern XI' compete alongside established sides from the south including elite Colombo schools, and in some instances win. Many participants bought into the reconciliatory spirit, with southern coaches encouraging their students to pair off with northern boys and share a room. The tournament attracted funding from a wide variety of local and international donors, much secured by famous players Sangakkara, Muralitharan, and Mahela Jayawardene, who also attended the tournament and interacted with the children.

The response to the tournament was overwhelmingly positive. All of the past participants I interviewed (coaches and players) noted it gave them fresh perspectives on their counterparts from the north/south, and forged new friendships, while some even had beneficial life outcomes. One informant from Jaffna now worked for the FoG full time on the back of his participation as a player in the 2012 edition. Despite this success, tournament organization has been hampered in the last few years, with a sponsor pulling out last minute in 2017, halting that edition. Despite their efforts, the FoG has struggled to make up the shortfall and has not held the tournament since. Political issues posed obstacles for holding the tournament in the north: as much of the land remains occupied by the army and land claims have not been resolved post-war, securing a ground to play on has been difficult. After the tournament stopped, the relevant government ministries apparently approached the FoG, questioning why this happened and offering support. Yet according to an informant, 'when we got back to them with the details we never heard back'. Again, this highlights the desire for association with cricket, yet little desire to work on it.

Notwithstanding, the Murali Cup is the marquee event in a wider sport programme run by the FoG. Much of their other work centres on their sports facility in the south of the island and focusses on developing talent from rural areas, then getting these talented athletes into the national sides of their respective sports. Even in the north, focus tends to be on finding talented sportspeople, developing an elite cricket squad, and enabling selection to the national side. Thus, even for NGOs like the FoG whose focus is primarily on rural development, progress tends to be measured in number of pitches laid, equipment bags given, and sports scholarships attained by their charges. Ultimately, it is easier for sponsors to support these measurable things too.

The efforts, aims, and motivations of these various actors further highlight the broadly causal approach to SDP in Sri Lanka. For many it is simply about sourcing funding, then finding someone to carry out implementation. For NGOs that are not involved in sport, it often remains an afterthought, tacked on to other projects. Even for the FoG, for whom sport is a central part of their work, the reconciliatory aspect of cricket has been diminished. They continue to focus on promoting rural athletes. In examining the motivations for stakeholders in this sector, the desire for proximity and prestige only adds to this sense of causality. While everyone remains very pro-sport, which is ostensibly a 'good thing' to do, and many people told me that 'it will give "good values"' to those in rural areas, this only further highlights the simplistic, causal approach: giving sport gives 'good values'. Invariably, I could never pin people down to what these values might be. The cricket sector is therefore sport development, *not* sport for development, and at this stage, FoG notwithstanding, certainly not sport for development and peace.

Establishing a Relationship between Sport and Reconciliation

While there is some logic to associating cricket with reconciliation, those trying to employ cricket have evidently found things difficult. The literature on SDP and reconciliation illustrates the complexities of assuming any relationship between cricket and reconciliation, and this contends there is also an inherent difficulty for scholars assessing such contexts.

Firstly, the 'mythopoeic' understandings of sport maintained by SDP practitioners are somewhat vague and idealistic, while the debate surrounding the use of sport as a development tool is not underpinned by a strong evidence base.[61] There is little consensus on if and how sport 'works'. As is evident from this chapter so far, the evangelical perspective on sport within the SDP movement has engendered a largely functional approach, resulting in some practitioners 'merely offering sport activities'[62] in the vain hope they will '"automatically" deliver . . . developmental outcomes'.[63] Many strategies remain predicated on an 'individual behaviourist' model which focusses on personal change,[64] and this method ignores the difficulties of achieving change at the structural level.[65] Even when SDP creates social change, it may 'strengthen hegemonic relations by reinforcing dominant social and economic hierarchies'.[66] Thus, the simplistic approaches commonly underpinning SDP reify 'sport' as something with its own power for change, effectively ignoring the multiple ways in which sport is experienced as a *social* phenomenon. In Sri Lanka alone, the massive diversity in forms of engagement with cricket suggests it is the nature of this engagement that has power, not the sport itself. Cricket in essence is not a monolithic entity.

Secondly, the issue of reconciliation in Sri Lanka is far from simple, as there are many different understandings of reconciliation operating at various levels. Sri Lanka is an ethnically and religiously complex island,[67] comprising a number of ethnic and religious categories, the boundaries of which have gained increasing inflexibility over time.[68] This indicates reconciliation is not about simply reuniting two opposing sides, and the characterization of the civil war as a 'Sinhala versus Tamil' conflict elides the involvement of other groups like the 'Moors' and the Christians.[69] Furthermore, different kinds of reconciliation are required; northern Tamils may desire greater accountability from the state, whereas Tamil Muslims may simply want to return to their homes and coexist again with their neighbours.[70] The ideas that contribute to the varied understandings of reconciliation come from an equally diverse set of influences. For example, the ethics of TRCs are often contextual and culturally specific, underpinned by local concepts of personhood and morality, 'born in communities working to address specific problems'.[71] Conversely, the notion of global human rights is often implicated in the local work of TRCs,[72] and certainly becomes part of the agenda in SDP contexts.[73] Altogether, Thiranagama notes that 'everyday relations cannot be successfully divorced from the larger orders that contour and shape them',[74] echoing that the concepts of the state, of the home, and of the community inflect notions of what reconciliation is. Evidently, reconciliation is not just one monolithic 'thing' either, but a multifaceted concept operating at a variety of levels, one embedded in a much wider set of ideas including ethics, personhood, ethnicity, and memory.

If sport is understood in vague and idealistic terms, and reconciliation is a fluid concept, it is futile to draw a causal relationship between the two. In short, cricket is *not* a panacea. Complex contexts like this highlight the inherent difficulty of assessing sport in terms of reconciliation—of trying to ascertain the relationship between two complex social phenomena. Yet cricket evidently has real positive effects for those who participate in it and is regularly invoked as something capable of enabling reconciliation. If the relationship is not causal, then how might scholars approach understanding this relationship?

Does Cricket 'Work'?

Despite these difficulties, there is a way forward. In the SDP literature, Lindsey et al. advocate contextualizing the perspectives of those engaged in SDP, to 'de-reify' concepts of sport,[75] while Coalter suggests researchers must focus 'on understanding the social processes and mechanisms that might lead to desired outcomes'.[76] I suggest that in order to push this SDP literature forward, it is necessary to move beyond the practical assessment of SDP and understand how sport interacts in society at the micro level, to focus explicitly on the individual. The anthropology of sport suggests that sports are both reflective and constitutive of society, drawing from and influencing other social phenomena outside of the sporting arena.[77] Cricket is therefore embedded in a much wider web of social meaning.

Following anthropologist Michael Carrither's characterization of rhetoric as commonplace acts of persuasion 'invoked for everyday purposes', which involve drawing from and mobilizing certain 'cultural schema' to negotiate the social world,[78] I argue that cricket is merely one of many 'cultural schema' present in Sri Lanka. Those engaging with cricket draw from this web of social meaning in order to understand their own actions and the actions of others. Sport is therefore not only a locus of discourse but is also a rhetorical tool, mobilized by those who participate in it for social gain in combination with other concepts. If sport generates and sustains a certain global discourse that interacts with similar local concepts (e.g. fairness, equality), then it is the way people employ this discourse that is of interest: one must examine the gaps between rhetoric and practice. Any analysis of cricket's potential import for reconciliation *must* focus on the rhetorical and idiomatic employment of sport in common social contexts as much as the specifically (limited) developmental context. I first look at some elements of cricket discourse in Sri Lanka before then suggesting some ways this is employed, and the potential ramifications of this.

Although it is debated whether sport as social phenomenon has ever been 'modern',[79] cricket certainly has traces of being a modernist enterprise, especially through its employment as a colonial tool associated with 'Muscular Christianity'.[80] Anthropologist Arjun Appadurai notes that as a 'hard cultural form' espousing particular Victorian 'class codes',[81] cricket promotes a strong sense of fairness and equality, going on to note that this 'code of fair play dictated an openness to talent and vocation in those of humble origins',[82] an inclusive ideology which appealed to regular Indians. Of course, 'no doubt aspects of this ideology of fairness are based on myth and romanticism'[83] and may be essentially empty signifiers, but few other sports 'formally prescribes the required "Spirit of the Game" '[84] in their rules, and the mythic quality of cricket's discourse has hardly been problematic for its uptake in the subcontinent. Indeed, I assert the invocation of this myth may be the primary draw: the spirit of the game is often discussed in the Sri Lankan media, while the Victorian notion of 'gentlemanly values' remains prevalent, particularly in coaching. Of course, the sporting event often takes place in a liminal space, positioned outside of yet in relationship to society,[85] and we must also pay attention to the 'multidirectionality of flows' of discourse, and not situate sporting ideology purely in the West.[86] Discourse is contested and negotiated locally in the cricketing arena. This all comments on sport as an agent of change in society and reflects it is precisely cricket's nature as a social phenomenon that makes it a problematic tool for reconciliation. In other words, it at once appears 'outside society', and is therefore powerful, yet is also 'of society' and therefore corrupt.

This dynamic most potently reveals the flaw in the rhetoric of 'One Team, One Nation'. As I have shown, the discourse of cricket in Sri Lanka is somewhat problematic, being driven by a very middle-class core of participants who believe it to be diverse and unifying. The nature of a sport like cricket in Sri Lanka is further problematic for reconciliation given that in order to reconcile, it must first divide into teams. This is pertinent given that this could reinforce the already 'hardening' boundaries of ethnic and religious categories in the country.[87] While many teams I encountered were multi-ethnic, within each there remained a dominant group. Furthermore, this ignores the complexity of the conflict in Sri Lanka, subsuming it into a simple binary opposition. Such an opposition may be unifying on the global stage, when there is a greater 'enemy' to oppose, as when Sri Lanka plays international matches. If people's primary engagement with cricket is on the level of the national team, then this is certainly a potential avenue for unification. However, this may break down on smaller stages—that is, national and even local—where oppositions are more likely to be created between groups. Overall, if cricket is employed as a rhetorical device, then this cannot function solely in terms of fairness and a presumed unifying nature. While such discourse is positive and can have benefits for those who employ it, it is hard to see how this rhetoric can directly address issues of reconciliation.

Rhetorical Employment

I invoke examples from my fieldwork in Sri Lanka to show how the employment of such a simplistic cricketing rhetoric on the national level shows some of these flaws in action, whereas the more complex rhetoric on the local, individual level highlights some of the potential benefits. Predominantly, I worked with a Muslim hardball team in central Colombo, and the specific background of the Muslim minority highlights the intricacy of these rhetorical issues. Muslims are a distinct minority 'ethnic group' in Sri Lanka, at about 10 per cent of the population; central Colombo holds a greater proportion, about a third of the city's total population.[88] Muslims have regularly been the target of majoritarian Sinhala Buddhist nationalism,[89] and post-war the Muslim community has been targeted more explicitly, especially in the aftermath of the Easter Sunday attacks, where various Muslims homes and businesses were damaged.[90] While Sri Lanka tends to conceive of Islam as a distinct ethnic category, within this there are numerous individual groups. The majority of Muslims are 'Moors', Tamils descended from traders, but other groups include Memons, Bohra, and Malay. This conveys the huge diversity even *within* Sri Lankan ethnic communities.

My informants were relatively well-off, generally multi-lingual, highly mobile people, who attended more prestigious schools and often travel to go on *Hajj* or *Umrah*. Perhaps tellingly, many of my informants identified themselves as Muslim first, then as Sri Lankan. Some said that they 'managed' their Islam in everyday actions in Sri Lanka, minimizing or maximizing aspects when necessary. It was possible to be a good Muslim and a Sri Lankan patriot, but this required personal negotiation. Islam sustains a transnational identity beyond Sri Lanka,[91] and thus the global discourse of Islam allows for Sri Lankan nationalism, but this proves it is not the only way of categorizing oneself in Sri Lanka.[92] This transnational identity is why Muslims are often denigrated by Sinhalese nationalists, who frame their nationality with reference to the Sri Lankan soil itself and therefore see Muslims as not belonging.[93] By trying to unify Sri Lankans, the 'One Team, One Nation' rhetoric therefore misses out on the complexity of modern global personhood, where persons relate to a far greater web of meaning in constructing their identity. While my informants were huge fans of Sri Lankan cricket, it seemed it did not represent them as strongly as other determinants might. 'One Team, One Nation' does not reflect the 'Sri Lankan identity' of many of these Muslims, then, and therefore elides the immense plurality in Sri Lanka. Any way of moving forward and negotiating nationhood in terms of cricket needs to take account of this complexity.

Despite these issues, my informants indicated cricket had some very real positive effects on their lives. Perhaps, looking more deeply at social relations, sporting discourse and the rhetoric used to mobilize it may work towards cultural change. Theologist Anna Scheid notes that reconciliation functions on a scale, indicating that interpersonal reconciliation between individuals may enable reconciliation between groups, working up the scale to the nation.[94] There may be promise in 'intrinsically value-free' things like sport, when concepts like fairness and equality, mobilized appropriately within the liminal space of the sporting arena, change the way persons understand one another, enabling a greater sense of unity in wider society. The cricketing arena remains one of only a few ostensibly meritocratic spaces in heavily hierarchical Sri Lanka, and I contend the way cricketing discourse is employed reveals how useful it is for teaching individuals to navigate the complexities of their world. In essence, sport may achieve things in changing culture that are potentially mostly imperceptible.

This can be seen in the way my informants went about their cricket, employing these tropes for their own benefit. In examining some of the intricate details of this rhetorical employment by my team-mates during cricket matches and training, I show that contextualization of SDP scenarios requires deeper analysis of individual engagement with sport. Cricketing discourse of fairness and equality was invoked by my team to create a meritocratic, egalitarian space. Hesitancy in leadership at training suggested a desire to maintain a space of equality, with decisions about activities made mostly by consensus, and all members invited to lead certain portions of training. Selection policy for matches was based on attendance, performance, and skill, in that order, aiming to put egality over meritocracy, although this did not always work in practice. Similarly, rhetoric invoked at matches by the captain and key players emphasized a team effort, working for each other, enjoying the game, and so on. Supporting those playing was heavily emphasized, even if one was not selected for matches; we often travelled with more than the eleven men needed. Tensions between egality, meritocracy, and established notions of hierarchy were always present, however. Certain talented players who rarely attended training were selected based on their skill, while others who were mainstays in organizing club activities seemed to gain selection regardless of their skill. Conversely, those more skilled players (therefore higher meritocratically) often used this to cement their position in the club, gaining hierarchical position—assuming leadership roles—through their cricketing exploits.

This conflict between maintaining fairness and being competitive as a team is familiar to any recreational sport team in the world. However, perhaps less typically of other recreational sporting contexts, my informants strongly highlighted how cricket was beneficial to their lives. Many of my informants were eager to note that because of cricket, they took increased confidence into the wider world; they said it helped them to make better decisions and to forge new connections with people who they might otherwise never meet. More importantly, yet less tangibly, there was a lot of discourse about learning about life. My informants often said things like 'respect the pitch'; 'control what you can control'; 'be patient, your time will come'. Cricket therefore taught one how to deal with difficult situations; how to bear hardships and overcome them. Finally, and perhaps most importantly, the cricketing space was often conceived of as an arena within which one 'could express oneself', an exhibition of talents that people may otherwise be unable to show. In all of this, cricket provided an arena for social negotiation. The liminal space of the cricket field allowed my informants to test the bounds of sociality, establish and contest relationships with others, create and maintain self-worth, and understand how better to succeed in life.

This concept of cricket (and sport) as an arena, a liminal space where a dense interplay of social meaning is raised, contested, and refined, shows that an anthropologically sensitive reading may be that cricket has effects on a much deeper social level. The sporting discourse of fairness and equality, functioning to create a space outside of their normal, hierarchically stringent lives, allowed my informants to experiment with sociality and establish better ways of dealing with their problems. If these positive effects are unintended consequences of cricketing rhetoric, this indicates one should perhaps not even really assess the relationship 'between' sport and reconciliation at all, but the employment of sport in navigating the social world and the ramifications this might have on concepts *like* reconciliation. The answer to 'does it work?' probably lies in deeper—potentially imperceptible—social change: the way my informants are changed as they interact with a complex social phenomenon like sport. Showing that people's lives are improved by sport on an individual level is not new, but this highlights the value of ethnographic work as it contends SDP should assess structural change on a more granular level.

In the Sri Lankan context, it also identifies some potential ramifications. It may be that representation of minorities in the national team will aid social unity, as many people's primary engagement is with the national team, and greater diversity in representation will enable people to feel more represented themselves. 'One Team, One Nation' remains a poor capture of Sri Lankan complexity if it remains stringently Sinhala Buddhist. Similarly, if cricket improves lives and enables better social relations within and across groups, then the apparently simplistic response of stakeholders in developing cricket and widening participation is actually a very good thing. It may not be that cricket has to forge relations between different groups but simply forge relations full stop. Most of my informants reported that cricket helped them to understand and interact better with others. Without understanding how rhetorical employment of sporting discourse affects the way cricket is conceived of by participants, any scholarly interpretation of SDP will remain limited.

Conclusion

The historical and cultural context of cricket in Sri Lanka conveys that there is a certain local logic to associating cricket with reconciliation. However, the framing of this association as a causal relationship—where cricket entails reconciliation—is flawed, and ignores much of the social complexity of a diverse country. Furthermore, the literature on SDP and reconciliation implies that there are inherent difficulties in ever ascertaining a relationship between two social phenomena like cricket and reconciliation. This all shows that cricket doesn't merely 'work' to enable reconciliation but is a complex phenomenon held within an intricate web of meaning. Cricket is replete with multiple discourses, and is furthermore an arena where such discourses are rhetorically deployed, contested, and refined by individuals. Cricket is not a monolithic entity, does not 'work' in any simple fashion, and is not a panacea.

I have argued that in order to understand any relationship between these two phenomena, to better contextualize SDP contexts, scholars must see sport embedded within broader social structures, and therefore look specifically at the social engagement with sport by informants, to see how they mobilize meaning for their own purposes. Whether forging new relationships, developing social status, or improving understanding of their life, those who engage in cricket do seem to gain positive effects that might support reconciliation. However, I suggest that if these effects are broadly unintended consequences, this indicates one should perhaps not even really assess the relationship 'between' sport and reconciliation at all but the employment of sport in navigating the social world and the ramifications this might have for concepts *like* reconciliation. The answer to 'does it work?' probably lies in deeper—potentially imperceptible—social change.

Moving forward, what this implies is that perhaps in the Sri Lankan context, cricket development and widening participation is far more beneficial than it initially appears. Representation may be a good thing if most people's engagement with cricket is the national team. Therefore, cricket suggests reconciliation is much more of an economic or class problem than other reconciliatory analyses allow. Cricket reveals that the middle-class hub of discourse does little to affect wider society. It tries to portray Sri Lankan cricket as inclusive, when realistically it tends not to be inclusive of the multiplicity of identities present in Sri Lanka. Hence, what is needed is potentially simply *more* cricket; real interaction with other groups, not merely imagined unity.

Notes

1. Sharika Thiranagama, *In My Mother's House: Civil War in Sri Lanka* (Philadelphia, PA: University of Pennsylvania Press, 2011), 256.
2. The diverse reconciliatory strategies employed in Sri Lanka are too numerous to cover fully here. Briefly, one should note Sri Lankan stakeholders recognize 'hard' reconciliation, i.e. political and legalistic work towards acknowledgement of alleged war crimes and reparations, and 'soft' reconciliation, the development of links between and across various ethnic, religious, and class divides. Who these

diverse peoples are and the way they can or should be brought together is often ignored: the vague and slightly imprecise nature of what soft reconciliation means in the Sri Lankan context is part of why it is bandied around so readily by various stakeholders. Much 'soft' reconciliation—especially that pursued by NGOs—is often subsumed within wider developmental goals: addressing rural/urban inequality, education, empowerment, etc. Cricket fits within this 'soft' category.

3. Yngve G. Lithman, 'Anthropologists on home turf: How green is the grass?', *Anthropologica* 46, no. 1 (2004).

4. Kumar Sangakkara, 'MCC spirit of cricket Cowdrey lecture', presented at the MCC Annual Dinner, Lords Cricket Ground, 2011.

5. Sangakkara, 'MCC spirit of cricket'.

6. 'Sri Lanka cricket launches 1 Team. 1 Nation', Sri Lanka Cricket, 8 March 2016, www.srilankacricket.lk/news/sri-lanka-cricket-launches-1-team-1-nation.

7. Sri Lanka Cricket, 'Cricket-aid fundraiser at Lord's', 2016.

8. Ethnically, Sri Lanka is majority Sinhalese (75 per cent), with distinct Sri Lankan Tamil (11 per cent), 'Moor' (Tamil Muslims) (9 per cent), and Indian Tamil (4 per cent) minorities (Census, 2012). See Nira Wickramasinghe, *Sri Lanka in the Modern Age: A History* (updated 2nd ed.) (New York: Oxford University Press, 2014) for a fuller explanation of how these categories developed and hardened during the British colonial period. Jonathan Spencer, Jonathan Goodhand, Shahul Hasbullah, Bart Klem, Benedikt Korf, and Kalinga Tudor Silva, *Checkpoint, Temple, Church and Mosque: A Collaborative Ethnography of War and Peace* (London: Pluto Press, 2015) is particularly informative about the ramifications of this complexity in the present.

9. Michael Roberts, 'Sri Lanka: The power of cricket and the power in cricket', in *Cricket and National Identity in the Postcolonial Age: Following On*, ed. Stephen Wagg (London: Routledge, 2005).

10. Michael Roberts, *Incursions and Excursions in and around Sri Lankan Cricket* (Colombo: Vijitha Yapa, 2011).

11. Muralitharan is an 'Indian Tamil', a descendent of migrants brought over by the British to work in the tea plantations. At the time of writing, Sri Lanka has not included a 'Sri Lankan Tamil' from the north in a cricket squad since C. Balakrishnan in 1969 (see Roberts, 'Sri Lanka: The power of cricket', 135).

12. Lyndsay Hayhurst, 'The power to shape policy: Charting sport for development and peace policy discourses', *International Journal of Sport Policy and Politics* 1, no. 2 (2009).

13. Bruce Kidd, 'A new social movement: Sport for development and peace', *Sport in Society* 11, no. 4 (2008); Fred Coalter, 'The politics of sport-for-development: Limited focus programmes and broad gauge problems?' *International Review for the Sociology of Sport* 45, no. 3 (2010).

14. Coalter, 'The politics of sports for development', 296.

15. John Sugden, 'Critical left-realism and sport interventions in divided societies', *International Review for the Sociology of Sport* 45, no. 3 (2010): 260.

16. Sugden, 'Critical left-realism'.

17. Coalter, 'The politics of sports for development', 296.

18. Sugden, 'Critical left-realism'.

19. Ibid.

20. Ibid., 262.

21. Bruce Kidd paraphrased in ibid., 262.

22. The 'Stolen Generations' were the Australian children of aboriginal descent, re-moved from their parents to be raised in White foster homes from the First World War to the 1970s. The government formally apologized to them in 2008. See Nayanika Mookherjee, Nigel Rapport, Lisette Josephides, Ghassan Hage, Lindi Renier Todd, and Gillian Cowlishaw, 'The ethics of apology: A set of commentaries', *Critique of Anthropology* 29, no. 3 (2009): 345–366.

23. Mookherjee et al., 'The Ethics of Apology'.

24. Nancy Scheper-Hughes, 'Undoing: Social suffering and the politics of remorse in the New South Africa', *Social Justice* 25, no. 4 (1998): 138.

25. Thiranagama, *In My Mother's House*; Spencer et al., *Checkpoint, Temple, Church and Mosque*.

26. Thiranagama, *In My Mother's House*, 12.

27. See Mythri Jegathesan and Kitana Ananda, 'What Sri Lanka needs now', *CNN*, 28 April 2019, www.cnn.com/2019/04/28/opinions/sri-lanka-attack-threatens-fragile-peace-ananda-jegathesan/index.html; Ahilan Kadirgamar, 'Don't give in to polarisation', *The Hindu*, 3 May 2019, www.thehindu.com/opinion/lead/dont-give-in-to-polarisation/article27016132.ece; Sharika Thiranagama, 'Perspective: For Sri Lankan Christians like me, the Easter attacks revived old ghosts', *Washington Post*, 30 April 2019, www.washingtonpost.com/outlook/2019/04/30/sri-lankan-christians-like-me-easter-attacks-revived-old-ghosts.

28. Priscilla Hayner, *Unspeakable Truths: Transitional Justice and the Challenge of Truth Commissions* (New York: Routledge, 2010), 190.

29. Richard Ashby Wilson, 'Anthropological studies of national reconciliation processes', *Anthropological Theory* 3, no. 3 (2003): 367–387.

30. See Sharika Thiranagama, 'Claiming the state: Postwar reconciliation in Sri Lanka', *Humanity: An International Journal of Human Rights, Humanitarianism, and Development* 4, no. 1 (2013): 98. The Lessons Learnt and Reconciliation Commission was widely criticized for being biased in the government's favour.

31. Nayanika Mookherjee, 'The aesthetics of nations: Anthropological and historical approaches', *Journal of the Royal Anthropological Institute* 17, no. 1 (May 2011): S1–20.

32. Niko Besnier and Susan Brownell, 'Sport, modernity, and the body', *Annual Review of Anthropology* 41, no. 1 (21 October 2012): 452.

33. There is a relative paucity of scholarship on this history, limited mainly to the work of Michael Roberts (see particularly *Incursions and Excursions*), S.S. Perera, *The Janashakthi Book of Sri Lanka Cricket, 1832–1996* (Colombo: Janashakthi Insurance, 1999), and Nicholas Brookes, *An Island's Eleven: The Story of Sri*

Lankan Cricket (Penguin: New Delhi, 2022). I have sought to support these texts with my own archival work, particularly on schools cricket.

34. Burghers are a minority Sri Lankan ethnic group descended from Portuguese and Dutch colonists, and are predominantly Christian. They retained influence in Colombo due to their hybrid position and relative wealth. See Roberts, *Incursions and Excursions* for a fuller explication of the Burgher relationship with cricket.

35. Brookes, personal communication.

36. Brookes, *An Island's Eleven*.

37. Roberts, 'Sri Lanka: The power of cricket'.

38. Brookes, *An Island's Eleven*.

39. Ibid.

40. Roberts, 'Sri Lanka: The power of cricket', 132.

41. Roberts, *Incursions and Excursions*, 22.

42. Dominic Malcolm, Jon Gemmell, and Nalin Mehta, 'Cricket and modernity: International and interdisciplinary perspectives on the study of the imperial game', *Sport in Society* 12, no. 4–5 (May 2009): 431–446.

43. Roberts, *Incursions and Excursions*, 22.

44. Sri Lanka Unites told me only around one hundred schools in Sri Lanka have more than one language medium. Most are either wholly Sinhala or Tamil.

45. The distinction I draw here is between the original game played with a leather ball and cricket played with a tennis/rubber ball.

46. Many of my informants, male and female, noted that many women are actually bigger fans than the men. Unfortunately, female participation in playing cricket remains very limited.

47. Tariq Jazeel, 'Urban theory with an outside', *Environment and Planning D: Society and Space* 36, no. 3 (1 June 2018): 412.

48. Many current national players began their cricket careers at small schools and moved to elite institutions in their late teens. Some only play for the big colleges in their final year and are known as 'imports'.

49. Aravinda De Silva and Shahriar Khan, *Aravinda: My Autobiography* (London: Mainstream Publishing, 1999), 38.

50. Jazeel, 'Urban theory', 415.

51. Roberts, 'Sri Lanka: The power of cricket'.

52. Jonathan Spencer, *Anthropology, Politics and the State: Democracy and Violence in South Asia* (Cambridge: Cambridge University Press, 2007) and *Sri Lanka: History and the Roots of Conflict* (London: Routledge, 1990).

53. 'Ceremony ahead of Sri Lanka's departure for ICC World Twenty20 2016', Island Cricket, 2016, www.islandcricket.lk/cricket_video/ceremony-ahead-of-sri-lan kas-departure-for-icc-world-twenty20-2016.

54. Benjamin Hildred, 'Is cricket "Sri Lankan"? Sport, values, and personhood in a post-conflict state' (Master's dissertation, University of Durham, 2017).

55. Andrew Fidel Fernando, 'Growing up with Murali'. *The Cricket Monthly*, 11 August 2020, www.thecricketmonthly.com/story/1228133/growing-up-with-murali.

56. Fernando, 'Growing up with Murali'.
57. 'Outstations' commonly refers to almost any area of the island which is outside of Colombo.
58. Kidd, 'A new social movement'.
59. Ajith Siriwardana and Yohan Perera, 'Suspend "Cricket Aid": COPE instructs SLC', *Daily Mirror*, 4 September 2019, www.dailymirror.lk/breaking_news/Susp end-Cricket-Aid:-COPE-instructs-SLC/108-173924.
60. Named after Muralitharan.
61. Sugden, 'Critical left-realism'; Coalter, 'The politics of sports for development'.
62. Ramón Spaaij, 'Building social and cultural capital among young people in disadvantaged communities: Lessons from a Brazilian sport-based intervention program', *Sport, Education and Society* 17, no. 1 (1 January 2012): 77.
63. Iain Lindsey, Tess Kay, Ruth Jeanes, and Davies Banda, *Localizing Global Sport for Development* (Manchester: Manchester University Press, 2017), 38.
64. Lindsey et al., *Localizing Global Sport for Development*.
65. Robert Huish, 'Punching above its weight: Cuba's use of sport for south–south co-operation', *Third World Quarterly* 32, no. 3 (1 April 2011): 417–433.
66. Simon Darnell and David R. Black, 'Mainstreaming sport into international development studies', *Third World Quarterly* 32, no. 3 (1 April 2011): 369.
67. See Spencer et al., *Checkpoint, Temple* and John Clifford Holt, *Buddhist Extremists and Muslim Minorities: Religious Conflict in Contemporary Sri Lanka* (Oxford: Oxford University Press, 2016).
68. Wickramasinghe, *Sri Lanka in the Modern Age*.
69. 'Moors' are Tamil Muslims—see Thiranagama, *In My Mother's House*; Holt, *Buddhist Extremists and Muslim Minorities*. The Christian community in Sri Lanka crosscuts various ethnicities including Tamil, Sinhala, and Burgher.
70. Sharika Thiranagama, 'The self at a time of war in northern Sri Lanka', *Journal of Historical Sociology* 26, no. 1 (March 2013): 19–40.
71. Anna Floerke Scheid. 'Interpersonal and social reconciliation: Finding congruence in African theological anthropology', *HORIZONS* 39, no. 1 (2012): 46.
72. Wilson, 'Anthropological studies of national reconciliation'.
73. Coalter, 'The politics of sports for development'.
74. Thiranagama, 'Claiming the state', 110.
75. Lindsey et al., *Localizing Global Sport for Development*, 48.
76. Coalter, 'The politics of sports for development', 311.
77. Lithman, 'Anthropologists on home turf'.
78. Michael Carrithers, 'Why anthropologists should study rhetoric', *The Journal of the Royal Anthropological Institute* 11, no. 3 (2005): 577–583.
79. Besnier and Brownell, 'Sport, modernity, and the body'; Ingrid Kummels, 'Anthropological perspectives on sport and culture: Against sports as the essence of Western modernity', in *Sport across Asia* (London: Routledge, 2013), 25–45.

80. Dominic Malcolm, Jon Gemmell, and Nalin Mehta, 'Cricket and modernity: International and interdisciplinary perspectives on the study of the imperial game', *Sport in Society* 12, no. 4–5 (May 2009): 431–446.

81. Arjun Appadurai, *Modernity at Large: Cultural Dimensions of Globalization* (Minneapolis, MN: University of Minnesota Press, 1996), 91.

82. Ibid., 92.

83. Malcolm et al., 'Cricket and modernity', 435.

84. Ibid.

85. Lithman, 'Anthropologists on home turf'.

86. Kummels, 'Anthropological perspectives on sport', 13.

87. See Wickramasinghe, *Sri Lanka in the Modern Age.*

88. Sri Lanka, ed., *Census of Population and Housing 2012: Key Findings* (Colombo: Department of Census and Statistics, Ministry of Finance and Planning, 2014).

89. See Holt, *Buddhist Extremists* and Rohan Bastin and Premakumara de Silva, 'Historical threads of Buddhist–Muslim relations in Sri Lanka', *Buddhist–Muslim Relations in a Theravada World*, eds. Iselin Frydenlund and Michael Jerryson (Singapore: Springer, 2020), 25–62.

90. See Michael Safi and agencies, 'Sri Lanka imposes curfew after mobs target mosques', *The Guardian*, 13 May 2019, www.theguardian.com/world/2019/may/13/sri-lanka-imposes-curfew-after-mobs-target-mosques; Meera Srinivasan, 'Dozens arrested after anti-Muslim violence in Sri Lanka', *The Hindu*, 14 May 2019, www.thehindu.com/news/international/one-killed-in-anti-muslim-riots-in-sri-lanka/article27123889.ece; and Thiranagama, 'Perspective: For Sri Lankan Christians like me', among others.

91. See Holt, *Buddhist Extremists* and Bastin and de Silva, 'Historical threads of Buddhist–Muslim relations'.

92. This also works similarly to sport, as in the 'the global cricket community'.

93. Bastin and de Silva, 'Historical threads of Buddhist–Muslim relations'.

94. Scheid, 'Interpersonal and social reconciliation'.

6

'On Top of the World' (?)

England and the 'National' Aesthetics of World Cup Cricket, 1999 and 2019

Claire Westall

The British Empire made national identities complex for those within its grasp, at home as well as overseas, and its effects continue to be seen in international sport. In the United Kingdom, we are used to British 'national' teams appearing in some sporting situations, as with the Olympic 'Team GB', and the UK's constituent home 'nations' performing separately in others. In cricketing circles, we are familiar with the imperial, then 'commonwealth', lineage of England's Test rivals, especially its oldest foe, Australia. We are also familiar with the different cricketing versions of 'national' representation England encounters internationally; from the Indian team's connection to a republic of a billion people to the ambition for a regional Caribbean 'nation' embodied by the West Indies team.[1] In addition, the England cricket team itself has never been a 'national' sporting team in any straightforward fashion.

It is in this context that this chapter examines the 'national' predicament expressed by cricket's England and then uses its consideration of the British-English cricketing 'nation'—pegged to Britain's creation and dissemination of imperial Englishness—as the backdrop for examining the aesthetic culture of the International Cricket Council's (ICC's) Men's World Cups of 1999 and 2019, hosted officially in England, and then England and Wales. More specifically, and in a similar vein to Ben Powis and Philippa Velija's useful analysis of the non-events and hollow 'diversity' presented within the 'Cricket Has No Boundaries' campaign,[2] the discussion compares the musical anthems and music videos used by the ICC and the England and Wales Cricket Board (ECB) for the 1999 and

Claire Westall, *'On Top of the World' (?)* In: *Cricket and Nationhood in the Twenty-First Century.* Edited by: Souvik Naha, Oxford University Press. © Oxford University Press 2024. DOI: 10.1093/9780191982576.003.0007

2019 tournaments, linking their complexities and 'national' signifiers to the long story of cricketing Englishness, British imperialism, and the demand to 'world' the game from a supposedly 'young' and 'diverse' London. What becomes clear is that even when the England team is seemingly 'on top of the world', as it was in 2019, and when the England team might also stand for a vibrant civic nation, English cricket continues to look insecure and its connection to England reads as uncertain. Indeed, contemporary cricket continues to rely upon nostalgic and imperial conceptions of Englishness—which England itself needs to move beyond—and it disclaims or side-steps the difficulties of a national England by selling cricket to the world as a product of multicultural British London.[3]

England as the British-Imperial Cricketing 'Nation'

Cricket is renowned for being a global sport that remains synonymous with England and a mythic sense of Englishness.[4] Despite the game's love affair with the story of its own beginnings, cricket's claim to England, as a 'nation', has been, and remains, fraught. Cricket's originary myth depicts its own English ancestry as stretching back to before the twelfth century—long before England annexed the Welsh Crown in 1284—as if ancient pedigree might protect the game, as well as England, from external forces (including Wales and Scotland) and 'modernizing' pressures. Generally, though, cricket historians now recognize that cricket has its roots in the 'pre-national' age of pan-European folk games, and that its relatively early formalization was a modern and economic undertaking that bore no relation to the 'spirit of the game' that later became Britain's cricketing shorthand for British-English ethical superiority.[5] In fact, cricket gained real popularity and patronage across the eighteenth century while the new, industrializing, and (particularly after 1707) imperial 'union' of Britain was developing as a world power. Importantly, though the game was notoriously bound to drinking and gambling, in this period cricket was cast as an innocent rural pastime as part of Britain's urban nostalgia for the English countryside—a nostalgia that was taking shape while simultaneously being made ready for exportation around the world as a kind of imperial idea of Englishness.[6]

In the mid- to late eighteenth century, cricket was adopted and formalized by the landed aristocracy and Britain's rising class of merchants.

These groups often acted together from a shared London base that was (and still is) thought of as distinct from an England outside of the city and as itself directly connected to the world beyond thanks to Britain's imperial networks. Mike Marqusee writes that the 'land-owning capitalists' who 'issued the Laws of Cricket from the Star and Garter', in London's Pall Mall in 1744 and 1774, were also the leaders of 'the world's first market economy on a national scale', and as they became 'engrossed in the work of empire-building' they 'took for granted their right to rule at home and abroad'.[7] The same 'set', let's say, established Lord's—initially in 1787 and then permanently in 1814—as the hallowed 'home' of cricket and of the game's self-declared 'custodians', Marylebone Cricket Club (MCC). Hence, cricket's formal and self-styled 'home' was a financially determined London that directed Britain's (then) expanding empire and, from Lord's especially, projected its vision of Englishness out onto the world it wanted to claim for itself. When cricket underwent its mid-Victorian reimagining, via 'Muscular Christianity' and *Tom Brown's School Days* (1857), it became a British 'institution' that signalled a newly sanitized Englishness, and it was understood to be the character-building training ground for the men of Britain's Empire.[8] This repositioning of cricket established the idealized figure of the British-English amateur gentleman—from the reformed public schools and Oxbridge—as central to Britain's mythology of Englishness.[9] Such amateurs were supposedly fit to lead professional cricketers, the England cricket team, and all those within the British Empire, regardless of any contrary and exposing sporting or political realities.[10]

As a recognizable *sport*, then, cricket never belonged to an England that was singularly 'national' as distinct from, or prior to, Britain—even if England has always been understood as the dominant force within Britain, the UK, and the British Empire, and even if cricketing games existed in England, especially southern England, well before modern Britain. In addition, cricket's leading (and legislative) figures were Britain's London-linked men of worldly economic and cultural means. Consequently, when deploying Marqusee's insightful quip about the '*lie*' English cricket 'tells itself about itself'—that is, about the 'cult of the honest yeoman and the village green, in the denial of cricket's origins in commerce, politics, patronage and urban society'[11]—we should remember that this 'lie' is a British 'lie' about cricket's Englishness, and also about England, that works to actively erase—or at least bypass—a 'national' England through its dissemination of an Englishness imagined by, and working for, Britain's cultural and economic imperialism, especially as managed through British institutions. We should also remember that, in a related fashion, the tussles between England, London, and the British-imperial state underscored by cricket's history continue to be played out in the UK's contemporary political and sporting landscape. Think, for example, of the complex ramifications of Brexit for cricket (as sporting practice and cultural signifier) which are helpfully unpacked by Dominic Malcolm and Richard Parrish.[12] Moreover, it is in this light, and through Britain's imperial vision of England and Englishness, that we should read the creation and branding of the 'England' cricket team.

By the 1740s, 'England' had become a regularly used team name, but it had no 'national' or representative standing. Instead, it was deployed by numerous ad hoc or roughly assembled teams. The 'England' label was indicative of the 'transient appellations of convenience' often chosen by wealthy patrons or entrepreneurial professionals to describe the players recruited to execute their cricketing-financial plans.[13] Making cricket's history digestible, Simon Hughes writes of the 'first proper account of a full cricket match' as coming in 1744 with Kent playing 'All England', then, in the 1770s, the famed Hambledon regularly beating an 'England' side made up of Kent and Surrey players, and, in 1793, an 'England XI' taking on an enormous 'Norfolk XXXIII'.[14] Hughes also states that a 'Proper' England team ('star-studded' rather than 'motley') came, in 1846, with William Clarke's travelling 'All England Eleven'.[15] However, Simon Wilde insists that '[n]one of the famous All England or other wandering XIs that toured the United Kingdom between the 1820s and 1870s saw themselves as representing the nation' (i.e. England), and that included Clarke's professional group and the famous amateur wanderers *I Zingari*.[16] It is clear from Wilde and numerous other cricket histories that the use of 'England' as a team name functioned as a kind of brand label to attract crowds to cricket and financialize their interest, most obviously through gate money, wagers, player income, and sports equipment businesses.[17] Similar interests underpinned early 'England' trips overseas during the same period, beginning with the 1859 tour to America under George Parr's leadership.[18] While James Lillywhite, a professional and member of the pioneering sports-business family, led 'England' on the 1876–1877 visit to Australia (in what became the first 'Test' series), it was the imperially minded, amateur captain-administrators—Lords Harris and Hawke, and Sirs Pelham Warner and H.D.G. Leveson-Gower—who drove the formation of a regular and representatively strong 'England' team. These leading figures often had business interests in the places they took their 'England' teams (as with Hawke to Argentina, for his railway interests, and Leveson-Gower to South Africa, for his coal investments).[19] And these men were also central to domestic county cricket in England and to cricket's imperial diffusion, with the two coming together in their ties to the MCC (where the 'role of the MCC cannot be underestimated when considering the growth and development of imperial cricket'[20]). For such amateur-leaders, 'England' was bound to personal, familial, and British-imperial wealth creation, and the 'England' team was, in effect, a sporting arm of imperial diplomacy for Britain. In fact, the built-in claim to ethical standards being upheld by Britain's 'England' and its amateur-leaders when hypocrisies were self-evidently on display was chiefly why the Bodyline Tour of 1932–1933 was so explosive for imperial—or newly 'commonwealth'—relations between Australia and Britain-as-England.

Alongside the rise of print culture and the patriotic impact of war, from the 1899–1902 Boer conflict on, Wilde describes Australia's competitive strength, cultural confidence, and more egalitarian sense of camaraderie as significant in the development of England as a 'national' team, especially after the Ashes defeat of 1882.[21] In addition, England adopted Australian-inspired markers of national identification. This included the creation, by R.E. Foster, of an England badge and cap in 1908, which took as much inspiration from Australia's 'baggy green' as it did from the England football team's uniform and Three Lions insignia.[22] Although Wilde's discussion of the Three Lions symbol and cricket's varying use of the Crown and Coronet is helpfully detailed, it misses the obvious problem of the Lions and Crown imagery marking the British monarchy, the ways in which England slides into Britain with such referencing, and how such slippage makes it hard to separate England from other Commonwealth cricketing 'nations' also wedded to the British monarchy. Indeed, as Wilde recognizes, cricket's commonwealth 'nations' were required to align themselves with the British monarchy in the early phase of the ICC—and the ICC was itself set up by the MCC in 1909, shortly after the MCC had taken control of the England team and its tours overseas, in 1903–1904.[23] With the MCC, as a private members' club, functioning in effect as 'England' for much of the twentieth century, the layering of personal/private, national, and imperial interests as the basis of 'England' was normalized in international cricket. So too was the positioning of 'England' as imperial Britain's competitive representative, standing as the first yet supposedly 'equal' international player whose 'commonwealth' brethren were still claimed as British 'dominions' (as laid out in the Balfour Declaration of 1926) and had to adhere to the authority of the 'Laws' passed in London—via Parliament politically and, in a cricketing context, the MCC at Lord's. Despite the MCC having to formally relinquish control of England in the 1960s in order to claim public funds for cricket, the England team were still an MCC-marked side while travelling until 1976–1977 and were wearing MCC colours while overseas all the way up until the winter tour of 1996–1997.[24] This meant that a private London club's claim to England-as-cricketing-nation could still be seen on the bodies of England cricketers in what was 'empire' well into the sport's neoliberal phase. A full change of attire and organizational leadership only came in 1997 with the creation of the ECB. However, this new entity maintained the supra-national and imperial version of England it had inherited, even though it came into being at the very moment New Labour made British devolution possible.

Today, as most England fans realize, the ECB is responsible for all forms of cricket in England and Wales, and it is the employer of 'centrally' contracted England players and support staff.[25] This means that the England team still formally represents England *and* Wales—that is, two of Britain's constituent 'nations' or two of the UK's constituent countries—despite Wales being treated as both a country/nation (like England) and a region (a part of England). When the new board chose to subsume the Welsh 'W' within the dominant 'E' of England in its abbreviated moniker, ECB, it reflected the position of Welsh cricket in relation to English cricket— where Wales is a country with a 'national' team that is not 'international' and has only one first-class club, Glamorgan, which plays its cricket in the English Country Championship and has actually played against touring sides like Australia and West Indies in 'quasi-international' matches as if standing in for an international Wales.[26] More broadly, it also mirrored the wider political situation for the Welsh—in which Wales has often been 'subsumed' within an elastic England, since Edward I in 1284[27]—and the legal situation for Wales—in which 'English law' is shorthand for the laws that apply to England and Wales because they are treated as a single jurisdiction, as established in 1536 and formerly articulated in the 1746 Berwick Act. The name ECB, then, is a neat little marker of the way in which 'England' has been understood elastically, in a British mode, as a 'national' unit that subsumes other 'nations' while also standing as seemingly distinct from—and above—the very nations it has erased from view through its own non-national position.

This 'Greater England' of a cricketing England–Wales structure helps prevent both England and Wales from having separate international cricket teams and, thereby, from having specifically 'national' identities on the world stage.[28] It also means that cricket's 'England' functions in much the same way as England does politically within the unevenly devolved and not-quite-postimperial British 'union'—as a kind of dominant yet invisible (and never formalized) unit that is imagined as equal to, or the same as, Britain, especially when seen from beyond the UK or sold to an international audience.[29] When, in the early 1990s, Marqusee wrote that '[i]n cricket, all components of the United Kingdom are supposed to be represented by "England"', he was roughly right, especially in the context of top-tier international Test cricket.[30] He was, though, making this point just a few years before British devolution, and as Ireland and Scotland were growing their claims to international cricket—with Ireland gaining ICC Associate status in 1993 and Scotland doing likewise in 1997, then, via the ICC Trophy, qualifying for the 1999 World Cup at the expense of Ireland. Scotland and Ireland now have well-established international teams, and Ireland has had Test status since 2017.[31] Nevertheless, England still operates as a kind of 'British' team, in part because it is still the highest-achieving team within Britain, and also because its British dimensions play out in player qualification issues (as is often noted) and in the (rarely explored) way the ECB and ICC market cricket by making use of an explicitly London-centred 'British-national' aesthetic. This is an aesthetic that includes a notably imperial sense of Englishness, refuses to understand England in national terms, and even helps inhibit the possibility of imagining (and growing) England into a postimperial and potentially progressive nation—in cricketing and in larger terms.

In many ways, we need to read this aesthetic and its rendering of contemporary cricket's British 'England' through the tensions between

Englishness and Britishness that evolved with empire and continue to play out at 'home' and 'overseas', especially as the elastic understanding of 'Greater England' was fundamentally important to the ethical claims to superiority of the British Empire. A notable source of help with this, and the most astute reading of cricket's place in the national and imperial negotiations between England/Englishness and Britain/Britishness, is still Ian Baucom's *Out of Place* (1999), as many of Baucom's insights remain relevant to cricket and England within an unevenly devolved Britain. Presenting the cricket field in England and 'out' in empire as an identity-inscribing locale, or *lieu de memoire* in Pierre Nora's terminology, Baucom argues that 'Englishness has been identified with Britishness' and that Britain's 'Englishness has also defined itself against the British Empire', first through its 'privileging of *English* soil' and second, 'from the 1960s onward, by largely abandoning spatial and territorial ideologies for a racial "discourse of loyalty" and coidentity'.[32] He understands that the British Nationality Bill of 1948 announced Britishness as 'coincid[ing] with the territory of the nation *and* the empire' so that ' "British" space was thus read as homogenous, interchangeable, everywhere alike, while "English" space remained unique, local, differentiated: a formula which permitted the empire to be that which was simultaneously *within* the boundaries of Britishness and *outside* the territory of Englishness'.[33] Baucom also explains the 1981 Nationality Act as 'render[ing] hegemonic a racial narrative of English identity' that had not previously been the 'official narrative' of Britain.[34] In what follows, I suggest that Baucom's understanding of British-English cricketing disruptions to 'national' identity can be seen in the aesthetic language used during the 1999 and 2019 World Cups, and that his conception of 'the colonial cricket field' as a complex site of 'the imperial dialectic of Englishness'[35] might be thought of as animating the unique combination of confidence and anxiety evident in England's cricket as well as in the musical 'selling' of cricket for World Cups played (predominantly) in England. In addition, Baucom's caution about the way Englishness, and England, remains protected and inaccessible to 'Others' because of the buffering and homogenizing international/imperial role of Britishness can help with a reading of cricket's links to, and use of, London-British claims to diversity and inclusion because these claims rely on the structures of race- and class-based exclusion that continue to cast England and Englishness as White/exclusive/

pure/inaccessible. In this way, the analysis to come is informed by, and hopefully contributes to, debates in recent cricket research about the intersections of race, class, and Englishness, but does so by concentrating on Britain's deployment of Englishness, its construction of a non-national cricketing England, and its performative insistence on London's internationally marketable diversity.[36]

Englishness, Eccentricity, and the Dull, Dull Failure of 1999

As Baucom makes clear, cricket in England is bound to nostalgia—nostalgia for an always already lost rural England, and for a worldly, imperial sense of British dominance that helped create that mythic rural image. Given that nostalgia is a kind of 'homesickness',[37] it makes sense—as in Baucom's argument—that the imperial diffusion of cricket, and ideas of England and Englishness, influence the way cricket and England connect with 'home'. Further, any idea of 'home' for England, and for cricket, must always negotiate with Britain—with imperial decline coming to England and cricket via Britain and its institutions. For example, Cate Watson describes the relationship between cricket, nostalgia, and the waning of empire by analysing the discursive effects of the BBC's Test Match Special (TMS). Watson pinpoints an 'aura of failure' as built in to England's cricket, and TMS's cricket coverage, suggesting this stems from England's very first Test match being a loss—to Australia during the 1876–1877 tour—and that this 'aura of failure' has only grown with the postimperial uncertainty of post-war Britain and post-war English cricket.[38] In short, international cricket for England began with failure in empire, and, later, there was a nostalgic twinning of imperial and cricketing failure in the way English cricket and cricket played by the England team were discursively packaged by the British state's broadcaster, the BBC. When Marqusee described the 'national malaise' of England and English cricket in the 1990s, England's malady came from a postimperial crisis of national identity (often expressed as imperial nostalgia) that was unfolding on the cricket pitch through the dire performances of the England team, as if the England cricketers of 1993 were 'bowed down not just by the burden of losing, but by the burden of representing their country'.[39] Also reflecting on the England team in the 1990s, Emma John has, more recently, described how during her teen years cricket was 'universally considered the most boring of sports', and 'England's cricketers were losers', recognized as such in the media and popular imaginary.[40] Despite becoming an England obsessive, John details her sense of the meaningless abundance of One Day Internationals (ODIs) and England's inability, in the 1990s, to play them in an aggressively competitive manner, stating that 'one-day cricket could actually be more boring than a five-day Test' because '[w]hen the opposition posted a good score, there was nothing more dull than watching England tramp stodgily after it, their defeat a foregone conclusion'.[41] Alongside a clash with her university exams, John's familiarity with England's dull failures meant that she adopted 'a total and utter disinterest' in the World Cup of 1999.[42] She even confesses to feeling 'a huge and perverse sense of pride that [she] had adopted such a gloomy demeanour from the start' when the entire competition-as-spectacle imploded in a shambolic manner and England crashed out in the group stages of the tournament for the very first (but not last) time.[43] In contrast to John, in 1999 I was a first year English Literature undergraduate who'd been raised on cricket (in an obviously minor way) and wanted to persuade those around me that the cricket World Cup was going to be an enjoyable affair—despite having to resort to alcohol and fancy dress to make my case. As it turned out, I was fantastically wrong. The 1999 World Cup encapsulated the sense of insecurity, failure, and postimperial uncertainty that dominated English cricket in the 1990s. In short, 'England 99', as the tournament was branded, was about a number of 'home-sicknesses', including the cricketing ailments of England that were evident when ODI cricket was brought back 'home', to a never-quite-national England, and the multiple ways in which the cricketing world was able to see a failing cricketing England as tied to a dull, nostalgic, and eccentric rendering of Englishness.

Having acted as World Cup hosts in 1975 and 1979 and then co-hosts with Wales in 1983, England was the (unsurprisingly) self-appointed 'home' of cricket's most celebrated of international competitions until the tournament moved to the Asian subcontinent in 1987 and then became a key prize in the power struggle between cricket's leading international boards (of India, Australia, and England).[44] Where the 1992 World Cup in Australia and New Zealand marked the emergence of 'modern' ODI cricket—in the vein of Kerry Packer's World Series, with coloured kits, day/night games, and a white ball— 'England 99' was the first time the ICC staked a strong claim to the image, marketing, and execution of the tournament, working with the (relatively new and Lord's-based) ECB to package cricket for the world's televisual consumption. In 1999 England were the dominant hosts, but a minor form of co-hosting was granted to Scotland, Ireland, the Netherlands, and Wales. This 'union' of host nations was part of an effort to reward the development of cricket within Britain and Europe, and to draw ICC Associate Members into the World Cup fold.[45] The effect, though, was a good number of awkward oddities for the 'nations' involved. While Scotland became the first Associate to host a World Cup match, Ireland and the Netherlands were hosts without participating national teams, and, as always, Wales was a co-host without being an international ICC cricketing 'nation' itself. Moreover, in typical British-cricketing fashion, Wales was omitted from the list of host nations when Prime Minister Tony Blair made his short (and seemingly underprepared) speech at the opening ceremony.[46]

That a British prime minister could forget about Wales might strike one as predictable, but when Parliament has just passed the Devolution Acts, including the Government of Wales Act (1998), and the Prime Minister is on the field at Lord's with a Welsh-born, former England captain—in (then) MCC President Tony Lewis—the erasure is more pronounced, and the imagined supra-national yet un-devolved England it is predicated upon becomes obvious. In addition, with Blair and Lewis flanked by two of cricket's leading neoliberalizers—Lord McLaurin, the ECB chairmen of Tesco fame, and the ICC president Jagmohan Dalmiya—a dark-suited foursome of world leaders (cricketing, economic, and political) stood to welcome the world to an England that was a 'national' oddity within Britain's new political arrangement, and was largely hidden from view because Lord's (with the MCC) and London were standing in for cricket and its England. When Blair made use of the fateful label 'carnival of cricket', it was clearly meant to tap into the 'Cool Britannia' moment, but much of the tournament's iconography felt wedded to the Thatcherite heritage industry and its imperial nostalgia. In fact, the tournament's carnival strapline was, as Tim Crabb and Stephen Wagg say, 'savagely ironic', standing as woefully misjudged in the context of 1990s English cricket and obviously exploitative in its grabbing at an earlier

(1970s and 1980s) understanding of West Indies cricket culture as part of a corporate effort to appeal to the British-Caribbean community and a 'multicultural Britain' that was meant to link cricket in Britain to a global audience.[47] Blair tried to help this cause when he claimed to remember (but was incorrect about) West Indies' Roy Fredericks hitting the 'first ball for six' in 1975.[48] A similarly hollow claim to international 'colour' (as a cricket 'carnival') and an accompanying enlarging of England as an erasing force were also evident in the 1999 corporate tournament logo. The logo depicted a multi-coloured outline of a bowler—said to be India's Debashish Mohanty—following through, with 'England 99' emblazoned underneath.[49] The erased or empty white centre of the bowler, and the subsumption of all the other hosts within the 'England' label, offered an international casting of cricket's England by the ECB and ICC as worldly and dynamic but also elastic, dominant, and apparently all-consuming in a way that (again) made England a cricketing-imperial signifier; that is, the British 'England' of empire rather than a specific cricketing nation, place, or team.

The 1999 World Cup is generally thought of as a humiliating flop for the ECB, the ICC, and cricket itself. Indeed, so much about the competition was wide of the mark—including the white duke ball which, being used for the first and last time, swung so much that a record 979 wides were bowled across the six weeks of the tournament, upsetting spread-betting forecasts considerably[50]—that criticism was abundant at the time and has only become more refined and insistent since. In the build-up to the 2019 World Cup, *The Cricketer* magazine summarized the general view when describing the tournament as 'a disaster from the start', with 'a wretched opening ceremony, a failed corporate strategy, unequipped match venues, a flawed tournament format, unexplainable mascots, a horrible summer strapline, unruly supporters, a terribly one-sided final [with Australia beating Pakistan by eight wickets] and a host nation [meaning England] out of its depth'.[51] The opening ceremony has received particularly negative attention, having been 'widely deemed the most embarrassing and underwhelming attempt at sporting pageantry ever seen'.[52] Even while the ceremony was taking place, England's Darren Gough captured the team's confusion and amusement on his own hand-held 'Gough Cam', as rain and then smoke obscured the minor spattering of fireworks, children ran on the soaked outfield with flags, and the green pitch at Lord's was made 'home' to giant white balls that looked like golf (rather than cricket) balls and were clearly inspired by the giant inflatable footballs used in the Euro 96 Opening at Wembley.[53] Unlike the fans at Wembley, though, the Lord's crowd were witnessing a failing on-field and televisual display of sporting 'worldliness' at 'home', and seemed unsure of what to expect or do in response.

Looking back, Gough's autobiography, *Dazzler* (2002), written 'with' David Norrie,[54] gives more detail about the troubled position of England in the build-up to the tournament, including the players' failed attempt to improve their tournament pay, the incompatibility of Simon Pack's military team directorship with the struggles of the England players, and how the England set-up was 'shell-shocked' by their early exit and had never understood the importance of upping their run-rate for tournament survival after they had only made 103 runs in their loss to South Africa.[55] In relation to this chapter specifically, three particular points in the book's explanation of the moment stand out. First, Gough claims that the opening ceremony was indicative of England's inability to act as big-event hosts thanks to 'tradition and natural reserve',[56] as if national characteristics prevented England and English cricket from offering competence, grandeur, and an effective welcome to the world, or at least the cricketing world it supposedly created and welcomed to Lord's. Second, Gough says that Neil 'Harvey' Fairbrother 'shouldn't have gone' to watch Manchester United in the Champions League Final against Bayern Munich, in Spain, during the tournament,[57] despite the 'Gough Cam' footage showing Gough, and others, making light of this at the time.[58] Interestingly, Fairbrother's odd kind of 'moonlighting' (with permission) underlined the length of the ICC tournament, the effect this had on players, and the European networks of sporting achievement football made appealing, even to professional cricketers playing for their country on the world stage. Third, the book describes how embarrassing it was that the England team, as hosts, had to attend a post-tournament World Cup Party at Buckingham Palace, where '[h]er loyal failures had to line up to meet H.M. the Queen' alongside the victorious Australian side.[59] Across the 1990s, then, failure was the hallmark of the England team, English cricket, and their World Cup, especially as they attempted to welcome, and negotiate with, the world (as the ICC and its membership), and as they stood before the authority of Britain/the UK (as marked by the Queen and Prime Minister). Moreover, this low point in England's cricketing reputation has been partly explained by the difficulties of Englishness or national character. And ideas of national character and imperial cricketing Englishness underpinned the music video used for the official World Cup song in 1999—itself another telling failure.

Almost every commentator deriding the 1999 tournament—Gough included—references the weird and disastrous official song, 'Everybody All Over the World', by Dave Stewart of Eurythmics. Critics highlight: the song not mentioning cricket or sport; it not being performed by Stewart at the opening ceremony; it being released the day after England were knocked out; and it failing to register in the UK singles chart.[60] Some of these shortcomings are relatively common for songs released for big sporting occasions, including the omission of sporting references. Even football's comparatively successful 1996 European Championships, held in England, had a downbeat ballad as its official song—'We're in This Together' by Simply Red's Mick Hucknall—which offered an abstract idea of coming together, made no explicit reference to football or sport, and actually described England as 'wash[ed]-up failures' in the eyes of the world.[61] While the music video with Hucknall concentrates on England's footballing history and the loyalty of England fans, his song failed to register with the crowd when he performed it at Wembley to open the tournament. Instead, it was the unofficial anthem of 1996, Baddiel, Skinner, and The Lightning Seeds' 'Three Lions', which contributed to an upturn in English national identification in the late 1990s (despite the 'Cool Britannia' markers of the track and its video).[62] Nevertheless, the popularity of 'Three Lions' and the problem of the not-quite-right Hucknall example were clearly not heeded by cricket's authorities. In fact, the 1999 World Cup song and its music video—fairly described as some of 'English cricket's more bizarre pieces of memorabilia'[63]—are premised upon ideas of eccentricity and sickness that relate back to imperial conceptions of cricket's Englishness and do nothing to identify a national England or England's cricket team.

With a chorus stating that 'everybody all over the world' should join the 'festival' (which sounds like 'best of all') because 'life is a carnival', and lyrics declaring the 'universe is just one song', Stewart's track offers an obvious call to international collectivity (akin to Hucknall's) that might suit a global sport that describes itself as apolitical (as cricket nearly always does).[64] That this call for an international celebration can be linked (even distantly) to a gentlemanly sporting adventure might partly explain why the song was later adapted to become the signature track for the 2004 Disney film *Around the World in 80 Days*.[65] If we are generous, we might suggest that there are nods to cricket's soundscape occurring musically, and through the contribution of Chucho Merchan particularly, in the seemingly crowd-inspired bursts of Ludwig van Beethoven's 'Ode to Joy', in the way mixed percussion joins up with blasts of brass (think Barmy Army), and in the use of steel drums (think West Indies and the Caribbean). Yet Stewart's lyrics say nothing sporting and his steady, almost ironically flat verses don't lend themselves to ideas of physical effort and achievement. In fact, in his lyrics heroes aren't physical/ sporting warriors but rather calm figures who 'come and go' as 'wise men watch the river flow'. It is instead 'electricity' that connects people—men and women, equally resilient—as it 'howls' and 'blows' through them, prompting the energetic rise necessary for the communal chorus that comes when there are 'no grey clouds inside your head'. In these lines the song gestures to the eccentric world of the music video; a cricketing miniaturization of the classic American film *One Flew Over the Cuckoo's Nest* (1975)—with similar characters, costumes, roles, and plot moves—that makes dark sense of the mental 'grey clouds' and the 'howl[ing]' electricity as that of electroshock therapy, originally described in Ken Kesey's 1962 novel, on which the film is based. In the music video, Stewart stands in Jack Nicholson's place as a kind of English McMurphy who leads his fellow asylum innates in a bid for freedom by stealing a bus, picking up a woman, and enjoying a moment of shared sporting action before being rounded up by the institutional authorities—represented onscreen by two female nurses, a male orderly and actors wearing 'Sheriff's Department' outfits. With this framing, the deadpan verses are the musical musings of Stewart-as-McMurphy 'inside' (perhaps drugged) as he plays guitar, and the more exuberant choral 'carnival' is the shared joy of escape, of getting 'out' and 'playing'. The replacement of the film's fishing trip with a cricketing excursion works to domesticate an American cinematic and literary classic via a recognizable trope of Englishness. It also offers a move 'out' of an American context—in which America stands as the first site of imperial failure and rejection (as well as the market the ICC/cricket really wants to penetrate)—and back 'inwards', as the asylum escape becomes a return to an open, green, and pleasant land of English sporting play. This movement pattern might even be read as a return to English soil after an American imperial-cultural adventure. And this already odd cultural coding only becomes more complicatedly bizarre on closer inspection.

The video opens with a closeup of a bat, batting gloves, and a score-board, as if formal cricket will be central to what follows. It then interlaces wicket-taking action from a junior cricket match with scenes of card-playing and puzzle-making in the asylum as Stewart begins to serenade the *Cuckoo's Nest* asylum group from behind his masking dark shades. Quickly making a run for it, Stewart then leads the inmates out onto a bus, which he briefly drives through London (past houses and shops), and via his girlfriend's home, until the escapees arrive at a green cricket pitch. This part is filmed at Hornsey Cricket Club—the club dating back past the 1870s and situated in Crouch End—and pulls cricket's London history, and urban-pastoral amalgamation, into view.[66] Simultaneously, with the scoreboard showing Hornsey having made 103, there is an un-canny pointer to England's lowest 1999 tournament score, which also is 103 but against South Africa, and it is as if the standard of the men's international team has already been met by London's cricketing boys and girls—children who seem capable (unlike their international seniors) of turning their 103 into a success (given that wicket-taking images are used). But success doesn't quite happen for this young team because their space is taken over by the asylum escapees in a scene of chaotic, perhaps 'crazy', sporting play. The apparently misshapen, grotesque, and misun-derstood male bodies of the 'inmates' are allowed to move, take up space, and run around haphazardly—as they use a wheelbarrow, bounce a bas-ketball, bowl a cricket ball, and wildly swing a cricket bat. Even the lead nurse (a Nurse Ratched figure) briefly swings the bat (in what reads as a reference to the film's sexual politics[67]) before reverting to type and over-seeing Stewart's removal by the police.

Across the music video, but especially in this cricketing sequence, white clothing is over-determined in the dress of the 'inmates', staff, and young cricketers, and this use of 'whites' stands in marked contrast to the inter-national cricketing moment in which England are wearing their coloured ODI kit at home for the first time. We might see the video's colour-coding as pulling sporting youth, state authority, and those marked as 'different' into an older, and distinctly imperial, claim to cricketing-English purity, innocence, and amateur elegance (when this colour-coding had long been relinquished for cricket World Cups). The importance of the colour palette is presented in racial terms too, with a Chief Bromden figure pictured pretending to sweep against the white-washed walls of his confinement, and with a Black 'inmate', draped in gold jewellery, bearing his gold teeth in a wide-mouthed grin to greet Stewart-as-McMurphy's White girlfriend. This man's performed combination of excitement and demure welcome is set to expose and undercut any idea of Black male threat in a way that is markedly like the supposedly 'colourful' marking strategies used to advertise the 1999 World Cup and attempt to attract Black spectator-participants to the matches.[68] This figure is an entirely British insertion into the otherwise American-inspired set of characters and so highlights the British vision shaping the video's aesthetic. And this British gaze is also evident in the way the video has at its critical core a British-imperial construction of English eccentricity, where games for those 'in white' are brief interludes for eccentrics caught between institutional containment and pre-determined failure—failure that, as the *Cuckoo's Nest* novel and film tell us, will lead to the euthanasia of freedom.

Eccentricity 'becomes a viable and necessary concept when culture begins to be perceived as having centres and margins', as was the case for Britain and England from the late eighteenth century.[69] As Rainer Emig explains, it also 'serves as a field of experimentation' as well as of 'tolerance and compromise in times of cultural self-interrogation'.[70] This was certainly the situation for England and its cricket in the 1990s. In his book-length study, *Englishness Identified: Manners and Character, 1650–1850* (2000), Paul Langford describes how the idea of eccentricity as an English national characteristic develops from around the 1770s—that is, as empire is taking off and cricket is being formalized—and is understood as linked to liberty, originality, and the need for a 'safety value' that doesn't become insanity but is allowed to rub up against the edge of madness.[71] For Langford, eccentricity is linked to the role of the amateur and a kind of politically 'soft' conservatism[72]—attributes that carry over into cricket's discursive culture. Eccentricity also plays a 'double function', as Julia Saville says, in that 'within English society it is the mask of oddity that unmasks hypocrisy, constituting earnestness and decency as the bedrock of a moral society', and, simultaneously, '[b]eyond the borders of England, within the broader empire, it takes the form of a rhetorical and affective excess that parades the Englishman's cultural difference even as it helps to stabilize and disseminate English moral values'.[73] By drawing on these readings of eccentricity—by Emig, Langford, and Saville—and connecting them back to Baucom, we might read Stewart's video as presenting the multi-functioning role of British-English eccentricity as it disrupts a domestic cricketing space after, and as, it regains its 'home', outside of the imperial space it previously made/claimed. In such a reading, the imperial/outer/marginal domain of the enclosed British-American institutional asylum is escaped yet also brought back 'home', to the urban-green cricketing ground of youthful endeavour. This cricketing space is then upended by older and seemingly eccentric men—men whose eccentricity might cast them as developmentally stunted, or as trapped in an arrested/detained mode of imperial development. Framed by the *Cuckoo's Nest* narrative, their eccentricities are set to expose the institutional and emasculating violence of the asylum and to point to the contaminating effects of imperial and carceral spaces—as if their 'insanity' has been created in the outer domain of state-imperial institutions and is revealed as benign and creative eccentricity—that works as physical self-expression—when repositioned 'at home'. It is also as if the men's identification with the cricket ground, including their touching the ground/soil, is a (re)connection with the green field as a site of Englishness. Such (re)connections act as evidence of their inner honesty, their trustworthiness, and even their innocence or purity, and these ideas are demonstrated through the acts of physical play that never become organized sport. In this way, the men never enter the space, structure, and discipline of cricket (as a *sport*) but remain free only when in contact with the cricket ground, and only in the context of an always-already known failure to escape the authority of the imperial state in a playful re-enactment of imperially imagined Englishness.

All this is fantastically troublesome, and not least because *One Flew Over the Cuckoo's Nest*—as novel and film—presents a serious attempt to bring an anti-psychiatry vision of institutional violence to the public. In the music video, though, the institutional construction of 'insanity' is no more dangerous than the soft imperial association of Englishness and eccentricity that Britain used to cast British-English men, especially in empire, as pillars of international liberty, originality, and freedom-creation. The eyebrow-raising reticence of Stewart-as-McMurphy when he is recaptured is a long way off the hollowed-out figure of McMurphy after his electro-treatment and as he is released into death by Chief Bromden. Moreover, in all this there is never a sense of cricket and England—the Englishness associated with the cricket pitch is almost dream-like in its promise of welcome for the eccentrics. Cricket is taken away from the young, organized cricketers, and from those deemed 'insane', and the cricket pitch becomes entirely empty after the inmates have been recaptured. Hence, it is (and was, in 1999) hard to imagine any positive message about cricket, England, and the World Cup being associated with this creative offering, and its aesthetic reads (and read, then) as if it were formulated in the early to mid-1980s, certainly before Caryl Phillips' *Playing Away* (1987), and not as after Euro 96 and within the New Labour, millennial moment of British devolution and growing English nationalism. It should not have been surprisingly, then, that when the World Cup came back to England in 2019, the ECB and ICC went all out to ensure that the popular reaction and tournament vibe was not—in the words of another Stewart song—'Oh no, not you again'.

Britain's London-without-England and the Triumph of 2019

If 1999 was a particular nadir for England's ODI cricket, especially as it was presented to the world from 'home', a new World Cup low came for the team when England again failed to make the knockout stages at the 2015 competition, with heavy group-stage losses to Australia and New Zealand (the joint hosts) as well as defeats by Sri Lanka and Bangladesh.[74] However, the immense turnaround that followed—between 2015 and 2019—with the Eoin Morgan, Andrew Strauss, and Trevor Bayliss phase of England's ODI redevelopment meant that by 2019 the team were genuine tournament favourites as the World Cup returned to 'England and Wales'. Collectively, England had become an attacking, risk-taking team that made strong use of the Twenty20 (T20) experiences and skills of their players.[75] As cricket writers often explain, the one-day game can seem relatively slow and less significant than T20 cricket—and most importantly, the playing and entertainment package that is the Indian Premier League (IPL)—but T20 also infuses ODI cricket with new batting and bowling techniques, as well as higher scores and destructive 'death' bowling.[76] These and related developments added to the expectations for the 2019 World Cup, and shaped England's own team selection and playing style, most obviously through the playing/captaining mentality of Morgan, the batting confidence of Jos Buttler and Jason Roy, the late inclusion of Jofra Archer, and the importance of spinners Adil Rashid and Moeen Ali to the squad. Moreover, the ECB and ICC knew that the 2019 World Cup presented a significant, perhaps pivotal, opportunity to raise the profile of cricket in England/the UK, and to develop links between English cricket and the game's global audience, most notably via the South Asian diaspora. And yet where the 1999 tournament was broadcast by both Sky and the BBC (in the BBC's last offering of live cricket for decades), the late kerfuffle over television rights and the need to show England in the final on terrestrial television underscored the ongoing problem of how to grow the popularity of the game, especially 'at home', when the financial benefits of exclusive—though international—broadcasting rights packages have been prioritized since the turn of the millennium.

Nevertheless, as if scripted by the media-marketing gods, the 2019 World Cup was packaged as a dramatic T20- or IPL-style 'hit' and became one (despite lower scoring rates and totals than expected). The England men's team lifted the trophy for the first time, and Ben Stokes became English cricket's unique 'special one', as Ian Botham named him.[77] Much had changed since 1999. Most importantly, the England team had gone from 'losers' to world champions, defeating New Zealand in the World Cup final—on 'home' soil, at Lord's, via a boundary count back, following a tied fifty-over match (with controversially awarded overthrows) and a unique tournament 'Super Over'. There are no words that can recapture the excitement of the 2019 World Cup final. Others have tried and there is no need (or space) to replicate such efforts here.[78] Instead, the focus in this section is on the over-looked aesthetic culture, music, and music videos employed to sell the 2019 World Cup—specifically Andrew 'Freddie' Flintoff's rendition of 'On Top of the World', and the official tournament anthem, 'Stand By', from Loryn and Rudimental. Examinations of these cricketing-musical texts demonstrate that while the England team had changed a lot between 1999 and 2019, there was not so much a change of marketing direction, from 1999 to 2019, but rather an improved execution of the sales-pitch required for an international cricket tournament speaking to the world from its British-London base. This base laid claim to a new, 'young', and 'diverse' audience, at 'home' in London—as part of an effort to shore up the game's financial future, domestically and internationally—by presenting them as already attached to a British-and-worldly big-event 'party' that merely coincided with cricket. And this musical-marketing effort not only removed cricket-as-sport from its frame of reference but also presented a built-in sense of imperial Englishness that continued to bypass, or erase, a national conception of England.

In August 2018, the ICC released a music video of Flintoff singing 'On Top of the World' to mark the opening of the ticket ballot for the 2019 World Cup.[79] While it was not an official music 'single', it was a telling part of the wider 'Are You In?' marketing campaign for the tournament and even carried over the carnival trope from 1999—declaring 'The World Cup Carnival Is Coming!'[80] The Flintoff track is an abridged reworking of the song, with the same title, by Imagine Dragons, a US pop-rock band from Las Vegas, who rose to popularity in 2012 and became the US billboard's 'breakout band' of 2013. They released 'On Top of the World' in 2013. The song is built around a sample from Steve Reich's 1972 'Clapping Music'—which is overlaid with nonchalant whistling that acts as a casual, everyday inclusion strategy—and also has its own sporting links with its appearance in FIFA 13 and ESPN's 2013–2014 National Basketball Association (NBA) coverage.[81] While the Imagine Dragons track itself is about success coming after years of struggle, and belief in future achievement, their official music video is about success being followed by disbelief, as it depicts but also satirizes the popular conspiracy theory that the Apollo moon landings of 1969 were faked, and that Stanley Kubrick references this fakery in later cinematic works.[82] In the official video, there is a kind of communal sense of euphoria and madness on display as the American public feasts on the televisual spectacle of a lunar landing even after it has been exposed as a Hollywood production, and a mass of female fans descend on the film studio when the astronaut-actors are shown to be the band. The band, then, are not 'on top of the world', looking down on earth from the moon, but are 'on top' of the world of music-and-fandom—with all that this seems to bring.

In the ICC reworking of 'On Top of the World', the earlier clap-whistle combination is supplemented by Flintoff tapping a teacup to make the necessary slide from an American cultural product to a recognizable trope of Englishness. The move also works to suggest that a quaint version of English applause and the consumption of tea (both associated with cricketing civility) are the background against which Flintoff performs. When Flintoff sings, the song's original opening references to interpersonal relationships have been removed, and the focus tightens to express the highs and lows of personal failure, triumphant recovery, and the forward momentum of life's journey, as if offering a metaphor for sporting/cricketing life: 'I've had the highest mountains / I've had the deepest rivers / You can have it all, but life keeps moving'. Separated from any idea of a cricketing team, the lyrics imply that Flintoff is describing his own past efforts—of the dues he's 'paid to the dirt'—and not being able to give up, having been 'been dreaming of this since a child'. With the chorus, he declares, 'I'm on top of the world, ay [. . .] been waiting on this for a while now [. . .] I'll take you with me if I can', as if it might be possible to share his journey to the top, and that the rise to the top comes after contact with the 'dirt', where, in this setting, 'dirt' reads as the soil of 'home' and cricketing competition. From here the song moves outwards by addressing the listener, and working to instil confidence and resilience in them, with Flintoff explaining that he knows 'it's hard when you're falling down' but 'get up now, get up'. The rationale for recovery is this singer's own success—'Cos I'm on top of the world'—and the cricketing star is allowed to instruct and/or inspire those listening to recover themselves because he is at the 'top'—perhaps setting an example or providing a space for them to join him.

In the accompanying ICC video for 'On Top of the World', Flintoff is the leader joined by others as his lyrical claim to a vertical rise to 'the top' is substituted, visually, with a horizontal journey that appears to traverse the land of Britain-England-London. However, England is only imagined through the lens of imperial Englishness (as empty, rural, quaint, village-like, and set against the international picture of the 'world' beyond, etc.), and it gets left behind by, because it is less significant than, an internationalized and cricketing British London that is the centre and climax of the video's celebratory journey. Flintoff begins his travels from the 'Boundary Café' and he moves through a sequence of British-English locations, leading an increasingly large and diverse dance troupe of cricket supporters to and then through London, eventually arriving at the Oval's Hobbs Gates ready for the coming tournament's opening game. This journey visually establishes the idea of an England outside of London as marginal, as on the 'boundary', and rearticulates the centrality of London as the 'home' of cricket, as well as the financial-cultural hub for a multicultural and cricketing Britain that doesn't understand itself as English or as part of England. From the opening, and with the appearance of a Barmy Army-inspired brass band, there is a binding of cricket and music, and early on Radio 1's Greg James—known for his cricket interests and work—is watching Flintoff's growing popularity and following. The video converts this connection between sport and music into an image of carnival as Flintoff is leading a mobile carnival caravan of costumed performers with the choreography of Del Mak using twenty-three actors/ dancers and around one hundred other fans. This conception of a 'cricket carnival' is writ large with performers wearing England shirts walking on stilts with comedically tall cricket pads as Flintoff's band of merry fans walk through a seemingly rural field of Englishness (complete with a background church spire) that might be said to allude to the conceptions of Englishness underpinning the singing of Jerusalem at cricket grounds from the mid-2000s. Despite the comedic excess of this trampling of Englishness by English-supporting cricketing bodies, there are moments when a broader, international referencing of cricketing fandom could be positive for England—as a team and cricketing nation acting with other cricketing nations. This idea is embodied by the cluster of dancers— men and women, Black and White—whose dancing bodies animate the St George's Cross or England cricket shirts of their costumes. It is also reinforced by the synchronized union of these England-identified fans with other dancers marked as representing the nations of cricket's world of international play. However, when Flintoff catches the ball hit by a young White batsman wearing a St George's T-shirt, that boy is inadvert- ently cast as 'out' (in cricketing terms) in a manner that seems to meta- phorically encode a jettisoning of England and a refusal to let him come to 'the top of the world' with Flintoff. It is as if England is caught out, then overridden by the dominance of London-as-Britain, which means that the earlier referencing to mothers and their sons as potential 'fans' is made moot for young White boys supporting England. And Flintoff isn't allowed to 'bowl to' this boy but rather is positioned as the boy's opposition-in-passing. This cricketing removal of a young, White male body identified with (or as standing for) England immediately precedes the video's opening out into a vision of multicultural London. The shift from the English fields of 'rural' life to the blocks of city flats and brutalist architecture that stands for London's working-class, urban living spaces makes this point clear. In addition, the drawing together of fans in team shirts, fancy dress, and face paint calls attention to the fun of ODI and T20 spectatorship but does so in order to link cricket's shorter formats to these London-lived spaces of urban domesticity. The long-running claim by the ICC and ECB to a Caribbean-infused cricket carnival is also reinforced with the appearance of a 'Carnival Cuisine' shopfront on the corner of Electric Avenue, as the film and dancing troupe moves through Brixton market. And it is in London, and at the Oval specifically, that ordinary citizens and cricket stars (Flintoff, Phil Tufnell, and Kumar Sangakkara) can mix, in a coordinated dance to welcome the world and kick off the cricket party.

That it is Flintoff leading this welcome to the world is important. He stands as a warm, well-known, and successful body of English cricketing achievement—as the iconic allrounder of the Ashes winning team of 2005—whose achievements did not lead to a 'worlded' tournament victory. His Lancastrian accent (obvious in the singing) signals his Preston upbringing, his state education, and his experiences of moving from county to country youth cricket. It also works to make audible an England that cannot be conflated with London-British life, despite London being Flintoff's musical-visual-cricketing destiny in the video. In fact, his seemingly ordinary connection to the national space of England, and its north, helps to complicate the otherwise obvious ICC/ECB-promoted British-London aesthetic that demands and animates inclusion by sacrificing, bypassing, or, as in the video, apparently leaving England, as place/space and as identified with a young White boy, behind. While this emphasis on London makes sense in some ways—and specifically with the Oval being the ground for the tournament's opening game as well as the place where short format cricket has proven most successful/lucrative in English cricket—the close of the video for 'On Top of the World' makes clear that this is not the only reason a London-British aesthetic dominates. In fact, when dancing ground staff and gatekeeping beefeaters close out the Flintoff video, they are kickstarting the aesthetic used for the 2019 World Cup's 'opening party'.

The aesthetic for the 2019 'opening party' was heavily indebted to 'London 2012'; that is, the look and cultural 'feel' created for the Queen's Diamond Jubilee celebrations and London Olympics of 2012 (an aesthetic reanimated for the Platinum Jubilee celebrations of 2022). The ICC promised that the 2019 tournament opening would be 'the most celebrated start to a World Cup ever' and located the 'party' on 'The Mall', with Buckingham Palace as its backdrop. Cricket, then, was being preemptively celebrated outside of any cricketing location in what was obviously an anxiety-bound and finance-orientated move that insisted on positioning the game as belonging to Britain's London. By escaping the confines of a green cricketing field, or a recognizable ground or pavilion, the tournament creators looked to shed the identity-inscribing pressures Baucom describes and opted instead for the iconography of Britain's 'landmark London', particularly as it had been used in 2012.[83] Indeed, in 2012 Pall Mall was the principal site of the Jubilee celebrations and part of the Olympic marathon route that erased the appearance of London-as-lived in favour of a tourist's-eye view of the televised capital. Roughly speaking, the iconic Pall Mall also marks the place where cricket's formalization by the wealthy occurred (see earlier), and where high-end shopping is married to the history of a non-cricketing ball and bat (or mallet) game called 'pall mall'. For the 2019 cricket party, 'The Mall' was repurposed as a temporary, and unconvincing, site of 'street cricket'. This gesture was meant to suggest that informality, as 'party', could replace ceremonial formality despite everything being tightly controlled—scripted and timed—and the location signalling British institutional wealth and imperial monarchy. As a cricketing 'street party', the opening event was also set to tap into—but quite explicitly usurped—narratives of improvised and adapted cricket associated with former colonial spaces, and/or with those outside of cricket's recognized establishments and grounds.

Flintoff's relatively 'soft' lad-cricketer image was central to this welcoming party, as he hosted the event alongside his (then) *Top Gear* cohost, comedian Patrick 'Paddy' McGuinness, and Shibani Dandekar, the Indo-Australian singer and presenter. These three celebrities introduced live music, the competing World Cup captains, and a host of stars—cricketing and otherwise—playing 'street cricket' in mini 'national' teams. This ICC/ECB orchestration struck as backward looking, with the marrying of 2019 to 2012's earlier aesthetic, as well as exclusive, especially in and through its effort to perform 'diversity' and 'inclusion'. The supposed celebration of cricket, music, and popular participation was poorly attended—with about 400 fans braving the rain[84]—and was also only available on subscription television (when the BBC-led coverage of 2012 had been crucial for the public imaginary). Moreover, cricket was never going to become the image of 2012 but it looked to emulate the 2012 aesthetic so as not to appear parochially English, or specifically cricketing in an established and thereby 'dull' manner that might point back to the 1990s and to English cricket's general reputation. The subsuming of England under a British-London banner, and the old British-imperial claim to the world via cricket's England, was even made visible in the decorating of 'the Mall', as the flags of the participating cricketing 'nations', including England's St George's Cross, were almost lost on screen amidst the abundance, and visual dominance, of Union Jacks (used as they had been in 2012 and would be again in 2022).[85] This was always going to strike as odd, and revealingly so, because where Britain's London—as capital—was the host *city* for the 2012 Olympics and where London's, and Pall Mall's, 'palace' stands as the official 'home' of the Queen, England and Wales were the 'national' cricketing hosts for the 2019 World Cup (so not Britain and not London) and so should have been central to the iconography used to welcome the world to its cricketing 'home'. Yet the cricketing authorities had doubled down on the idea of London-as-Britain being the international 'home' of cricket (without England or by minimizing England) by reclaiming the Mall for a non-cricketing version of cricket and by removing cricket from any association with the land of England. It was clear that there was an erasure or minimizing of England within a dominant British-London aesthetic as if this would head off, or remove, issues of nationalism, race, and imperial prejudice when, in fact, this move was helping to underline and animate the continuation of such pressures.

At the opening 'party' (and unlike 1999), the official World Cup song was performed by its primary artists. The onlooking crowd were also shown how to perform the dance moves from the accompanying music video. The official ICC World Cup song, by Loryn, featuring Rudimental, was released on 18 May 2019 and titled 'Stand By'—as if the power of anticipation was a key marketing idea. 'Stand By' has nothing to connect it lyrically to cricket or sport, and makes no claim to England or any specific sporting place. While it notes that 'there's a million other people here tonight', its call to 'Stand By' is about a personal relationship, about the absence of a loved one, and the desire to reconnect with an out-of-sight body (the kind of content erased from the ICC's use of 'On Top of the World'). Musically, we might say that its party-based dance rhythm is not unlike the previous two World Cup anthems (of 2011 and 2015). We might also note that it is fantastically more 'of its moment' than Stewart's 1999 track, thanks, in large part, to the skill of Rudimental, the drum and bass band from Hackney who rose to prominence in 2012 when their single 'Feel the Love' (featuring John Newman) became a hit during the 'Jubilympic' summer. The titles of Rudimental's three albums carry their key promotional ideas about music and its connection to their own sense of located identities—with *Home* (2013), *We the Generation* (2016), *Toast to Our Differences and Distinction* (2019), and *Ground Control* (2021). They have often used relatively young/unknown singers to make their tracks, and this was the case with Loryn. The ICC press release described the Loryn–Rudimental partnership as 'celebrat[ing] the cultural diversity of the United Kingdom', despite the voice coming from an almost unknown Canadian singer, and despite England and Wales (not the UK or London) hosting the tournament.[86] It also quoted Steve Elworth, managing director of the 2019 competition, as saying: '[i]t is important to acknowledge the power of music in sporting environments—from a motivational platform for players to providing a common voice for fans to celebrate together [and] I am sure we will see the official song at the absolute heart of this tournament'.[87] And the catchy and well-crafted track was certainly ubiquitous during games and on the Sky coverage. The same press release also cited members of Rudimental and their explanations for the track, with Piers Aggett saying, '[c]elebrating our diversity is a key message of the band. Obviously, we've all got different heritages, we're from London—one of the most diverse cities in the world and we like to celebrate our differences. That's our vibe'.[88]

This idea—of being together in and as an international London—is at the centre of the music video for 'Stand By'. Where, in 'On Top of the World', the presence of Flintoff helped to signal England despite his cricketing-marketing journey prioritizing London, the video for 'Stand By' severs any connection between cricket and England-as-place.[89] Instead, it concentrates on the build up to, and enjoyment of, a summer party for a 'young' and 'diverse' crowd in London, and it bookends this celebration with images of older, seemingly first-generation immigrants who appear to retain nostalgic cricketing connections. The video opens with soft-focus seemingly warming shots of a remembered boyhood of beach cricket, apparently in the Caribbean, and it closes with a white cricket ball being caught by a Black pensioner playing dominoes outside a London pub and remembering this cricketing childhood. In addition, the video depicts a teenage White boy stealing a white cricket ball from a barber shop coded as British Asian, and in which cricket is the communal entertainment (on the TV) of an older male collective of South Asian heritage that disapproves of the boy's incursion and theft. When outside, this young White boy briefly throws the ball to some friends, but they never play cricket. No-one does. Instead, the ball becomes a prop that leads us to the dancing group and is part of their dancing, as the World Cup trophy sits casually in the back of the shot. While the same White boy later appears to connect with a Black peer in the takeaway shop—via music as he performs clichéd awkward-amusing dance moves—he is far from the young multicultural 'party' of a London that is abstractly in support of cricket but has no link to the game established in the video.

The danger that this video signals cricket's marketing interest in making 'Cricket for People Who Don't Like Cricket' seems relatively obvious.[90] And this line of thinking might be ironically echoed by the chorus of the track: 'you ain't gon' learn to love me that's no lie'. What the video does offer is a multicultural/multi-ethnic London-based idea of youthful celebration and exuberance, with flats and bikes and street scenes, where cricket is only nostalgically linked to seemingly first-generation migrants. The video quite obviously makes no link between the party crowd and cricket as a sport, and even the passing references to flag-linked fandom are brief. But in addition to this kind of anti-cricket selling of cricket, there is a troublesome relationship with England in the music video. The video only references England explicitly in a minimal fashion, with one female fan's face-painted St George's flag. However, the teenage White boy omitted from the main party appears to stand as a marker of White/male/England that is working class, and he is positioned first as an intruder and then as someone excluded seemingly without knowing it. With his body standing as distinct from the dancers, the video ultimately suggests that Britain's London will hold the party, without England, and in the place of England, and at the same time will celebrate a multi-racial, multi-ethnic London in a way that positions England as both White and absent. In doing so, it problematically enables the idea of England as untouched by those understood as 'diverse' and from 'outside' the very England that is itself cast 'out'. This effectively works to point up the imperial dialectic of Englishness, as in Baucom's argument, wherein England stands as distinct from British space and as untouched by those 'global' bodies found in Britain's capital city as well as in Britain's former imperial locations. England, then, slides into a racialized and excluded 'White' (and typically male) space by default, without actively participating, and is characterized in this way while being rendered absent in terms of team, place, or nation. For all the strengths of Loryn, Rudimental, and the song, this selling of cricket as London-British clearly comes from a place of insecurity—insecurity about what England can stand for when appearing on Britain's version of the world stage, even when the England cricket team are set to do well (and do!).

Insecurity at the Top, Even While Briefly 'On Top'

While the insecurity of England and English cricket appeared entirely in keeping with the dull sense of failure—political and cricketing—of the 1990s, by 2019 what became clear was that even when England are 'on top of the world' in cricketing terms, English cricket still reads as insecure, and its decision-making authorities behave as if this insecurity is guiding their future planning. For example, while it seemed like the 2019 World Cup itself was supposed to reverse the shrinking of cricket in the English or British imaginary, if it was going to do this, it had to do so in the context of the ECB's announcement of 'The Hundred', the new short format tournament that was (and is) meant to reinvigorate the game in England but partly functioned, prior to the World Cup in 2019, as a distracting 'hedge-bet' just in case the tournament was more like 1999 than anyone wanted. The announcement undermined the achievement of the World Cup winning England women's team of 2017 and reduced the significance of the impending competition for the England men's team. It also prompted Michael Henderson and Duncan Hamilton to give book-length expression to many of the insecurities about English cricket and the perpetually terminal decline of county cricket that we might readily associated with Britain's imperial image of Englishness and cricket's England (as bucolic, superior, pure, and in need of protection from the financializing pressures of modernization that forget the game's roots).[91]

When England's men were eventually victorious in 2019, much was made in the media of the international and mixed cricketing and personal backgrounds of the England squad (of Morgan's Irishness, of Stokes' early childhood in New Zealand, of Jason Roy's childhood in South Africa, of Archer's relatively recent arrival from the Caribbean, and of the Muslim faith of Adil Rashid and Moeen Ali). And Morgan, as captain, contributed to such narratives.[92] In the media storm, praise for the team and its diversity tended to emerge from two opposing camps, and their encampments were either side of the Brexit line. As Jonathan Liew recorded in *The New Statesman*, while Brexiteers jumped on the idea of a kind of 'England plus Commonwealth' victory coming without Europe (forgetting Morgan's Irish standing), their approach to praising England was opposed by others celebrating the 'unique' diversity of a team that might be said to reflect the contemporary 'nation it represents' and the 'very best of these isles' in a British multicultural mode.[93] Yet, in each of these views, England is understood as the cricketing version of Britain, and is read in the context of Britain's postimperial position, including its nostalgia and its contemporary investment in a London-centred idea of diversity and inclusion. So, while English votes pushed Britain 'out' of Europe, it is Britain or, better, the UK (and not England alone) that left the European Union, and it is Britain or the UK, as 'these isles', and its Britishness that is understood as identity-category of inclusion for players like Archer, Ali, and Rashid. Indeed, Ali and Rashid will almost always be labelled England players and 'British Asians' or 'British Muslims', where the British marker works, again as in Baucom's argument, to separate them from England-as-nation and from their 'home'.

While there is much to be said (and is being said) about race and cricket, especially in the context of the situation with Yorkshire County Cricket, and while there are many reasons not to simply revert to the idea of the soil as a determinant of national identification (as well as every reason not to give legitimacy to the 'Tebbit test'), we should identify the England team with England and mark the ways in which players belong to England, find homes in England, play cricket in England, and are not 'British' as soon as they are understood as 'different' or 'diverse'. That England and its cricket team might be understood as domestically heterogeneous and national, as postimperial and successful, is worth holding on to, and this might be easier to do if its claim to being a nation were not so readily subsumed in cricket, and elsewhere, by British-imperial claims to the world, and marketable conceptions of British 'diversity'. Indeed, the insecurity of English cricket is most obvious when it hides England behind a London-British aesthetic that continues to work imperially, as it did in 2019.

Notes

1. See, for example, the body of work on West Indies cricket and nationhood by Hilary Beckles, including *The Development of West Indies Cricket Volumes 1* and *2* (London: Pluto, 1998) and *A Nation Imagined: The First West Indies Test Team* (Kingston: Ian Randle, 2003).
2. Ben Powis and Philippa Velija, 'Cricket has no boundaries with NatWest? The hyperreality of inclusion and diversity in English cricket'. *Sport in Society* 24, no. 8 (2021): 1510–1525.
3. Some of the ideas presented here were first aired at the 'Music and Sport: Knowing the Score' conference held at Leeds Beckett University in June 2019. Thanks go to the organizers of that conference and those contributing to the questions and discussions, including those who engaged with my paper. Thanks also go to the editor of this volume, both for his patience and his scholarly suggestions.
4. While all histories of the game make this point, particularly useful readings of cricket's Englishness can be found in: C.L.R. James, *Beyond a Boundary* (Durham, NC: Duke University Press, 2013 [1963]); John Simons, 'The "Englishness" of English cricket', *Journal of Popular Culture* 29, no. 4 (1996): 41–50; Ian Baucom, *Out of Place: Englishness, Empire and the Locations of Identity* (Princeton, NJ: Princeton University Press, 1999); Anthony Bateman, *Cricket, Literature and Culture: Symbolising the Nation, Destabilising Empire* (London: Ashgate, 2009), 23–28; and Dominic Malcolm, *Globalizing Cricket: Englishness, Empire and Identity* (London: Bloomsbury, 2013).
5. Mike Marqusee, *Anyone but England: An Outsider Looks at English Cricket* (London: Aurum Press, 2005), 47. Also see, for example, Derek Birley, *The Willow Wand: Some Cricket Myths Explored* (London: Aurum, 2000 [1979]); Derek Birley, *A Social History of English Cricket* (London: Aurum, 1999); and Roland

Bowen, *Cricket: A History of Its Growth and Development throughout the World* (London: Eyre & Spottiswoode, 1970).

6. Bateman, *Cricket, Literature and Culture*, 23–28.

7. Marqusee, *Anyone but England*, 49.

8. Claire Westall, '"But it's more than a game. It's an institution": Cricket, class and Victorian Britain's imperial Englishness', in *The Making of English Popular Culture*, ed. John Storey (New York: Routledge, 2016), 32–46. Also see, for example, J.A. Mangan, *The Games Ethic and Imperialism: Aspects of the Diffusion of an Ideal* (London: Frank Cass, 1988); Mangan, *The Cultural Bond: Sport, Empire and Society* (London: Frank Cass, 1992); and Brian Stoddart and Keith A.P. Sandiford, *The Imperial Game: Cricket, Culture and Society* (Manchester: Manchester University Press, 1998).

9. As well as Mangan's work, see, for example, James, *Beyond a Boundary*; Simons, 'The "Englishness" of English cricket'; and Richard Holt, 'Cricket and Englishness: The batsman as hero', *The International Journal of the History of Sport* 13, no. 1 (1996): 48–70.

10. Stephen Wagg, 'Never the gentleman: Caste, class and the amateur myth in English first-class cricket, 1920s–1960s', *Sport in History* 37, no. 2 (2017): 183–203; Simon Wilde, *England the Biography: The Story of English Cricket 1877–2019* (London: Simon & Schuster, 2019); and Duncan Stone, 'Deconstructing the gentleman amateur', *Cultural and Social History* 18, no. 3 (2017): 315–336.

11. Marqusee, *Anyone but England*, 71 (original italics).

12. Dominic Malcolm, 'Cricket, Brexit and the Anglosphere', *Sport in Society* 24, no. 8 (2021): 1274–1290; Richard Parrish, '"You're out!": Cricket and Brexit', in *Sport and Brexit*, ed. Jacob Kornbeck (Abingdon: Routledge, 2022), 131–142.

13. Marqusee, *Anyone but England*, 69.

14. Simon Hughes, *And God Created Cricket: An Irreverent History of the English Game and How Other People (Like Australians) Got Annoyingly Good at It* (London: Doubleday, 2009), 6, 11, 23–24.

15. Hughes, *And God Created Cricket*, 42.

16. Wilde, *England the Biography*, 38.

17. See, for example, Birley, *A Social History of English Cricket*; Marqusee, *Anyone but England*; Hughes, *And God Created Cricket*; and Wilde, *England the Biography*.

18. For more detail, see, for example, Birley, *A Social History of English Cricket* and Birley, *The Willow Wand* (London: Aurum, 2000 [1979]).

19. Wilde, *England the Biography*, 81–82. Wilde gives far more detail and more example cases, and such research is a highlight of his impressive book—to which I am heavily indebted in this part of the discussion.

20. Mike Cronin and Richard Holt, 'The imperial game in crisis: English cricket and decolonisation', in *British Culture and the End of Empire*, ed. Stuart Ward (Manchester: Manchester University Press, 2001), 111–127 (118).

21. Wilde, *England the Biography*, 38.

22. Wilde, *England the Biography*, 107–114.

23. Wilde, *England the Biography*, 81. The ICC was initially the Imperial Cricket Conference, then later, in 1964, the International Cricket Conference and, from 1989, the International Cricket Council.
24. Wilde, *England the Biography*, 63, 111–114.
25. The ECB website explains in full its own remit, responsibilities, and make-up: www.ecb.co.uk/about/who-we-are/our-members.
26. Wilde, *England the Biography*, 192. The same point is made by several other scholars, including Stephen Wagg in this collection.
27. John Curtice and Anthony Heath, 'Is the English lion about to roar? National identity after devolution', in *British Social Attitudes: Focusing on Diversity—The 17th Reported*, eds. Roger Jowell et al. (London: The National Centre for Social Research, 2000), 155–174, 155.
28. A similar point is made by Dominic Malcolm in 'Malign or benign: English national identities and cricket', in *The Changing Face of Cricket: From Imperial to Global Game*, eds. Malcolm, Jon Gemmell, and Nalin Mehta (Abingdon: Routledge, 2010), 183–198, 189.
29. For discussions of England's position within the UK after devolution, see, for example, Arthur Aughey, *The Politics of Englishness* (Manchester: Manchester University Press, 2007); Arthur Aughey, 'Anxiety and injustice: The anatomy of contemporary English nationalism', *Nations and Nationalism* 16, no. 3 (2010): 506–524; John Curtice, 'A stronger or weaker union: Public reactions to asymmetric devolution in the United Kingdom', *Publius: The Journal of Federalism* 36, no. 1 (2006): 95–113; David Richards and Martin J. Smith, 'Devolution in England, the British political tradition and the absence of consultation, consensus and consideration', *Representation* 51, no. 4 (2015): 385–401; and Ben Wellings, *English Nationalism and Euroscepticism: Losing the Peace* (Oxford: Peter Lang, 2012).
30. Marqusee, *Anyone but England*, 34.
31. See John Gemmell, 'Naturally played by Irishmen: A social history of Irish cricket', in *The Changing Face of Cricket: From Imperial to Global Game*, eds. Dominic Malcolm, Jon Gemmell, and Nalin Mehta (Abingdon: Routledge, 2010), 17–33.
32. Baucom, *Out of Place*, 12.
33. Ibid., 10, original italics.
34. Ibid., 24.
35. Ibid., 39.
36. See, for example, Sam Berkson, 'Is cricket for "everyone"? Reflections on the 2021 Ollie Robinson scandal', *Race and Class* 63, no. 2 (2021): 82–88; Michael Collins, 'Englishness, cricket and racial thinking', *The Political Quarterly* 93, no. 1 (2022): 95–103; Thomas Fletcher, David Piggott, and Julian North, 'The "blazer boys" were getting all the chances': South Asian men's experiences of cricket coaching in England', *Sport in Society* 24, no. 8 (2021): 1472–1492; and Powis and Velija, 'Cricket has no boundaries with NatWest?', as well as others cited elsewhere in this piece and appearing in this collection.

37. Ashley E. Reis, 'The wounds of dispossession: Displacement and environ-mentally induced mental illness in Ken Kesey's *One Flew Over the Cuckoo's Nest*', *ISLE: Interdisciplinary Studies in Literature and Environment* 23, no. 4 (2016): 711–729, 719.

38. Cate Watson, 'Test match special, Twenty20 and the future of cricket', in *Twenty20 and the Future of Cricket*, ed. Chris Rumford (Abingdon: Routledge, 2013), 73–84 (77).

39. Marqusee, *Anyone but England*, 26.

40. Emma John, *Following On: A Memoir of Teenage Obsession and Terrible Cricket* (London: Bloomsbury, 2017), 43, 4.

41. John, *Following On*, 190.

42. Ibid., 203.

43. Ibid., 204.

44. See, for example, Tony Cozier, ed., *History of the World Cup* (Alton: Wisden, 2006).

45. Followers of cricket and its World Cup tournaments will be familiar with debates about the size of the tournament, in terms of length, and in terms of the number of participant teams.

46. Tony Blair's speech: www.youtube.com/watch?v=KisItSfYHzA&t=610s.

47. See Tim Crabbe and Stephen Wagg, ' "A carnival of cricket?": The cricket World Cup, "race" and the politics of carnival', in *Cricket and National Identity in the Postcolonial Age: Following On*, ed. Wagg (Abingdon: Routledge, 2005), 204–222, 204.

48. www.youtube.com/watch?v=KisItSfYHzA&t=610s.

49. www.paviliontales.com/story-behind-the-icc-world-cup-1999-logo.

50. Matthew Engel, 'World Cup 1999', in *History of the World Cup*, ed. Tony Cozier (Alton: Wisden, 2006), 136–147, 140. Also see http://news.bbc.co.uk/1/hi/sport/1999_cricket_world_cup/349794.stm.

51. *The Cricketer*, 9 May 2019, www.thecricketer.com/Topics/world_cup_2019/world_cup_moments_no.28_england_humiliated_in_1999_before_official_song_is_released.html.

52. Hughes, *And God Created Cricket*, 203.

53. This 'Gough Cam' moment can be seen online: www.youtube.com/watch?v=IyVjExrZE7c.

54. *Dazzler: The Autobiography* (London: Penguin, 2001) is credited to Darren Gough with David Norrie (who is acknowledged as Gough's ghost writer for earlier *News of the World* pieces). Hence, in this discussion Gough is named as the primary 'voice' of the book, though it is clear that Norrie is the controlling authorial hand at work.

55. Only Scotland posted a lower total in the tournament.

56. Gough, *Dazzler*, 216.

57. Ibid., 219.

58. 'Gough Cam': www.youtube.com/watch?v=PvGTjv9vgho.

59. Gough, *Dazzler*, 220.

60. See, for example, Gough, *Dazzler*; Hughes, *And God Created Cricket*; Wilde, *England the Biography*; and *The Cricketer*, 9 May 2019.

61. Mick Hucknall, 'We're in This Together', www.youtube.com/watch?v=TmQQ J8FQioc, accessed 5 May 2022.

62. See Westall, 'Memories are made of this', in *1966 and Not All That*, ed. Mary Perryman (London: Repeater Books, 2016), 276–290, 281–282.

63. Nicolas Freestone, 'Life is a carnival: The story of the 1999 Cricket World Cup official song', 9 February 2016, https://njfreestone.wordpress.com/2016/02/09/life-is-a-carnival-the-story-of-the-1999-cricket-world-cup-official-song/amp, accessed 5 May 2022.

64. Dave Stewart and Churcho Merchan, 'Everybody, all over the world', www.yout ube.com/watch?v=jOxJrxBE38o, accessed 5 May 2022.

65. Dave Stewart, 'Everybody, all over the world [*Around the World in 80 Days*]', www.youtube.com/watch?v=MeT7iMlG_yM, accessed 5 May 2022.

66. It was filmed before a fire destroyed the club house and it had to be rebuilt. See Nicholas Giles and Vikki Rimmer, 'From ashes to "The Ashes": Cricketing colts rejuvenate ashen club', *BBC Online*, 24 September 2014, www.bbc.co.uk/london/content/articles/2007/07/19/hornsey_flames_feature.shtml, accessed 5 May 2022.

67. See, for example, Michael Meloy, 'Fixing men: Castration, impotence, and masculinity in Ken Kesey's *One Flew Over the Cuckoo's Nest*', *Journal of Men's Studies* 17, no. 1 (2009): 3–14.

68. Crabbe and Wagg, ' "A carnival of cricket?" ', 205.

69. Rainer Emig, 'Eccentricity begins at home: Carlyle's centrality in Victorian thought', *Textual Practice* 17, no. 2 (2010): 379–390 (380).

70. Ibid., 380.

71. See Paul Langford, *Englishness Identified: Manners and Character, 1650–1850* (Oxford: Oxford University Press, 2001), 289 and 301–305.

72. Langford, *Englishness Identified*, 302–304.

73. Julia Saville, 'Eccentricity as Englishness in *David Copperfield*', *Studies in English Literature, 1500–1900* 42, no. 4 (2002): 781–797 (795).

74. See, for example, Andrew Roberts, *A History and Guide to the Cricket World Cup* (Philadelphia, PA: White Owl, 2019) and Cozier, *History of the World Cup*.

75. See Nick Hoult and Steve James, *Morgan's Men: The Inside Story of England's Rise from Cricket World Cup Humiliation to Glory* (London: Allen & Unwin, 2020).

76. See, for example, *Twenty20 and the Future of Cricket*, ed. Chris Rumford (Abingdon: Routledge, 2013).

77. Botham label is cited everywhere, including on the cover of *Ben Stokes on Fire: My Story of England's Summer to Remember*, by Stokes with Richard Gibson (London: Headline, 2019).

78. As well as the mass of media coverage at the time, *The Times* pulled their tournament write-ups into a book: Richard Whitehead, ed., *England's World Cup: The Full Story of the 2019 Tournament* (Cheltenham: The History Press, 2019).

79. ICC, 'The Cricket World Cup carnival is coming!', 7 August 2018, www.youtube. com/watch?v=UFONbWly3Ds&t=3s, accessed 5 May 2022.

80. See, for example, 'ICC Cricket World Cup 2019—Are you in?', www.youtube. com/watch?v=4XStGKdW_yg, accessed 5 May 2022.

81. IMDB, 'Imagine Dragons: On Top of the World', www.imdb.com/title/tt6971582, accessed 5 May 2022.

82. See Imagine Dragons, 'On Top of the World (official music video)', 13 November 2013, www.youtube.com/watch?v=w5tWYmIOWGk, accessed 5 May 2022. IMDB carries the same (self-evident) explanation of the video: www.imdb.com/ title/tt6971582.

83. This term is borrowed from Andrew Higson in *Film England: Culturally English Filmmaking since the 1990s* (London: I.B. Tauris, 2011), 85. Also see Claire Westall and Michael Gardiner, *The Public on the Public: The British Public as Trust, Reflexivity and Political Foreclosure* (Basingstoke: Palgrave Macmillan, 2015) and Gardiner and Westall, 'The last great British summer for England', www.opende mocracy.net/en/opendemocracyuk/last-great-british-summer-for-england.

84. See, for example, Andy Bull, 'Sodden World Cup opening ceremony puts antici- pation in deep freeze', *The Guardian*, 29 April 2019, www.theguardian.com/sport/ 2019/may/29/world-cup-opening-ceremony-cricket.

85. See, for example, www.youtube.com/watch?v=M_nfQZPCDzw&t=107s.

86. www.icc-cricket.com/media-releases/1211942.

87. Ibid.

88. Ibid.

89. www.youtube.com/watch?v=Tt5BybCUY5E.

90. See Barrie Axford and Richard Huggins, 'Cricket for people who don't like cricket: Twenty20 as expression of the cultural and media zeitgeist', in *Twenty20 and the Future of Cricket*, ed. Chris Rumford (Abingdon: Routledge, 2013), 16–29.

91. See Michael Henderson, *That Will be England Gone: The Last Summer of Cricket* (London: Constable, 2020); Duncan Hamilton, *One Long and Beautiful Summer: A Short Elegy for Red-Ball Cricket* (London: Quercus, 2020).

92. See, for example, Morgan, 'England's multicultural World Cup winners: Different strokes for different folks', Wisden, 10 August 2020, https://wisden.com/alman ack/englands-multicultural-world-cup-winners-different-strokes-for-different- folks-by-eoin-morgan, accessed 5 May 2022.

93. Jonathan Liew, 'As England's multicultural team celebrated at Lord's, it felt as if we were getting somewhere at last', *The New Statesman*, 17 July 2019, www.newst atesman.com/culture/sport/2019/08/england-s-multicultural-team-celebrated- lord-s-it-felt-if-we-were-getting, accessed 5 May 2022.

7

Brand It Like Ben Simmons

Gen-F(ranchise) and the Americanization of Australian Cricket

Tom Heenan

On 17 February 2019, Melbourne franchises the Stars and Renegades clashed in the Big Bash League (BBL) final before 41,000 fans at Marvel Stadium. The match attracted much media interest and did not disappoint. Watched by a peak television audience of 942,000, the Renegades struggled to 5/145 off their twenty overs.[1] In reply, the Stars' Ben Dunk and Marcus Stoinis posted a ninety-two-run opening stand. The Stars then lost 7/19 off thirteen balls and fell seventeen runs short of victory. As the Renegades players celebrated, television cameras focussed on a young boy in Stars merchandising. He was among many Stars and Renegades supporters decked out in their teams' brands and was crying because his franchise had lost. He was also among the family demographic that Cricket Australia (CA) had lured to the game through Twenty20 cricket. The demographic was not raised on Test or fifty-over cricket, but the BBL. Their allegiance was not primarily to country or state, but franchise. They signified a generational shift in Australian cricket's fan-base. Twenty20 was their game, and they were Australian cricket's future.

The Stars and Renegades had established a keen rivalry. The Stars were packaged as flashy and from Melbourne's leafy, middle-class eastern suburbs, and their home ground was the establishment's Melbourne Cricket Ground (MCG). The Renegades were supposedly working-class outliers from Melbourne's grittier western suburbs who entered home-fixtures to blasts of the rock band AC/DC. Unlike Melbourne's Australian rules football clubs, the franchises had not grown from the city. The football clubs were rooted in places and communities and had retained some of

Tom Heenan, *Brand It Like Ben Simmons* In: *Cricket and Nationhood in the Twenty-First Century.* Edited by: Souvik Naha, Oxford University Press. © Oxford University Press 2024. DOI: 10.1093/9780191982576.003.0008 their tribal identities. The Renegades and Stars were merely brands and their rivalry confected by the franchises, CA, and the media to broaden cricket's market. Although the boy's tears were real, they were shed for a brand without place or tradition. He signified cricket's new, neoliberal Gen-F(ranchise) (Gen-F) whose allegiances are not organically rooted in club culture but manufactured by marketers. His loyalties were shaped by strategies tested in the Indian Premier League (IPL) and influenced by North American sport entertainment. The boy was just another consumer. He may have followed the National Basketball Association's (NBA's) LeBron James, Steph Curry, or Melbourne's own Ben Simmons with the same teary-eyed intensity as Stars captain Glenn Maxwell, but from CA's perspective he was there to buy and wear the merchandise.

He was an important cog in cricket's new neoliberal agenda. Drawing on Schumpeter, David Harvey contends that neoliberalism is a continuation of capitalism's drive for 'creative destruction'.[2] It dismantles old narratives and institutions, and values above all else entrepreneurial flair and profit-driven markets. The city-based, franchised BBL was a seismic expression of this. Fans morphed into consumers, while stadia were transformed into Ritzer's 'cathedrals of consumption', structured to maximize product placement and revenue.[3] Players became performers in a Disneyfied entertainment spectacle that involved big hitting, pyrotechnics, and promotions of the latest superhero. The game's traditions were either commodified or shelved, not required in the new three-hour entertainment 'fests', marketed for families and packaged for primetime television. With cricket participation rates and attendances stagnating in a cluttered and competitive Australian sporting landscape, CA introduced the BBL to capture the Gen-F market. Cricket's summer calendar was restructured to accommodate the competition. The goal was to lure a new generation of fans and participants, especially women and girls, and the Women's Big Bash League's (WBBL) establishment was crucial in achieving this. Fostering greater women's participation, either as spectators or players, became an important part of CA's Gen-F strategy.

But the strategy involved the phased destruction of the old to herald the new. The old state and Test-match summers were not to be completely obliterated—only partially. The WBBL and BBL were meant to complement the Test and fifty-over formats. Instead, as British journalist Tim Wigmore noted, 'for many Australians, [the BBL] is now the main event of the cricketing summer'.[4] By 2017, it numbered among the world's top ten sports leagues, according to *Forbes*, and was 'changing the professional sports paradigm'.[5] In reality, it was cannibalizing cricket's longer formats and alienating traditionalists who saw Twenty20 as 'trashing' the game's heritage. But Twenty20 bolstered CA's finances, proved an effective bargaining chip in broadcast rights negotiations, and gradually colonized the summer. The pandemic's onset merely solidified its hold. In the future, CA will rely more on BBL revenues and the Gen-F market. This reliance has been built on a long-term, fifteen-year strategy of phased creative destruction that used Twenty20 to strengthen cricket's revenue and supporter bases and secure its long-term future.

Inventing the Bash

In December 2010, CA released a report, *A Good Governance Structure for Australian Cricket*, written by the Australian Football League (AFL) commissioner, Colin Carter, and businessman David Crawford. Crawford was an influential figure in the corporatization of Australian sport, having conducted similar reviews of the AFL and Australian soccer. He and Carter identified specific challenges that Australian cricket faced globally and locally. The global market had changed with the IPL's introduction and its privately owned team franchises. Crawford and Carter contended that the revenues flooding into the IPL 'will increasingly attract the best talent and pose challenges to Australian cricket'. It risked becoming 'a feeder league that provides players to lucrative competitions elsewhere'. Locally, cricket also faced challenges from multiculturalism. A quarter of major cities' populations were not Australian-born, with many migrating from non-cricket-playing countries. If the trend continued, Carter and Crawford argued, cricket would struggle to attract fans and participants. When combined with the competition from other sports and entertainments, cricket needed to 'strengthen [its] capacity to win its share of public support'.[6]

The report confirmed what CA already knew. In August, it had convened a roundtable involving board members, players, and administrators to discuss cricket's current state and future direction. They agreed that cricket was not attracting women and children, and strategies were needed to lift their numbers. Migrants gravitated to soccer, and with the A-League's formation in 2005, it became a competitor in the summer market. Also required was an overhaul of domestic cricket. The Sheffield Shield should be retained because it was integral to player development, though it cost a reported AU $10 million annually to support. To offset these costs and attract a new family demographic, the roundtable agreed on the introduction of an eight-team, city-based Twenty20 competition, which would replace the existing state-based Big Bash (BB).[7]

Introduced in January 2006, the BB had proved popular with fans, though players and some administrators considered it not serious enough. Twenty20 lacked an international presence, according to CA chief executive James Sutherland, and unlike the domestic limited overs competition or the Sheffield Shield, it did little for player development.[8] Sutherland's attitude shifted in February 2005 when Australia defeated New Zealand in a Twenty20 international in Auckland before 30,000 fans. The following January, CA introduced the BB. The two-week competition was widely dismissed as a marketing stunt, but four of its seven games attracted crowds over 10,000. Recognizing the BB's popularity, CA increased the season's length in 2006–2007, though the view persisted that Twenty20 was not real cricket.[9] It was reinforced when New South Wales (NSW) selected the popular rugby league star Andrew Johns for two games.[10] Twenty20 was cricket's fun format, tailored for non-cricketing audiences. As Cricket NSW chief executive David Gilbert remarked: 'Twenty20 is about promoting the game . . . Nobody loses sleep if they win or lose.'[11]

Attitudes changed as the format's popularity and revenues grew. An Australia–South Africa Twenty20 international at the Gabba in January 2008 drew 38,000 and an estimated television audience of 2.5 million. Heavy metal rock accompanied batters to the wicket, while players' nicknames were plastered on their backs. But the game was a money-spinner. With the 2007 Twenty20 World Cup in South Africa, the format became a fixture on cricket's international calendar.[12] Many Australian players expressed concern that Twenty20 fixtures added to their workloads. It was a sticking-point in the players' negotiations with CA over the 2007 Memorandum of Understanding (MoU). The additional workload coincided with CA pushing to reduce the player payment pool from 25 per cent to 20 per cent of total revenue. The parties agreed that revenues from

Twenty20 internationals be used to support cricket's development and attract new fans, but also to allow players to retain their 25 per cent share.[13] With the deal sealed, Twenty20 gained player credibility and a permanent spot in CA's calendar.

Tests and One Day Internationals (ODIs), however, remained the main formats. As CA's corporate affairs manager Peter Young explained, 'Twenty20 has to find a place that complements but does not compromise Test and ODI cricket.'[14] But the global cricket market was changing. Emerging were players who earned lucrative livings on the Twenty20 circuit. By 2008–2009, New Zealanders Brendon McCallum and Daniel Vettori, and West Indians Chris Gayle, Dwayne Bravo, and Kieron Pollard, had signed with BB teams. They were the Bash's first imports and signified the creative destruction that was occurring in cricket's global labour market. Emerging was the Twenty20 freelancer, contracting his services to teams and franchises. The British journalist Steve James branded them 'itinerant T20 mercenar[ies]' whose 'loyalt[ies] were limited only to their back pockets'.[15] But cricket authorities did not discourage the freelance-player market's development. By 2008, Sutherland wanted more name-freelancers 'to make the tournament a bigger bash'.[16] But the Bash was operating in a changed global Twenty20 market dominated by the Board of Control for Cricket in India (BCCI).

Too 'Middle-Aged, Middle-Class and White'

Cricket always has had a great capacity for creative destruction. Historically, it has been an ever-shrinking game. From the end of the timeless Tests to the latest shrunken fad, The Hundred, cricket administrators have seemed obsessed with reducing game-time to attract fans and broadcasters. As enthusiasm waned for the fifty-over game, the trimline Twenty20 was concocted to boost interest and revenues. In 2002, the England and Wales Cricket Board (ECB) added it to a crowded county schedule. As the ECB's marketing manager, Stuart Robertson, remarked, English cricket needed a younger audience. The current crop was 'disastrous': too 'middle-aged, middle-class and white', as well as old and male.[17] Twenty20 was the answer and the idea caught on, especially in South Asia. Behind the strategy was a power shift between media organizations and cricket's governing bodies. As media determined the fates of governments, so too did they shape cricket's direction, and it was most apparent in India.

In 2007, Indian media magnate Subash Chandra established the rebel Twenty20 International Cricket League (ICL) for his network, Zee-TV. Chandra raided South Asian and global cricket for players, and though the ICL only lasted two seasons, it highlighted Twenty20's marketability and threatened the BCCI's monopoly of Indian cricket. As a counter, the BCCI established the IPL in 2008 with backing from the International Cricket Council (ICC), cannibalizing the ICL and bolstering India's financial and political dominance. Fed by Indian capital, an assertive nationalism, substantial media and entertainment empires, and a widespread Indian diaspora, the IPL boomed and was accorded space in the international calendar, while other cricket-playing countries became labour feeders to cricket's now dominant market.

The IPL was Sutherland's benchmark for the revamped BBL. But he realized that Australian cricket could not compete with the IPL because of its smaller market and capital base.[18] Whereas cricket was India's dominant sport, it competed against the football codes for media space, sponsorships, and fans in Australia. But the IPL had significant ramifications for Australian cricket. The money on offer induced players to end their international careers prematurely to play in the IPL and other Twenty20 leagues. The initial 2008 IPL player auction was a labour market game-changer, netting US $1.8 billion.[19] The International Cricketer's Association head, Tim May, suggested that players were now paid their real market value, and so gravitated to where their services were better rewarded.[20] In a survey of twenty-five contracted Australian players, the Australian Cricketers' Association (ACA) found that 67 per cent were prepared to sign a Twenty20 contract. According to the player union's chief executive, Paul Marsh, Australian players were 'well paid . . . [but] the IPL . . . provides more money for less work [and] . . . [t]hat's a proposition most people would accept in a heartbeat'.[21]

With financial and political power shifting to the subcontinent, CA's scope was limited. Like the IPL, CA wanted a free window in the international calendar for the BBL, and a sufficient revenue stream to lessen its financial dependence on the Indian and Ashes tours. Sutherland realized that the BBL—like the IPL—could not solely rely on cricket to sell its

product. The game had to be packaged in bite-sized, three-hour entertainment chunks and sold to a younger, Gen-F audience who were more
likely to wear Air-Jordans and Yankee caps than CA merchandising.
Required was a marketing strategy that targeted cricket's missing demographic: mums and kids. Among boys under the age of fifteen, cricket
ranked seventh in their list of preferred sports, while for girls it was four-
teenth.[22] The BBL's project manager, Mike McKenna, recognized that this
demographic had to be engaged to protect 'the future of the game'. A bite-
sized Bash with pyrotechnics, bursts of AC/DC, and Disneyesque entertainment was concocted to lure families, secure the game's revenue base,
and lessen CA's dependency on India.

To achieve this, CA tapped into the American sports marketing and
entertainment industries. In 2008, a CA delegation visited the USA and
met with the Chicago-based Property Consulting Group (PCG). PCG
had developed marketing strategies for Dana White's Ultimate Fight
Championship and Major League Baseball (MLB).[23] The Group's head
of innovation and co-founder, Dan Migala, knew little about cricket but
became a key figure in formulating the BBL's marketing strategy. Migala
had used glitz, 'glam', and pizazz to bolster fan engagement for MLB
franchises and their sponsors. The inventive Migala had convinced the
Chicago Cubs to change Wrigley Field's timer from '7:11' to '7-Eleven'
to spotlight the sponsor's brand-name. While visiting Australia in 2011,
he attended an Australia–England ODI at the MCG. He noticed that
while bars remained open throughout play, ice-cream vendors shut once
demand from kids dropped. The next day, he told CA officials that the
vendors' actions highlighted 'the reason why we need the [BBL] to get
kids interested in cricket again'.[24] The ODI was not tailored for them but
for an adult, male, beer-drinking demographic.

Migala believed that the BBL 'should deliver entertainment that
also happens to have a cricket match involved'.[25] The strategy, he cautioned, 'wasn't going to be all things to all consumers'. As Belzer notes,
it was 'counter-intuitive' in that it alienated traditional fans to attract the
mum-with-kid cohort. Migala emphasized that CA had to 'own families' through a three-stage strategy encompassing growth, engagement,
and transaction. But the overriding ingredient was fun. CA needed to
ask families and kids: what would they do for fun if they owned a cricket
club? Scheduling and access were crucial. Seasons must coincide with

school holidays, while admission costs should be kept low to encourage entry for families and kids. Partnerships with major entertainment companies were essential. The BBL was to be not just a game but a Disneyfied entertainment experience featuring screen-franchise favourites.[26] Migala arranged for CA to visit the NBA's Portland Timberwolves, MLB's Texas Rangers, and the National Football League's (NFL's) Seattle Seahawks and Dallas Cowboys to examine how they engaged with women and children. Superheroes were used to keep kids entertained, while the Cowboys had partnered with a nail polish company to entice women to games.[27] The BBL adopted many of these strategies. CA invested $20 million in a League that would extend over forty-three days and encompass the December to January school-holiday period.[28]

CA had hoped that the BBL might attract foreign investors. Private investment in franchises with licence sales had added US $724 million to the BCCI's coffers. Sutherland valued BBL franchises at AU $36 million each, benchmarking them against the National Rugby League's Brisbane Broncos. Some CA officials dreamt that franchise values could balloon to $90 million in five years if opened to foreign investors, though there was a catch.[29] Investors were only allowed a minority 49 per cent share in franchises, with the state cricket associations retaining a controlling interest. Reportedly, investors from Delhi and Mumbai had expressed interest in franchises, as well as US and Chinese consortia.[30] But Sutherland was concerned about the overall impacts of private ownership.[31] External owners would be entitled to a share of sponsorship and television rights' revenues and, as McKenna noted, could compromise CA's not-for-profit tax-free status. They could also influence the competition.[32] Franchises could become offshoots of the more powerful and wealthier IPL, or attract owners whose views differed from CA's. As McKenna later revealed, 'we . . . talked to people who were interested in buying, [but] their strategic objectives in investing in the league were at odds with ours'.[33]

'The Goose That Laid the Golden Egg'

The BBL commenced on 16 December 2011 without foreign owners, Indian players, and a free-to-air broadcast rights deal, as well as concerns that fans would not embrace the city-based franchise model. It had an AU $1 million salary cap per team, far below the IPL's inaugural US $5 million cap. The season opener between the Sydney Sixers and the Brisbane Heat attracted only 13,000, sparking concerns about the League's viability. Journalist Gideon Haigh declared that it must perform 'significantly better' to justify CA's AU $20 million investment. Haigh held well-founded fears that the BBL might 'cannibaliz[e] or dilute[e]' the game's traditional formats.[34] Although Sutherland assured traditionalists that 'Twenty20 cricket should not compromise international cricket', his phrasing was far from convincing.[35] An unnamed CA 'insider' told Melbourne's *Herald Sun* that Tests and one-day cricket were 'dying . . . and everyone knows Twenty 20 is the future of the game'.[36] It was apparent in the season's scheduling. CA had sought an international-free window in January for the BBL, but was hamstrung by the ICC's Future Tours Program. Under the programme, international fixtures were scheduled in advance, and took precedence over the BBL, limiting top Australian players' appearances. Without local stars, the BBL was of less value in the free-to-air broadcast market. Pay-TV provider Foxtel held the broadcast rights, which restricted the BBL's reach. The rights were due for renegotiation in 2013 and CA wanted a free-to-air deal to extend the League's market, but poor scheduling and periodic absences of leading Australian players limited its value to networks.

The League's major coup was the Melbourne Stars' recruitment of the forty-two-year-old Shane Warne. Warne had captured as many headlines for his off-field indiscretions as he had for his wicket-taking ability. After four seasons with the IPL's Rajasthan Royals, Warne retired at the end of the 2011 season.[37] But he was lured back by the Stars in November for a reported AU $100,000. Warne assured he was not playing for the money. He wanted to '[p]ut something back into the game [and] to help out the kids'.[38] It was the perfect marketing pitch that the kid-friendly BBL needed. Warne had the celebrity status and savviness to promote the BBL as family-friendly entertainment; and he came with a celebrity girlfriend, the English model and actor Liz Hurley. When the Stars and Sydney Thunder met in their season opener at the MCG on 17 December, Warne, Hurley, and their children made a stage-managed entry. Hurley even tossed the coin. As she kissed Warne and left the ground with the children, the image reinforced that despite their celebrity, they and the BBL were all about family and kids.[39]

A crowd of 50,000 was expected, but only 23,595 turned up.[40] The broadcast figures were more promising, averaging 488,000 viewers on Foxtel, breaking the previous Twenty20 record of 316,000 set during the 2009–2010 BB final. But the lower-than-expected crowds persisted, with the thirty-one-game season attracting only 17,750 per game. An unconcerned Sutherland suggested that the moderate attendances were 'more than offset by the TV audience'. The next broadcast rights deal, and not the gate, was Sutherland's focus. CA wanted to build sizeable television audiences to attract interest from free-to-air broadcasters, though the BBL continued to underwhelm.

The 2012–2013 season commenced with reports that the BBL had accrued losses of AU $10 million. State associations were AU $1.85 million 'in the red', while the Adelaide Strikers and Brisbane Heat's losses tallied AU $655,000 and AU $545,000 respectively. The sole franchise to return a profit was the Melbourne Stars, attributable in part to the Warne–Hurley 'soapie'.[41] Warne remained the BBL's most bankable commodity. During the Stars–Renegades derby at the MCG, he clashed with West Indian freelancer, Marlon Samuels, in a finger-wagging, bat-throwing incident that attracted much media 'oxygen' and highlighted that the Bash was serious cricket.[42] But attendances had dipped. Crowds for the thirty-five-match season averaged 14,366, while television audiences, restricted by Foxtel's limited reach, attracted 230,000 viewers per game.[43] This was rectified in June 2013, when the free-to-air Ten Network secured the BBL rights for a lowly AU $100 million over five years.[44] Although the deal was underwhelming, the impact was immediate. The additional revenue allowed CA to increase team salary caps to AU $1.05 million and double its investment in the BBL to AU $40 million. As Stensholt noted, the money would be spent on 'marketing and promotion' and providing funds for cash-strapped franchises.[45] As McKenna revealed, AU $4 million was spent on 'target[ting] shopping centres and transit places, where mums and families will see it'.[46] With increased audience numbers, KFC, Unilever, AAMI, and Holden jumped onboard. Whereas franchises had initially struggled for sponsors, only the Perth Scorchers and the Hobart Hurricanes commenced the 2013–2914 season without one.

With free-to-air access, the season marked a turning-point. By mid-January, the BBL had averaged 1.04 million viewers over thirty evenings, an increase of 16 per cent on 2012–2013. Ten's main competitor in the January window, Seven West Media, had paid AU $40 million per year for the Australian Open tennis. At AU $20 million, Ten's ratings rivalled those of the Open, prompting the network's chief executive, Hamish McLennan, to dub the BBL 'the deal of the century'.[47] Sutherland boasted that BBL attendances and ratings now rivalled those of the Ashes. Averaging 910,000 viewers nightly, total season ratings had increased fourfold on 2012–2013, while total attendances were up from 502,807 to 657,227. Consequently, average match attendances rose from 14,366 to 18,778, with notable growth in females and first-timers to the game.[48] Primetime ratings rose by 26 per cent, and the effect on Ten's financial bottom-line was immediate.[49] Although the network recorded a loss, half-yearly results to 28 February saw revenues increase by 7.8 per cent to AU $331 million, which McLennan suggested stemmed mainly from Ten's investment in sport.[50] Despite the BBL's growth, it still had not recorded a surplus. Sutherland admitted, '[i]t will be a long time before we recoup the money from it, but in a strategic sense it is starting to pay dividends and the benefit of being on free-to-air has turbocharged the Big Bash League'.[51]

The growth continued in 2014–2015. Total attendances topped 840,000, with average crowd sizes increasing to 23,000, an 18 per cent lift on the previous season. According to CA, 21 per cent of attendees were new to the game. Ratings slightly rose to 925,000 per primetime game, which Sutherland attributed to an overly cluttered January to February sports market, in which the BBL competed for 'eyeballs' against Asian Cup football and the Australian Open.[52] Seven of the eight franchises were now posting surpluses, the Hobart Hurricanes being the exception, while the best-attended franchise, the Melbourne Stars, registered a AU $129,401 surplus on revenues of AU $5.51 million, a marked improvement on the previous year's AU $163,000 loss on AU $4.5 million.[53] But traditionalists railed against the BBL's crass Americanized commercialism. The pyrotechnics, fried-chicken bucket hats, ear-splitting music, and 'snogcam' had seemingly sidelined the game. As *The Australian's* Will Swanton declared: 'We don't want the biggest party in town. We want to watch some cricket'.[54] Swanton was almost a lone traditionalist voice howling at the floodlights. In their creatively destructive wisdom, CA marketers were convinced that without the party, cricket had little future.

Questions persisted about the BBL's place in the summer calendar, and whether it was cannibalizing the game's other formats. CA continued to 'spin' the line that the BBL complemented the international season. Although national teams were given precedence on player selection, the Sheffield Shield was now a sideshow and labour feeder to the more lucrative BBL. While traditionalists criticized the Shield's shabby treatment and the summer's scheduling, Sutherland argued that 'there is no perfect solution'. Extending the BBL into December provided it with a pre-Christmas window free from other sports. Sutherland reminded critics that the BBL was laying the foundation for a 'sustainable future' that would 'maintain [cricket's] relevancy in Australian society'. It, and not the Shield, was the game's future.[55]

This view was reinforced during the 2015–2016 BBL season, when total crowd numbers topped the million mark for the first time. The average attendance per game of 25,539 outnumbered the daily crowd numbers for the West Indies and New Zealand Test series.[56] In its fourth season, the BBL was ranked the seventh highest-attended sport competition globally, rivalling MLB, Italy's Serie A, Japanese baseball, and Australia's domestic football codes. The season highpoint was an MCG crowd of 80,833 for the Melbourne derby, which surpassed the Boxing Day attendance of 52,000 for the Melbourne Test. Television audiences peaked at 1.3 million, an increase of 19 per cent on the previous season and 25 per cent on 2013–2014.[57] As a result, Ten recorded its highest metropolitan free-to-air ratings for four years, which boosted advertising revenues by 26 per cent on the previous year.[58] According to BBL boss Anthony Everard, the competition recorded an AU $4 million surplus, with AU $2.5 million coming from merchandise sales and increased sponsorship revenues. The eight teams had secured sponsorships worth AU $13 million, five of which were over AU $1 million. Two seasons before, only two franchises had achieved that mark.[59] The season was marred by an incident involving the high-profile Renegades freelancer Chris Gayle who made inappropriate comments to Ten journalist Mel McLaughlin during a boundary-rope interview. Everard promptly branded the comments 'offensive and inappropriate' for a 'league [that] is all about its appeal to kids, families and females'.[60] Gayle was fined AU $10,000 and his contract was not renewed.[61] As Everard stated, the incident 'gave us the chance to affirm that the BBL is about engaging with women and children.[62] The incident was a momentary sexist glitch in an otherwise profitable season. In mid-January, CA posted revenue projections of AU $1.32 billion for the four-year cycle ending 2016–2017. It was a substantial rise on the preceding cycle's AU $736 million.[63] To paraphrase journalist Russell Gould, CA had stumbled on 'the goose that laid the golden egg'.[64]

'Wringing . . . the Cash Cow'

In August 2016, CA staged a three-day cricket conference. The agenda included the BBL and international cricket's futures, and strategies to boost the game's popularity.[65] The conference coincided with the release of CA's national census. Cricket was now Australia's leading participation sport with 1.3 million players and was evolving into a more diverse game. Growth had occurred in many of the areas identified by Carter and Crawford as deficient. Women's participation rates had increased by 9 per cent to 314,936 players over the past year. They now comprised 'a quarter of [cricket's] playing base'. Growth had also occurred in multicultural (28 per cent) and indigenous (40 per cent) participants, and those with disabilities (70 per cent). The census was released after international and BBL attendances had topped 1.7 million for the 2015–2016 season, the highest on record. The main contributor was the BBL with total attendances of 1,030,495, again placing it among the world's best-attended competitions.[66]

Growth and diversity were also to the fore in CA's 2017–2022 strategy. Released in September 2017, the strategy had a twist. Sutherland maintained that the BBL's role was 'to bring new people to the game and graduate their interests to Tests'. Therefore, it complemented rather than compromised international cricket.[67] But this was not the gist of the five-year strategy. The BBL now was a priority area in junior and female cricket's development.[68] This came at a cost to Test cricket and the Sheffield Shield. Sutherland acknowledged that both had a 'proud history'; yet, he added, '[h]istory . . . does not guarantee continued success'. It would come from the new strategy, he suggested, that would meet the 'challenges and [CA's] ongoing responsibility to the future of the game'.[69] The strategy clearly prioritized the BBL over the struggling Shield, which was not surprising. In 2015, CA chair, Wally Edwards, and Sutherland had considered expanding the BBL season by axing the Shield final. Although fourteen games were added to the BBL, the final was retained, protected under the CA–ACA MoU.[70] Edwards and Sutherland's move clearly contravened the 2011 Argus Review into poor performances by the Australian Test and ODI teams. The review recommended strengthening the Shield to rebuild Australia's Test and ODI stocks.[71] But the review coincided with discussions over the BBL's introduction, which, as Hogan noted, were 'financially . . . more significant' than Argus' recommendations.[72] CA's mantra was to give fans what they wanted, which increasingly was the Bash.[73] Other than the Ashes and Indian series, Test cricket had its place but was of decreasing importance, while ODIs were in decline, and the Shield and domestic limited-over competition drained CA's finances.

The BBL was becoming the game's 'cash cow' and future, and broadcasters had begun to question if cricket's traditional formats provided value for money. International cricket still contributed 70 per cent of national boards' revenues, but as the Nine's Hugh Marks suggested, networks preferred the BBL.[74] Nine had held the cricket rights since 1979–1980, but was questioning their worth. In 2014, Nine's investment house, UBS, estimated that the network lost AU $30–40 million annually on its cricket coverage. UBS analyst Eric Choi recommended that unless Nine secured 'more cricket . . . at no additional cost', it should 'step away from the cricket contract'.[75] Hence, CA extended the 2017–2018 BBL season from thirty-two to forty matches with an earlier commencement date in December. The increased BBL content would be a useful bargaining chip in future broadcast rights negotiations. The season was further increased to fifty-nine games in 2018–2019, prompting one commentator to remark that CA was trying 'to wring more out of its cash cow', though it denied that this was the case.[76] The BBL would not determine broadcast rights, Everard claimed. The deal would be based on 'how we can . . . make the game more popular'.[77] The most popular and valuable format, however, was the BBL. Undermining its value were the season's scheduling problems, now exacerbated by an extended BBL. The mid-December Perth Test clashed with the BBL's start-date, while its January fixtures coincided with the ODI series against Pakistan, stripping the competition of leading Australian players. The scheduling reflected the major flaw in

CA's strategy. The game's formats competed against each other for players and media space, limiting the BBL's talent pool and marketability.

The problem stemmed from CA's underestimation of the Twenty20 market. Initial expectations were of an average viewership per game of 500,000, but ratings now exceeded 1 million.[78] The BBL had achieved the unexpected, breathing life into a moribund domestic cricket scene. As Ten's head of sport, David Barham, remarked: 'if you'd said five years ago a domestic cricket competition would do that, no one would have believed you . . . There wasn't a whole lot of other people bidding for it'.[79] With 8 per cent growth during the 2017–2018 season, average attendances peaked at 30,114, shifting the BBL to fifth on the global table.[80] For Everard, the family strategy had 'well and truly exceeded expectations', extending 'the fanbase beyond the traditional market and demographics'.[81] Its success led journalist Greg Baum to lament: 'the question is no longer whether the BBL is good for the game. It is whether it is the game'.[82]

The BBL was now a highly sought-after sport-media product. With the new broadcast and digital rights deals due to be finalized by April 2018, CA expected upwards of AU $850 million over a four-year period.[83] It would be a marked improvement on the previous deal between Nine and Ten of AU $590 million over five years.[84] Ten hoped to retain the BBL rights. Under Barham, the network had engineered the BBL's ratings success, but it was poorly positioned to secure the rights. In June 2017, Ten went into voluntary administration.[85] Prowling for scraps was the pay-TV provider, Foxtel. A part-owner of Ten, the Telstra-Murdoch-owned provider held the rights to the major football codes and wanted to build its summer content with cricket. With Nine reconsidering its options, and CBS acquiring Ten in November, CA altered its broadcast requirements. Only select content needed to be on free-to-air TV, notably Tests and some internationals, but not all BBL games.[86] The change opened the way for a joint partnership between a free-to-air network and Foxtel, which required some exclusive content to attract new subscribers.[87] When the new deal was announced in April 2018, Foxtel and CA were the main beneficiaries. The six-year, AU $1.182 billion deal with Seven West Media and Foxtel marked a 64 per cent increase on the previous deal.[88] Foxtel had secured the broadcast and digital rights to all international and BBL cricket for AU $100 million per annum. [89] Foxtel was required to introduce an exclusive cricket channel—a determining point in the negotiations, according to Sutherland—and a standalone digital platform.[90] For its annual instalment of AU $75 million, Seven West secured the rights for Tests, women's internationals, and forty-three of fifty-nine men's BBL games.[91] Seven's chief executive Tim Worner suggested the deal would be 'the foundation of our company for the next five years'.[92] The most important selling-points were the BBL's advertising slots. As Worner noted, 'the 30 seconds between overs in a T20 . . . [are] a very high-engagement commercial break'.[93] The slots placed the BBL among the most valuable pieces of sports-media real estate in the Australian summer.

Gen-F Cricket

In 2016, CA executives travelled to the USA, visiting the Mascot Games in Orlando, Ringling Brothers Circus, and Disney on Ice. They wanted to see how these events and organizations engaged with and retained their major fan-base, families and children, and transformed them into consumers.[94] The trip coincided with Kim McConnie's appointment as BBL head. After twelve years as the head of sports marketing with PepsiCo in New York, the Brisbane-born McConnie was well qualified to advance the BBL's American-styled, sports-entertainment strategy. As part of her PepsiCo brief, McConnie had organized the NFL's Super Bowl Halftime Show. She believed that 'sport and entertainment [were] merging, and that's what people want'. Fans had to be kept engaged, even when players were off the park.[95] As McConnie explained, '[t]he thing that really struck me in the US was the depth of fan engagement'.[96] Social media was employed to connect fans to player content and club merchandise.[97] So too were partnerships with global entertainment empires. McConnie wanted greater connectivity with Disney, Warner Brothers, and Nickelodeon to better engage with the Gen-F market. Fan engagement would extend beyond the field and match-day activities and into the children's entertainment market. Before the 2016–2017 season, CA and Nickelodeon agreed to produce the kids' programme, *Crash the Bash*. Distributed on Ten and Nickelodeon pay-TV, it was promoted through *Crash the Bash* drink-breaks and match-day activities, as well as Teenage Mutant Ninja Turtles promotions. McConnie's appointment had little to do with cricket. She was to transform the BBL into 'one of the best family entertainment options in the country'.[98]

But McConnie and CA faced some significant challenges. The BBL and cricket in general were losing traction. Fairfax reported a 19 per cent drop in television ratings for the 2017–2018 Ashes series in comparison to the 2013–2014 figures, while CA was yet to net a return on its BBL investment.[99] Expenditures over five seasons had totalled AU $187 million for a return of AU $154 million, yet Sutherland still held that the BBL was 'the shape of things to come'.[100] Leagues had been established in South Africa, the Caribbean, and Bangladesh, fuelling a more competitive Twenty20 market. Scheduled in the same window, the Bangladesh Premier League was proving attractive to high-profile freelancers with its shorter season and higher salaries. According to Melbourne Stars' freelancer Kevin Pietersen, overseas players felt that the two-month Australia season was too long.[101] By continually expanding the season, CA had reduced the BBL's attraction to name-players. Earlier editions had attracted local stars like Warne, Hussey, and Lee, complemented by imports such as Kallis, Jayawardene, McCullum, Vettori, and Flintoff. But the standard of imports had declined and star Australian players like Smith, Starc, and Warner bypassed the tournament because of international commitments or concerns about excessive workloads. Smith and Warner's Twenty20 priorities lay in the IPL, each having signed contracts worth AU $2.4 million, which exceeded the AU $1.6 million salary cap of BBL franchises.

But the major weakness was the absence of star Indian players. CA allowed Australian cricketers to play in the IPL. Given the AU $16.28 million salary cap, which was six-fold the BBL's, it was hard to stop them.[102] However, the BCCI ruled that its players were required for the Indian domestic season which clashed with the BBL. Their absence lessened the BBL's star quality and the value of its international broadcast rights.[103] CA suggested the BBL was prospering without them. Imported stars made 'marginal differences to TV ratings', claimed Everard. [104] But the lack of star-power was beginning to affect attendances. Since the competition's 2016–2017 average peak of 30,114 per game, attendances had dropped to 25,946 in 2017–2018.[105] The trend continued in 2018–2019, with average attendances further dipping to 20,512.[106]

Perhaps the major factor in the competition's decline was the narrowness of the BBL's marketing strategy. Cricket had been reduced to a game within a broader entertainment package structured for Gen-Fs and not the wider cricket public. Arguably, the Migala-based strategy of alienating cricket's traditional base to appeal to a family demographic had reached its end-point. To paraphrase cricket writer Malcolm Knox, CA's 'fatted calf' had lost its 'novelty'. Unlike Test cricket, the BBL could not draw on a long and rich history to sustain it. Twenty20, like its demographic, was still in its infancy. As Knox perceptively noted, the BBL 'always [had to] be fresh and young' or else it was 'stale'. McConnie found that the constant need to reinvent the BBL posed challenges. It was always 'continu[ing] to evolve'.[107] But the BBL had not evolved with its demographic. As Gen-Fs matured and moved on, the BBL remained forever infantile, which contributed to its declining attendances.

Another factor was CA's conflicting agendas. In trying to juggle several formats within a six-month window, CA was cannibalizing its 'cash cow'. Players were pulled from franchise fixtures for international duties, robbing the BBL of drawcards and competitive integrity. During the concluding stages of the 2017–2018 season, the Melbourne Stars lost several players to national team duties. Consequently, the Stars lost their final two matches, prompting chairman Eddie McGuire to call on CA to 'ma[ke] th[e] BBL really "fair dinkum"'.[108] The matter remained unresolved. In 2018–2019, the BBL ran parallel to a four-Test series against India, two Tests against Sri Lanka, and several ODIs. Missing from the BBL were major drawcards David Warner, Steve Smith, Pat Cummins, and Mitchell Starc. By January, Aaron Finch, Kane Richardson, Marcus Stoinis, and Adam Zampa had been withdrawn for ODI duties. D'Arcy Short and Alex Carey were then pulled from their franchises to prepare for a Twenty20 tri-series against England and New Zealand.[109] The scheduling meant that many top Australian players would miss the BBL semi-finals and final. Renegades captain Finch suggested that the clashes were 'unfortunate' but unavoidable.[110] The clashes reignited calls for a BBL window clear of international fixtures to ensure the best players were available.

The problem reflected the deep divide within Australian cricket between allegiances to franchise and country. The latter encompassed the traditionalist stream with its storied history, while the former comprised the Gen-Fs with their Americanized entertainment, 'fried-chook' bucket hats, franchised merchandise, and bite-sized cricket. The streams competed for talent and space in the cricketing calendar. Although the divide seemed irreconcilable, it reflected a cricketing culture in transition, as Twenty20 became the main game and Australian cricket renegotiated its place in changing local and global sporting landscapes. With competition mounting from other sports for market-share, CA had punted on Twenty20 as the format best suited to sustain the game's future. Nowhere was the punt more successful than in the women's game, which was less mired down by cricket's long and overly revered history.

The Curtain-Raisers

Cricket was long perceived as a game not for women. Although they played it and had a rich history, they remain invisible in much of Australia's cricket writing. Supposedly, the game was for men, and a woman's place was cutting the sandwiches and pouring the afternoon teas. This changed markedly with the BBL, as CA cultivated women as fans and participants. By the 2015–2016 season, 38 per cent of cricket's television audiences were women. Most were in CA's target demographic; under twenty-five or in the twenty-five to forty-nine age-group.[111] To increase female engagement and promote cricket as the first-choice sport for girls, Sutherland announced in February 2015 that an eight-team WBBL would commence in 2015–2016. The announcement followed the national team's ODI and Twenty20 World Cup victories, and a successful Ashes campaign. Teams would be aligned with current BBL franchises, maximizing the latter's profile while rationalizing costs. But the structure reduced the WBBL to a curtain-raiser competition for the men's BBL.

Sutherland wanted Twenty20 to become 'the premium format of the women's game'.[112] His comment reflected the broader drift in Australian cricket towards Twenty20 with its Gen-F demographic. But the WBBL was entering a rapidly evolving women sport's market. By September 2015, women comprised a quarter of cricketers and Australia rules footballers.[113] The football codes and netball were establishing elite women's competitions that would be the WBBL's main competitors for players, sponsors, and media space. To grow, the WBBL had to attract talent and professionalize, paying players competitive rates with other sports. The national team, the Southern Stars, were well paid by women's—not men's—standards. High-profile players, such as Meg Lanning, Ellyse

Perry, and Alyssa Healy, pocketed annually around AU $100,000 each. But lower-tiered players received only AU $10–17,000.[114] Most combined cricket with outside employment, so games were scheduled at weekends to lessen absences from work.[115] To compensate, CA raised the player payment fund by AU $600,000 to AU $2.26 million in mid-2015.[116]

To boost the WBBL's profile, CA and Ten entered a cost-sharing arrangement. Ten agreed to broadcast eight WBBL games on its secondary channel, ONE HD, during the 2015–2016 season.[117] As with the BBL, the ratings were unexpectedly high. The early rounds attracted average audiences of 216,000, surpassing the men's domestic ODI competition, the Matador Cup (96,000), and the National Basketball League and A-League.[118] The season's highest rating game was the Stars–Renegades Melbourne derby, which topped its timeslot with an average audience of 372,000, peaking at 439,000. With ratings of 231,000 per game, the season was an unexpected triumph.[119] From CA's perspective, it not only 'showcase[d] the women's game' but also emphasized that cricket was 'a sport for girls'.[120] Its success was recognized in October 2016 when the ICC awarded Australia the 2020 Twenty20 World Cup. According to CA chair David Peever, the WBBL had established that there was 'an audience for women's cricket both live and on prime-time television'. For the first time, the World Cup would be a standalone tournament, separate from the men's.[121] As Peever noted, this would move women's cricket 'from the shadow of the men's game'.[122]

Locally, however, women's cricket still lived in that shadow and an increasingly competitive women's sports market. The WBBL scrambled for athletic talent against netball, soccer, and the newly formed Australian Football League Women (AFLW). To remain competitive, CA lifted the player payment pool from AU $2.83 million to AU $4.2 million for the 2016–2017 season. Sutherland wanted 'fully professional playing careers within five years', but recognized that this could not be achieved until women's cricket was 'revenue positive'.[123] The most 'compelling offer . . . for talented young female athletes', he contended, was full professionalization.[124] Already there were promising signs. By late 2016, female participation had increased by 8 per cent, with over 30,000 players, and the WBBL was a major contributing factor.[125] Cricket's AU $4.2 million player payment pool far exceeded the AFLW's AU $2.3 million, though both were less than netball's AU $5.4 million. The WBBL's AU $7,000 minimum wage was less than football's AU $8,500, and well behind netball's AU $27,375. At the elite level, cricket offered far greater rewards. Whereas marquee AFLW players earned annually AU $27,000, and elite netballers AU $67,000, Australian cricketers could net from AU $40,000 to $100,000.[126]

CA wanted the WBBL to be the female equivalent of the IPL, attracting the world's top players. This was boosted prior to the 2016–2017 season, when the BCCI permitted Indian players to join the competition.[127] By the season's commencement, an influx of internationals had bolstered franchises and added substance to CA's boast that the WBBL was 'the world's best domestic women's T20 league'. The influx and presence of top Australian players was reflected in the high ratings.[128] Of the season's twelve televised games, ten were scheduled for Ten's main channel be-cause of the competition's unexpected popularity.[129] The opening double-header between the Renegades and Strikers attracted 267,000 viewers in a Saturday afternoon timeslot, while the night match between the Stars and Thunder on Ten's main channel averaged 432,000 viewers, peaking at 637,000. The game was the first standalone women's fixture broadcast at primetime on a commercial channel and was a ratings suc-cess.[130] Throughout the season, WBBL ratings averaged 239,000 per game, outperforming the much-vaunted AFLW's 192,000.[131] But the fi-nals highlighted that women were still cricket's second-class citizens. The WBBL finals were curtain-raisers to the BBL's. The women's games were scheduled according to the location of the BBL's finals. As Everard ex-plained, joint scheduling allowed Ten to cut production costs, while the women got 'the opportunity of a free-to-air broadcast'. But the scheduling robbed higher-finishing WBBL teams of a right accorded to their BBL counterparts; to play finals on their home grounds. This discrimination persisted into subsequent final series, strengthening the argument for a standalone WBBL.[132]

The controversy was part of a wider discrimination against women which surfaced during the 2017 dispute between CA and the ACA over the MoU. Although CA continued to push for full professionalization, the ACA campaigned for greater income security.[133] It held that women should be included in the 26 per cent share received by male players from CA's total revenues of AU $380.8 million. But the discrimination went deeper. The ACA, and not CA, underwrote many expenses incurred by women players, including health insurance.[134] Players were not entitled to parental leave and were required to declare if they were pregnant before signing contracts as 'a safety precaution'. Reportedly, the minimum pay for Australian male players was AU $270,000, including superannuation. Their female counterparts received a minimum of AU $40,000, excluding superannuation.[135] Although CA pushed for individual contracts and women to be paid from a smaller revenue pool, the ACA's position prevailed. As Fairfax reported, the female player pool increased from AU $7.5 million to AU $55.2 million, providing much sought-after financial security for top players, the revenue base for full professionalization, and increased impetus for a standalone WBBL.[136]

The 2017–2018 season confirmed Twenty20's place as the premier women's format and the WBBL as the world's top competition, with twenty-three players from six countries joining the eight franchises.[137] Again, the season exceeded expectations. The opening weekend's doubleheaders attracted a combined crowd of 8,726, while the Saturday-night clash between the Sixers and Stars was watched by an average audience of 422,500, peaking at 629,000.[138] Overall, ratings for the first four games increased by 24 per cent on the 2016–2017 season.[139] With attendances now totalling 151,931, there was an established demand for the WBBL and renewed calls for a standalone competition based on the BBL's format.[140]

Sutherland suggested giving the WBBL its own window early in the 2018–2019 season, but it clashed with a cramped international schedule.[141] The WBBL was pushed into December to January, coinciding with the BBL. The new broadcast rights-holders, Foxtel and Seven, broadcast twenty-three WBBL games, an increase of eleven on the previous season.[142] Boosted by Australia's Twenty20 World Cup victory in the West Indies, ratings increased by 10 per cent, and attendances by 45 per cent, on the previous season.[143] But the season was hamstrung by clashes with international commitments that saw the early departures of Indian, English, South African, and New Zealand players. The WBBL remained the BBL's little sister. It had gained a standalone final series at last, but its season was shorter than the men's, finishing on 26 January—Australia Day—and not in mid-February. Furthermore, the WBBL final was scheduled as an early morning televised curtain-raiser for the men's Australia-Sri Lanka Test. The 10am timeslot diminished the final's stature and reinforced the WBBL's curtain-raiser status. The final at Sydney's small Drummoyne

Oval was a turning-point, however, drawing a capacity crowd of 5,386 and an average viewing audience of 479,000, peaking at 812,000.[144] There was now substantial interest in the WBBL to justify a standalone Twenty20 season as a curtain-raiser to the standalone Twenty20 World Cup.

The Bug in Section N42

On 8 March 2020 Australia met India in the women's Twenty20 World Cup final at the MCG before a crowd of 86,174. It was the highpoint of an otherwise low summer. The Australia–New Zealand Test series was disappointing, with the home side far too good. Interest in the BBL had further deteriorated, with average crowds falling by 2,000 per game to 18,000, while the rain-drenched final at the Sydney Cricket Ground (SCG) drew a mediocre 10,129. Even interest in the WBBL plateaued. The first standalone season was plagued by player unavailability because of clashes with international fixtures. Crowds dropped and average audiences dipped to 191,000 per game, though women's interest in cricket remained high.[145] Six of every ten new cricketers were women, while the world's top players were the focus of the season's main event, the Twenty20 World Cup.[146]

The Australians were pre-tournament favourites but were unconvincing in the group stage, losing to India, and scraping through a rain-affected semi-final against South Africa. India were more impressive and entered the final as favourite. The pre-game hype centred not on the game but on the American singer Katy Perry. The 2015 Super Bowl Halftime Show headliner belted out her signature anthem *Roar* as cameras panned the packed MCG, focussing on mothers with their Gen-F daughters. With the Americanized entertainment over, the Australians easily accounted for the Indians, mainly due to an opening stand of 115 by Healy and Beth Mooney. The tournament crowned the Australians as the world champions and Twenty20 as the premier women's format. As the Australian players joined Perry onstage during the post-match concert, they were unaware that the event had dodged a viral bullet. Watching in Section N42 was a person infected with coronavirus.[147]

The virus was a game-changer, throwing Australian cricket into financial turmoil and reinforcing Twenty20's increasingly dominant position in the local market. Three days after the final, the World Health Organization declared a global pandemic. Although Australia was removed from Asian and European epicentres, the impact was immediate. International and domestic air travel stopped, as did national and international sport. The ODI series against New Zealand was abruptly curtailed, as was the Sheffield Shield season, while the women's white-ball series against South Africa was cancelled.[148] So too were the Bangladesh and Zimbabwe men's series, while doubts were raised about Australia's white-ball tour of England in June.[149] Because the pandemic hit in March, CA seemed better placed than the football codes to 'ride out' its financial impact. By October, CA hoped that the virus would be contained and normality would return with the men's Twenty20 World Cup and the money-spinning Indian tour. CA chief executive Kevin Roberts, who had replaced Sutherland in October 2018, was cautiously optimistic that cricket had the reserves and tour standing agreements to withstand the pandemic. But, he cautioned, '[w]e're in uncertain times and it's difficult to project precisely what will transpire over the next number of months'.[150]

By April, prospects of a return to normality were bleak. With the economy contracting and restrictions on travel, CA braced for a 50 per cent decline in revenues.[151] Consequently, Roberts stood down 80 per cent of CA staff, claiming that the organization could be insolvent by August.[152] The cuts were part of a reported AU $40 million job reduction exercise. As CA had recently secured an AU $50 million loan, questions were asked if the cuts were necessary.[153] A major concern was the estimated AU $300 million revenue loss if the 2020–2021 Indian series was cancelled.[154] Doubt was also cast over the future of the men's Twenty20 World Cup in October. The ICC was hopeful that the Cup would proceed, but the logistics of moving fifteen teams into and around Australia during a pandemic suggested that it too would be cancelled.

By June, the *Australian Financial Review* was reporting that CA had lost 40 per cent of its cash assets on failed investments in the stock market. Roberts confirmed that CA had taken a significant hit, but that it would not affect the operating budget.[155] Yet, he confessed that the game was in bad financial shape, despite CA having recently commenced its new broadcast rights deal and reported revenues of AU $399 million for the 2018–2019 financial year. But, reportedly, CA had lost AU $90 million through the devaluation of its share portfolio; seen unpaid player payments grow from AU $23 million to AU $58 million; and seen its cash assets butchered from approximately AU $199 million to AU $26 million.[156] The resultant cuts filtered through Australian cricket's federated structure. State associations had their funding slashed by 25 per cent, resulting in substantial job losses.[157]

The 'belt-tightening' also reignited tensions between Roberts and the ACA. Roberts sought reductions in contracts for male and female cricketers at international and domestic levels, and the sticking-point again was the revenue-sharing agreement. As self-proclaimed 'partners of the game', the ACA was prepared to accept cuts if the Indian tour was cancelled.[158] But the ACA head, Alistair Nicholson, wanted evidence of the pandemic's impact on revenue estimates to justify cutting the players' payment pool. Roberts pointed to a AU $170 million slump in cash assets, but Nicholson remained unconvinced. Australia had hosted England and India in recent summers, and signed an AU $1.2 billion media rights deal. With players facing a reported 50 per cent pay cut, Nicholson argued that they should not suffer financially for CA's mismanagement, especially when its executives had only sliced their salaries by 20 per cent.[159] Suspicions deepened that the pandemic was being used to mask CA's mismanagement and justify an across-the-board rationalization of the administration and game.

By June, the Australian batting coach, Graeme Hick, had been axed, while men's national coach, Justin Langer, and his women's World Cup winning counterpart, Mathew Mott, were on reduced hours.[160] CA's new chair, Earl Eddings, described the reductions as 'gut-wrenching' but emphasized that the financial position was not as dire as initially suggested.[161] CA had not recorded stock losses, nor was it almost 'insolvent', but it did have a revenue shortfall of between AU $80 million and $120 million.[162] His comments fuelled speculation that formats would be cut from the 2020–2021 schedule. As the Sheffield Shield was a major cost, reports circulated that it would be cut from ten to eight rounds and the final scrapped.[163] Women players feared that momentum generated during the World Cup would be lost.[164] Rumours persisted that the WBBL season would be reduced by sixteen games and the standalone window scrapped.[165] But Eddings emphasized that international and domestic competitions would be retained, though this would be dependent on the virus.[166] To cut either the WBBL or BBL ran counter to the Gen-F strategy and would diminish cricket's future sustainability. But with international and state borders closed, the 'cash cows' faced diminished seasons, living and playing in bio-bubbles, and without name international freelancers.[167] Questions remained about whether this would be sufficient to satisfy broadcast rights-holders who had paid substantial sums for high-quality media content.

Cricket at a Crossroads

In mid-June, Roberts tendered his resignation to CA's board. His tenure was marred by the pandemic and disagreements with the states and players. But Roberts had faced a deeper, irreconcilable crisis. Australian cricket was at a crossroads. Too many formats competed for media space and players. The pandemic-induced economic contraction forced CA to consider rationalizing its formats to meet broadcasters' demands for a lengthier and higher-quality BBL. Roberts' 'interim' replacement was Britisher Nick Hockley, who had worked on the organizing committees of the 2012 London Olympics and the 2015 cricket World Cup, as well as the women's Twenty20 World Cup. Hockley carried none of Roberts' baggage. He wanted all stakeholders 'pointing in the right direction', which meant mending relations with the states and the ACA.[168] He reached an agreement with the latter on the player payment pool. Pre-pandemic revenue projections were retained, though both parties agreed to adjust them if the Indian tour was cancelled.[169] Hockley confronted an uncertain international market and an assertive BCCI. In mid-July, the ICC confirmed that the men's Twenty20 World Cup would be postponed until 2021. It was an 'inevitability', Hockley explained, because of the virus, but the postponement placed added financial pressure on CA.[170] Given its budgetary problems, the four-Test Indian series needed to proceed to bolster revenues. Once again, CA was dependent on the BCCI's largesse.

Within its home market, the financial and structural problems remained unresolved. There were too many formats in a small yet cluttered sports market. The Sheffield Shield and the domestic fifty-over competition burdened the balance sheet, while international fixtures continued to cannibalize the most popular format, Twenty20. The traditional Test-match format provided a short-term revenue fix with the Indian series, but the BBL and WBBL offered longer-term financial solutions. Their increasing importance was evident in the release of the 2020–2021 Twenty20 schedule. The standalone WBBL season was retained. The fifty-nine-game fixture commenced in mid-October, but was compacted into three weeks. The final, on 26 November, was scheduled a week before the BBL's start, reinforcing women's curtain-raiser standing in the game. The extended sixty-one-game BBL season coincided with the Indian ODI and Test series. The season's conclusion on 6 February, with its five-game, American-styled play-off series, was tailored for the Gen-F market.[171] Twenty20 now extended from October to February and ran head to head with Test and international white-ball cricket. Because of their international commitments, Australia's best players were forced to bypass the BBL or make an occasional cameo appearance.

This arrangement did not suit the major rights-holders, Seven West and Foxtel. Seven alleged that they did not receive the BBL product agreed to in their contract with CA. The network's new managing director, James Warburton, was particularly forthright, claiming that Seven overpaid for the rights. He acrimoniously branded CA as 'the most incompetent administration I have ever worked with'.[172] With the pandemic intensifying, Warburton considered the rights were further devalued and so he sought a 40 per cent reduction on Seven's annual AU $82 million instalment for the remainder of the contract.[173] If none was forthcoming, the network threatened to seek the contract's termination in the Federal Court. Major concerns were CA's scheduling and its impact on the BBL's quality. Clashes with international fixtures lessened the competition's drawing power because Australia's top players were unavailable. Although CA offered Seven a $20 million discount, it was rejected. The matter then went before an independent arbitrator, the Australian Chamber for International and Commercial Arbitration, which ruled that Seven was only entitled to a $5.2 million discount.[174]

This 'stoush' had been brewing for some time. It was attributable to CA's repeated failures to address changes in cricket's market. Seven considered Twenty20 cricket's most commercially viable format with its value being diminished because of CA's scheduling failures. Although Seven agreed to 'absolutely support cricket's [2021–2022 Ashes] summer', CA still confronts the longer-term prospect of either bolstering the BBL's substance or facing costly legal battles with its free-to-air broadcaster. The matter remains a potential watershed that may determine the game's long-term future. It pits media power against the autonomy of a sporting body to operate its sport as it sees fit. At issue is the right of the media organization to determine the content, especially in cases where it considers that the content differs from what was agreed to in the contract. The Seven matter was compounded by a contracting and competitive media market, worsened by the pandemic, which caused many media organizations to reassess downwards the amounts paid for sporting rights.

Behind the legalities is a clash of cultures, which cricket administrators have failed to resolve. The IPL's success reshaped cricket. A quick rupee could be made from shortening the game, Americanizing the product with a twist of Bollywood, and luring the best players from across the globe on cashed-up contracts bolstered by substantial media and corporate revenues. National and regional boards jumped on the Twenty20 'gravy train' without much thought given to its impacts on cricket's other formats, the international calendar, and the game's traditions. Cricket was refashioned as Americanized entertainment and marketed to a new generation of fans—the Gen-Fs—influenced by the globalization of USA franchised sport. Teams became brands, top players were recast as celebrities, and cricket was repackaged as family entertainment.

CA swallowed this mantra. It wanted a show to attract the-brand-it-like-Ben Gen-Fs. Administrators clumsily attempted to juggle formats, trying to retain rusted-on, Test-watching traditionalists, while capturing a younger demographic through the Bash, but they failed. Twenty20 attracted revenues and became the main game. As the baby-boomers grew up with the ODI, the Gen-Fs have grown with Twenty20 and the BBL. In thirty years, CA's creative destructors will have their wish. The Bash will be the only game in town. It won't be as global as the IPL, but Australians will be proud when one of their own shines on cricket's biggest stage, Mumbai's Wankhede Stadium. Warburton and other media entrepreneurs will have got their way. In the coming stage of the creative destructive process, media organizations will determine the scheduling and content, while players and commentators will be entertainers and product-placers in Disneyfied spectaculars. In providing the money, the media will control the game; and in the media's market-driven free-for-all there will be winners and losers. Women will still be cricket's curtain-raisers, while the Gen-Fs will be the new traditionalists, writing their place into the game's new history. The old traditionalists will be long gone, and the Ashes and other long-form relics reduced to historical curiosities from a pre-Gen-F age before the bite-sized Bash and pandemic, and before media entrepreneurs stepped in to save the game.

Notes

1. David Knox, 'Ratings', *TV Tonight*, 17 February 2017, https://tvtonight.com.au/2019/02/sunday-17-february-2019.html.
2. David Harvey, 'Neoliberalism as creative destruction', *The Annals of Political and Social Science* 610 (2007): 22–44.
3. George Ritzer, *The Globalization of Nothing 2* (Thousand Oaks, CA: Pine Forge Press, 2007), 12.
4. Trevor Wigmore, 'The rise and rise of the Big Bash League', *Telegraph.co.uk*, 20 December 2017, www.telegraph.co.uk/cricket/2017/12/20/rise-rise-big-bash-league-will-attract-fans-ashes-secret-behind.
5. Tom Lowrey, 'Big Bash wary of growing too big too fast', *ABC Premium News*, 17 December 2017, www.abc.net.au/news/2017-12-17/big-bash-league-wary-of-growing-too-big-too-fast/9265540.
6. David A. Crawford and Colin B. Carter, *A Good Governance Structure for Australian Cricket* (Melbourne: Cricket Australia, December 2011), 4.
7. Chris Davies, 'Twenty20: Is it the right vision for the future of cricket?', *Sporting Traditions* 24, no. 1–2 (November 2007): 43–55.
8. Peter English, 'Twenty20 and the changing face of Australian cricket', *Sport in Society: Culture, Commerce, Media, Politics* 14, no. 10 (December 2011): 1371.
9. Ibid., 1369–1372.
10. Davies, 'Twenty20', 49.
11. *Sydney Morning Herald*, 'Joey's surprise code switch', 28 June 2006, www.smh.com.au/sport/cricket/joeys-surprise-code-switch-20060628-gdnun5.html.
12. Davies, 'Twenty20', 50.
13. Ibid., 52.
14. English, 'Twenty20', 1372.
15. Steve James, 'The Twenty20 affect: Have bat will travel', *Sunday Telegraph*, 25 January 2009, 11.
16. Ben Dorries, 'Even bigger bash targets Stars', *The Advertiser*, 25 October 2008, 116.
17. English, 'Twenty20', 1371.
18. Sanjjeev Samyal, Derek Abraham, and Seth Gautam, 'Can't get bigger than the IPL', *Daily News & Analysis Mumbai*, 30 October 2010.

19. Colin Agur, 'A foreign field no longer: India, the IPL and the global business of cricket', *Journal of Asian and African Studies* 48, no. 5 (October 2013): 548.

20. Chloe Saltau, 'Flintoff's early test declaration is bullish news for Australia's T20 season', *The Age*, 17 July 2009, 4.

21. Brett Stubbs, 'Explosion of talent: Battle of tribes in T20 Big Bash', *The Mercury*, 29 December 2009, 45.

22. Daniel Lane, 'How the Big Bash League became the 21st century's World Series Cricket', *Sydney Morning Herald*, 3 January 2016, www.smh.com.au/national/nsw/how-the-big-bash-league-became-the-21st-centurys-world-series-cricket-20160102-gly4s6.html.

23. *ABC Premium News; Sydney*, 'Big Bash wary of growing too big too fast', 16 December 2017, www.abc.net.au/news/2017-12-17/big-bash-league-wary-of-growing-too-big-too-fast/9265540.

24. Liam Blackburn, 'We won over the sceptics, The Hundred can too', *stadiumastro*, 16 May 2019, https://english.stadiumastro.com/sports-others/bbl-marketing-expert-we-won-over-sceptics-hundred-can-too-13504301.

25. Tom Heenan, 'How the Big Bash League took Australia's sporting landscape by storm', *The New Daily*, 2 January 2017, https://thenewdaily.com.au/sport/cricket/big-bash/2017/01/02/big-bash-league-popularity.

26. Jason Belzer, 'Why the Big Bash is changing the professional sports paradigm', *Forbes*, 22 January 2016, www.forbes.com/sites/jasonbelzer/2016/01/22/why-australias-big-bash-league-is-changing-the-professional-sports-paradigm/?sh=5c45834c0e2f.

27. Jeff Whalley, 'Smashing tradition', *Herald Sun*, 23 January 2015, 64.

28. Malcolm Conn, 'Big Bash opens up pot of gold', *Weekend Australian*, 30 October 2010, 41.

29. English, 'Twenty20', 1373–1374; Agur, 'A foreign field', 543.

30. English, 'Twenty20', 1374.

31. Peter English, 'Investors offered 33% stake in Big Bash teams', *ESPNcricinfo*, 29 October 2010. www.espncricinfo.com/story/australian-news-investors-offered-33-stake-in-big-bash-teams-484079.

32. Jesper Fjeldstad, 'Big Bash smashes conventional boundaries', *Sunday Telegraph*, 31 October 2010, 65.

33. Chris Barrett, 'Now it's time to privatise, argues players' chief', *Sydney Morning Herald*, 13 January 2016, 48.

34. *ABC News Victoria (ABC1)*, 17 December 2011.

35. *ABC News Queensland*, 29 October 2010.

36. Phil Rothfield and Michael Horan, 'India cash cow foreigners set to splurge for a share of our Big Bash', *Herald-Sun*, 28 October 2010, 94.

37. Ben Dorries, 'Bigger bash nod: Warnie hand up for new Twenty20 comp', *Herald Sun*, 5 January 2010, 59.

38. *World News Australia* (SBS Melbourne), 8 November 2011.

39. Andrew Wu, 'Come in spinner: Big Bash brings test tweakers out of woodwork', *Sydney Morning Herald*, 3 December 2011, www.smh.com.au/sport/cricket/come-in-spinners-big-bash-league-brings-former-test-tweakers-out-of-woodwork-20111202-1obay.html.

40. Jesse Hogan, '"There's no logic to bashing crowd sizes" says Brayshaw', *Sydney Morning Herald*, 21 December 2011, www.smh.com.au/sport/cricket/theres-no-logic-to-bashing-crowd-sizes-says-brayshaw-20111221-1p5od.html.

41. Peter Lalor, 'Big Bash League a $10m gamble: T20 competition puts large hole in cricket Australia budget', *The Australian*, 7 December 2012, 40.

42. *Ten 5PM News*, 7 January 2013.

43. John Stensholt, 'Big Bash investment doubled', *Australian Financial Review*, 16 December 2013, 34; Jesse Hogan, 'Big Bash a hit with fans', *The Age*, 7 January 2014, 39; BBL Crowds, *Sessions, BBL/02*, https://bblcrowds.com/bbl%7C02.

44. John Stensholt, 'Ten bashed for a six on digital cover of summer cricket', *Australian Financial Review*, 26 September 2013, 22; Andrew Wu, Jon Pierik, and Dominic Bossi, 'The turmoil adds to uncertainty for Cricket Australia', *Sydney Morning Herald*, 15 June 2017, 40.

45. Stensholt, 'Big Bash investment doubled', 34.

46. Ibid.

47. Chris Barrett, 'Ten's BBL serves it up to Seven's Australian Open', *Sydney Morning Herald*, 17 January 2014, 8.

48. Paul McIntyre, 'Network hopes Winter Olympics coverage will top Big Bash ratings success', *Australian Financial Review*, 10 February 2014, 37; BBL Crowds, *Sessions, BBL/03*, https://bblcrowds.com/bbl%7C03.

49. McIntyre, 'Network hopes'.

50. *AAP Finance News Wire*, 'Ten loses $8m in first half', 10 April 2014.

51. Peter Lalor, 'Big Bash launches its critics over the fence with fourfold growth', *The Australian*, 17 January 2014, 28.

52. John Stensholt, 'BBL heading for $4m total profit', *Australian Financial Review*, 14 December 2015, 34; John Stensholt, 'Growing crowds bolster Big bash coffers', *The Australian Financial Review*, 19 January 2015, 32.

53. John Stensholt, 'Big Bash into black', *Australian Financial Review*, 15 December 2014, 34.

54. Will Swanton, 'Somewhere in partyland there was a little cricket played', *The Weekend Australian*, 20 December 2014, 37.

55. Lalor, 'Big Bash launches its critics over the fence with fourfold growth', 28.

56. Andy Bull, 'T20 Blast ticket sales hit new high—So why does the competition feel unloved?' *The Guardian*, 14 May 2015, 2.

57. Miriam Webber, 'Big Bash soars to new heights', *Sydney Morning Herald*, 30 December 2016, 12; Tiffany Dunk, 'How the Bash became so big', *The Advertiser*, 11 January 2016, 19; John Stensholt, 'BBL heading for $4m total profit', *Australian Financial Review*, 14 December 2015, 34; Belzer, 'Why the Big Bash'.

58. Jake Mitchell, 'Big Bash a winner for Ten's revenue', *The Weekend Australian*, 16 January , 2016, 23.

59. Jeff Whalley, 'Buoyant Big Bash backers bid', *Herald Sun*, 23 January 2016, 5; Stensholt, 'BBL heading'.

60. *The Guardian*, 'Chris Gayle tells reporter: Your eyes are beautiful', 5 January 2016, www.theguardian.com/sport/2016/jan/04/chris-gayle-reporter-drink-blush-network-ten-big-bash-melbourne.

61. Russell Gould, 'Gayle a whisper in Aussie Circles', *The Mercury*, 4 December 2017, 45; *ABC News*, 'Chris Gayle fined $10,000 by the Melbourne Renegades', 5 January 2016, www.abc.net.au/news/2016-01-05/chris-gayle-fined-melbourne-renegades-bbl/7069194.

62. Whalley, 'Buoyant Big Bash'.

63. Ibid.

64. Russell Gould, 'Bash is the golden goose', *Herald Sun*, 28 December 2016, 68.

65. CRICKET.com.au, 'Australia sets sights on the future', 13 August 2016, www.cricket.com.au/news/australian-cricket-conference-outcomes-2016-james-sutherland-david-peever/2016-08-13.

66. CRICKET.com.au, 'Cricket becomes Australia's No. 1 sport', 23 August 2016; Gaurav Bhatt, 'Solid cricket with a touch of controversy: The rise of the Big Bash League', *Hindustan Times*, 21 January 2016, www.hindustantimes.com/cricket/solid-affordable-cricket-with-a-touch-of-controversy-the-rise-of-the-big-bash-league/story-cdcxvWpMseTEDK82BkcYZJ.html.

67. Russell Gould, 'Big Bash cash has boss talking up golden future', *The Advertiser*, 28 December 2016, 73.

68. Darren Walton, 'BBL can't beat Test cricket: Sutherland', *AAP Bulletin Wire*, 6 January 2017.

69. CRICKET.com.au, 'Big Bash, women focus of new strategy', 7 September 2017, www.cricket.com.au/news/australian-cricket-strategy-2017-22-big-bash-league-world-t20-james-sutherland/2017-09-07.

70. Peter Lalor, 'Shield final kept safe from Big bash league expansion', *The Australian*, 9 October 2018, 32.

71. *AAP Sports News Wire Service; Sydney*, 'CA overlooks Argus review recommendations', 16 November 2016.

72. Jesse Hogan, 'Argus identified as the man to put the Australian cricket team on course', *Sydney Morning Herald*, 5 February 2011, 42.

73. Rob Shaw, 'Ashes saga still burns', *The Examiner*, 12 September 2017, 35.

74. Simon Wilde, 'Growth of T20 means cricket is facing the acid test', *The Times*, 8 January 2017, www.thetimes.co.uk/article/growth-of-t20-means-cricket-is-facing-acid-test-pfkh86m39.

75. Jennifer Duke and John McDuling, 'Ratings fall for Ashes hit sports deal', *Canberra Times*, 17 March 2018, 28; Nick Tabakoff, 'Sporting bubble bursts', *The Weekend Australian*, 29 April 2017, 19.

76. Mitchell Bingemann, 'Big Bash a smart hit for cashed-up Cricket Australia', *The Australian*, 29 January 2017, 36.

77. Daniel Cherney and Jon Pierik, 'Bigger bash may enter the twilight zone', *The Age*, 28 January 2017, 46.

78. Robert Craddock, 'TV talks becomes dash with cash to secure Bash', *The Mercury*, 30 January 2017, 37; Max Mason, 'Despite grand final dip, Ten rides BBL was as rivals eye TV rights', *The Australian Financial Review*, 30 January 2017, 31.

79. Mason, 'Despite grand final dip'.

80. Ben Horne, 'Big Bash hits rival out of the park', *The Mercury*, 31 March 2017, 59.

81. Craddock, 'TV talks'; Jon Pierik, 'Bigger bash set for next season', *Sydney Morning Herald*, 28 January 2017, 48.

82. Greg Baum, 'Today the boundary rope: Tomorrow—the world!' *The Age*, 14 January 2017, 51.

83. Jennifer Duke, 'Cricket Australia needs better TV innings', *Sydney Morning Herald*, 27 March 2018, 25.

84. Tabakoff, 'Sporting bubble bursts'.

85. Robert Craddock, 'Ten may lose Big Bash rights over cash crisis', *The Mercury*, 25 April 2017, 34.

86. Max Mason, 'Cricket Australia's engages on all free-to-air broadcast rights deals', *Australian Financial Review*, 10 April 2018, 26.

87. Max Mason, 'Nine and News Corp in tie-up talks on cricket', *The Australian Financial Review*, 26 February 2018, 30.

88. Marc C-Scott, 'Seven and Foxtel snag rights, meaning more content but maybe not for free', *The Conversation*, 13 April 2018, https://theconve rsation.com/seven-and-foxtel-snag-cricket-rights-meaning-more-cont ent-but-maybe-not-for-free-94976.

89. Max Mason and John Stensholt, 'Summer shake-up as cricket changes channel', *Australian Financial Review*, 14 April 2018, 43.

90. Ibid.; Joe Aston, 'Rear window', *Australian Financial Review*, 16 April 2018, 40.

91. Mason and Stensholt, 'Summer shake-up'.

92. *Seven News (Seven Network)*, 13 April 2018.

93. Max Mason, 'Seven promises 13 mega days of cricket this summer', *Australian Financial Review*, 16 July 2018, 3.

94. John Stensholt, 'How the Big Bash League has become the hottest sports compe-tition in town', *Australian Financial Review*, 18 December 2016, www.afr.com/ companies/sport/how-the-big-bash-league-has-become-the-hottest-sports-competition-in-town-20161215-gtbsb8.

95. *The Mercury*, 'Bowling up super show for fans', 8 December 2017, 68.

96. Ibid.

97. Ben Horne, 'Big Bash theory', *Courier Mail*, 14 October 2017, 92.

98. *B&T Magazine*, 'KFC BBL announces renewed partnership with Nickelodeon', 14 November 2017.

99. Duke and McDuling. 'Ratings fall'.

100. Russell Gould, 'Call for inquiry as Big Bash League's $33 million loss revealed', *The Northern Territory News*, 1 June 2017, 36; Rob Forsaith, 'BBL won't grow bigger than tests, CA boss', *AAP Bulletin Wire*, 25 December 2017.

101. Daniel Cherney, 'Kevin Pietersen worried expanding the Big Bash will stop overseas players from coming', *Sydney Morning Herald*, 25 January 2018, www.smh.com.au/sport/cricket/kevin-pietersen-worried-expanding-the-big-bash-league-will-stop-overseas-players-from-coming-20180125-h0o e50.html.

102. Andrew Wu, 'IPL spending spree to over-shadow one-dayers', *The Canberra Times*, 26 January 2018, 61; *The Mercury*, '$2 million IPL boost to Aussie', 6 January 2018, 71.

103. Malcom Knox, 'Is it just me or have we reached peak Big Bash League?', *Sydney Morning Herald*, 6 January 2018, 42.

104. Andrew Wu, 'Big Bash does fine without international stars: TV chief', *Sydney Morning Herald*, 26 January 2017, 36.

105. Daniel Cherney, 'Big bash schedule to be shaped by fans: Cricket', *The Age*, 3 February 2018, 51.

106. Dhiman Sarkar, 'Finch backs call for shorter Big Bash League season', *Hindustan Times*, 25 February 2019, www.pressreader.com/india/hindustan-times-st-noida/20190225/282097752991996.

107. Cherney, 'Big Bash schedule'.

108. Jon Pierik, 'Stars boss wants tough talk to fix BBL scheduling clash', *Sydney Morning Herald*, 23 January 2017, 35; Dean Jones, 'Players should have the freedom of choice', *Sydney Morning Herald*, 28 January 2017, 48.

109. Paul Woodhams, 'Call-up puts stars in doubt for BBL finish', *The Canberra Times*, 17 January 2018, 37.

110. Jon Pierik, 'Finch laments missing big guns'. *The Canberra Times*, 11 January 2018, 37.

111. Tiffany Dunk, 'How the Bash became so big', *The Advertiser*, 11 January 2016, 19.

112. *AAP Sports News Wire*, 'Eight teams in new women's Big Bash', 19 February 2015.

113. Jennifer Browning, 'Elite female athletes switch sport to earn WBBL training contracts', *ABC Premium News* (Sydney), 3 September 2016.

114. *Herald-Sun*, 'Women play for peanuts compared with men', 21 November 2015, 7.

115. Eliza Sewell, 'Lanning a star for WBBL', *Herald-Sun*, 11 July, 2015, 65.

116. Eliza Adno, 'Aussie women get their chance to join cricket bash for cash', *Courier-Mail*, 11 July 2015, 11.

117. Chris Barrett, 'WBBL blasts A-League out of the park in TV ratings', *Sydney Morning Herald*, 22 December 2016, 46.

118. Ibid.

119. James Buckley, 'Women's Big Bash League to launch female cricket into professionalism', *Sydney Morning Herald*, 7 December 2016, www.smh.com.au/sport/cricket/womens-big-bash-league-to-launch-female-cricket-into-prof

essionalism-20161209-gt7qdu.html; Jesse Hogan and Tom Decent, 'Win all round: CA and Ten agree deal on WBBL finals', *Sydney Morning Herald*, 7 January 2016, 44.

120. Chris Barrett, 'WBBL blasts A-League out of the park in TV ratings', *Sydney Morning Herald*, 21 December 2015, 46.

121. James Buckley, 'Cricket Australia considering standalone final for next year's WBBL final', *Canberra Times*, 20 January 2017, www.canberratimes. com.au/story/6037367/cricket-australia-considering-standalone-final-for-next-years-wbbl-final.

122. ICC, 'Outcomes for the ICC board meeting in Cape Town', 14 October 2016, www.icc-cricket.com/news/183664; Julian Guyer, 'Women's World Twenty20 to be stand-alone event', *AFP International Text Wire Live in English*, 14 October 2016.

123. Sam Landsberger, 'Pro option for cricket women', *Herald Sun*, 18 June 2016, 86.

124. Ibid.

125. Fiona Bollen, 'Delivering the male', *The Daily Telegraph*, 10 December 2016, 101; Adam Collins, 'Women's Big Bash League sprinting after tentative, but successful, first steps in season one', *ABC Premium News Sydney*, 6 December 2016.

126. AAP, 'AFL: How the AFL women's pay deal stacks up', *AAP Sports News Wire; Sydney*, 10 November 2016.

127. Shalini Gupta, 'After giving permission for WBBL, BCCI mulling over women's T20 league', *The Hindustan Times*, 12 June 2016, www.hindustantimes.com/ cricket/after-giving-permission-for-wbbl-bcci-mulling-over-women-s-t20-lea gue/story-H074YcjP9DcPAJCGZL5kbI.html.

128. Eliza Sewell, 'Ready for the big time', *The Advertiser*, 8 December 2016, 64.

129. Scott Bailey, 'Women to kick off BBL', *AAP Sports News Wire; Sydney*, 7 June 2016, 8.

130. Will Knight and Adrian Warren, 'WBBL boasts big early TV audience', *AAP Bulletin Wire; Sydney*, 11 December 2016.

131. Ben Horne, 'Big Bash hits rival out of the park', *The Mercury*, 31 March 2017, 59.

132. James Buckley, 'Surging WBBL primed to play a standalone final next season', *Sydney Morning Herald*, 21 January 2017, 43.

133. Scott Bailey, 'MOU push to help WBBL stars', *AAP Sport News Wire; Sydney*, 19 August 2016, 8.

134. Peter Lalor, 'Finally a living wage for some', *The Australian*, 7 October 2016, 36.

135. Eliza Sewell, 'WBBL a boost to players' pay bid', *Herald Sun*, 7 January 2016, 68.

136. Daniel Cherney, 'Understanding how the game has changed: The agreement reached in the aftermath of cricket's pay dispute', *The Age*, 1 February 2018, 41.

137. James Buckley, 'Stronger international contingent spices up third season of third season of WBBL', *Sydney Morning Herald*, 8 December 2017, 39.

138. James Buckley, 'WBBL ignites as records tumble', *Sydney Morning Herald*, 11 December 2017, 37.

139. Callum Godde, 'Sydney WBBL teams to charge for tickets', *AAP Sports News Wire: Sydney*, 4 October 2018; Dana McAuley, 'Big Bash boom for Ten's summer ratings', *The Weekend Australia*, 23 December 2017, 23.

140. James Buckley, 'Standalone WBBL gains momentum after Sydney miss on home finals', *Sydney Morning Herald*, 6 February 2018, 40.

141. Jon Pierik, 'More matches needed in WNCL says Haynes', *The Age*, 2 March 2018, 42.

142. Daniel Cherney, 'Big Bash is to be shaped by the fans', *The Age*, 3 February 2018, 51.

143. Megan Maurice, 'Woman's cricket the winner in WBBL semis', *The Guardian*, 20 January 2019; Jason Cloat, 'Players in the WBBL final not only women scoring in cricket', *Australian Financial Review*, 26 January 2019, 11.

144. Caden Helmer, 'Players back standalone WBBL move', *Canberra Times*, 1 February 2019, 45; Fiona Bollen, 'Blackwell says WBBL warrants prime-time slot', *Daily Telegraph*, 28 February 2019, 62.

145. *The Australian*, 'WBBL final series could be expanded', 16 December 2019, 23.

146. Megan Maurice, 'Recent Australian dominance whets the appetite for WBBL season', *The Guardian*, 16 October 2019.

147. Xavier Voigt-Hill, 'Coronavirus and cricket: Everything that's happened so far', *The Cricketer*, 21 March 2020, www.thecricketer.com/Topics/zimbabwe/coronavirus_and_cricket_everything_that_has_happened_so_far_news_updates_covid-19.html.

148. Ibid.

149. Rob Forsaith, 'Coronavirus update: Aussies' Test tour of Bangladesh postponed', *7 News.com.au*, 10 April 2020, https://7news.com.au/sport/cricket/aussies-test-tour-of-bangladesh-postponed-c-968229.

150. *Reuters*, 'Australia's tour of Bangladesh postponed due to coronavirus', 9 April 2020, www.reuters.com/article/uk-health-coronavirus-cricket-australia-idUKKCN21R1IY; Daniel Bettrig, 'Cricket Australia guards cash and venues ahead of coronavirus winter', *ESPNcricinfo*, 17 March 2020, www.espn.com.au/cricket/story/_/id/28914287/cricket-australia-guards-cash-venues-ahead-coronavirus-winter.

151. Scott Bailey, 'Cricket Australia sets up plan to keep numbers', *The Canberra Times*, 27 June 2020, 69.

152. Scott Bailey and Rob Forsaith, 'Shortened WBBL an option for this summer', *The Canberra Times*, 19 May 2020, www.canberratimes.com.au/story/6762612/shortened-wbbl-an-option-for-this-summer; Ben Horne, 'Anger shifts to CA board', *The Daily Telegraph*, 19 June 2020, 91.

153. Andrew Wu, 'The big crash: Cricket in firing line amid brewing pay dispute', *Sydney Morning Herald*, 18 April 2020, www.smh.com.au/sport/cricket/the-big-crash-cricket-australia-in-firing-line-amid-brewing-pay-war-20200418-p54l1f.html.

154. Daniel Cherney, 'CA bracing for 50 percent revenue dip', *The Age*, 9 April 2020, 38.

155. Joe Aston and Myriam Robin, 'Rear window', *Australian Financial Review*, 21 April 2020, 40; Peter Lalor, 'CA chair says cash lost on stock market', *The Australian*, 23 June 2020, 24.

156. Aston and Robin, 'Rear window', 40; Wu, 'The big crash'.

157. Lalor, 'CA chair'; Chris Barrett and Andrew Wu, ' "Gut wrenching": Assistant coach Hick axed as CA slashes 40 jobs', *Sydney Morning Herald*, 18 June 2020, 31.

158. Wu, 'The big crash'.

159. Ibid.

160. Ibid.; Peter Lalor, 'Shield, WBBL in savage cost cuts', *The Australian*, 7 May 2020, 24.

161. Lalor, 'CA chair'; Barrett and Wu, ' "Gut wrenching" '.

162. Lalor, 'CA chair'.

163. Lalor, 'Shield, WBBL'.

164. Daniel Bettrig, 'Cricket Australia contracts delayed by coronavirus planning', *ESPNcricinfo*, 30 March 2020, www.espn.com.au/cricket/story/_/id/28969297/ cricket-australia-contracts-delayed-coronavirus-planning.

165. Bailey and Forsaith, 'Shortened WBBL'; Lalor, 'Shield, WBBL'.

166. Barrett and Wu, ' "Gut wrenching" '.

167. Martin Smith, 'WBBL will play big role saving the summer: Ellyse Perry', *Cricket.com.au*, 29 April 2020, www.cricket.com.au/news/ellyse-perry-wbbl-womens-big-bash-league-coronavirus-indian-tour-broadcast-crowds-ratings/2020-04-29.

168. 'Interim chief Hockley looks to reset Australian cricket'. *AFP International Text Wire in English*, 21 June 2020.

169. Peter Lalor, 'New Cricket Australia: Boss ready to compromise on cuts as states maintain the rage', *The Australian*, 8 July 2020, 22; Peter Lalor, 'No longer at such a loss', *Sunday Telegraph*, 5 July 2020, 67.

170. Peter Lalor, 'Covid-19: ICC announces postponement of 2020 T20 World Cup', *IANS English*, 20 July 2020; Daniel Cherney, 'Top stars expecting leave pass for IPL', *The Age*, 22 July 2020, 32.

171. ABC News, 'Big Bash fixtures reveal 61 game season: WBBL to retain standalone status', *ABC Premium News; Sydney*, 15 July 2020.

172. Steve Larkin, ' "It's a train wreck": Seven Network would drop contract', *The Canberra Times*, 29 August 2020, 62.

173. Daniel Brettig, 'Why the Ashes schedule won't shift despite England player threats', *The Age*, 16 September 2021.

174. Jon Pierik, 'Seven takes Cricket Australia to arbitration but court action could loom', *Sydney Morning Herald*, 6 October 2020, www.smh.com.au/sport/cricket/game-on-seven-takes-cricket-australia-to-arbitration-20201006-p562ci.

html; James Madden, 'Cricket's TV war: Future of Seven's coverage under a cloud after network's paltry discount from Cricket Australia', *The Australian*, 13 March 2021, www.theaustralian.com.au/sport/cricket/future-of-cricket-cover age-under-a-cloud-after-seven-gets-paltry-discount/news-story/c35a254b1 59b25200518578e19667940.

8

Nationalism on the 'Back Foot'
but Still Not Out

T20 Cricket in the West Indies, 2006–2019

Roy McCree

Introduction

Since the early twentieth century, cricket has been an integral component of West Indian nationalism, regionalism, identity, and anti-imperialism. Invariably, West Indian cricket and cricketers came to represent these lofty ideals, as well as a form of symbolic political capital (i.e. nationalism and regionalism), whose principal *raison d'être* was not just resisting historical modes of domination but also strengthening West Indian sovereignty, citizen empowerment, and unity across its various islands and the different ethnic groups who inhabit the region.[1] Against this background, and based on the use of documentary sources (notably media reports, relevant research literature, and League statistics), this chapter has two major objectives. Firstly, it examines how the commercialization of cricket in the region through the emergence of the Caribbean Premier T20 League (CPL) in 2013, fashioned along the lines of American franchise sport, has provided a context for deconstructing, disturbing, and reinforcing the traditional notions of nationalism or national and regional identity, which the game has symbolized in the region. In particular, CPL has done so by enabling both West Indian and non-West Indian cricketers to play for as well as captain teams associated with islands of which they are neither nationals nor citizens. Secondly, the chapter examines the significance of the social tensions and conflicts resulting from the manner

Roy McCree, *Nationalism on the 'Back Foot' but Still Not Out* In: *Cricket and Nationhood in the Twenty-First Century.*
Edited by: Souvik Naha, Oxford University Press. © Oxford University Press 2024.
DOI: 10.1093/9780191982576.003.0009

in which West Indian cricketers have participated in regional CPL teams and the West Indies national team, especially the criticism that they have surrendered their political consciousness for 'cash consciousness'.[2] The chapter explores these issues surrounding the role of commerce in eroding the sense of national belonging, which have gained much attention in the international media landscape since the early 2010s, using the framework of sociologist Pierre Bourdieu's theory of economic and symbolic capital.

Bourdieu, Capital, and Sport

In his study of society, Bourdieu identified four fundamental and related forms of capital—economic, social, cultural, and symbolic—which shape human action and the character of social relations. Economic capital refers to material wealth, which, in the context of sports, would include such elements as sponsorship, endorsement contracts, match fees, and the like.[3] Social capital refers to having the right contact, social connections, or a network of social relations that could include 'friends, families and workmates'.[4] Cultural capital refers to the possession of certain educational credentials, aesthetic tastes, and habits (notably in music and art). Finally, symbolic capital refers to 'a reputation for competence and an image of respectability and honourability'.[5] Bourdieu saw the state as the assemblage of several forms of capital: 'the culmination of a process of concentration of different species of capital'.[6] These 'different species of capital' embodied in the state included economic capital (with its monopoly over taxation and influence over markets and trade), cultural capital (e.g. state-sanctioned education system), 'informational capital' (the collection, storage, and dissemination of data like the national census and official notices), and juridical and military capital.[7] The dialectical intertwining or interconnectedness of these various forms of capital is evident in the fact that economic capital can be 'converted' into cultural capital (through educational qualifications) and vice versa, while social capital can be 'converted' into economic capital and vice versa. In addition, Bourdieu associates symbolic capital with other forms of capital but refers in particular to issues of 'recognition' and 'value' which could be conferred by the state or other 'agents'.[8] Relatedly, as the primary site of various forms of capital and with the power to sanction, recognize, or legitimize human actions, the state did not just have symbolic capital but 'is the site par excellence of the concentration and exercise of symbolic power'.[9]

This study uses symbolic capital in two separate but related senses. On the one hand, it can refer to the general reputation and image of cricket players and, on the other, it can refer to players as broader symbols of the nation and region which would be seen as symbolic political capital. This symbolic political capital or power would be equated further with the peculiar manifestations of nationalism in the form of national colours, music, and geographical territory. Political capital, on the other hand, refers particularly to the control of the state. Nationalism here refers to an affective attachment to a particular collectivity called a nation which can be seen as 'a territorially distinct aggregation of peoples who live under one common, central political authority (called the state)'.[10]

Scholars have applied Bourdieu's concepts of the field, *habitus*, and capital to the study of a range of issues in sport.[11] In a rare study to have applied Bourdieu's notions of capital to examine nationalism and the exercise of state power, Sullivan et al. show how the Chinese state has used sport, football in particular, as a form of symbolic power or capital to advance its nationalist and internationalist political and economic agenda. Organizing and patronizing sport (e.g. staging the Beijing Olympics) have helped China maintain a form of legitimacy at home and abroad that is embedded in economic capital.[12] This chapter argues that the same forms of capital can also undermine nationalism and regionalism, which it demonstrates through a study of the implication of T20 franchise cricket involving several small island states within the Caribbean, further complicating the scholarship on cricket's role in defining, framing, and developing the region since the early twentieth century. Figure 8.1 illustrates how this circuit or figuration of capital, to borrow from Elias, and the interrelated or multidirectional nature of its different forms works in the context of Caribbean cricket.[13]

Evolution of Caribbean T20 Cricket

Global T20 cricket now represents one of the more commercialized and deterritorialized forms of the game compared to the two other major

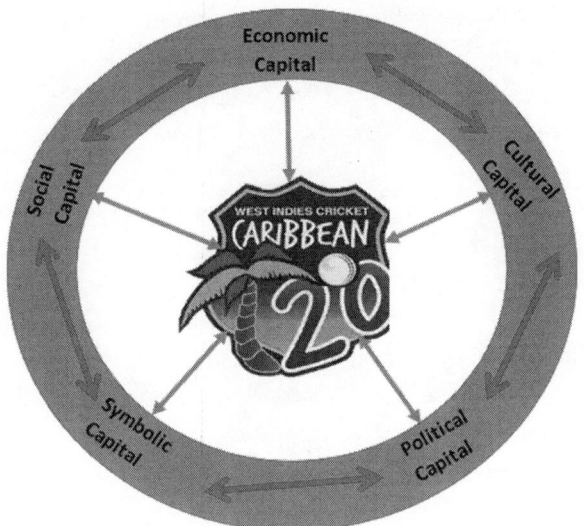

Figure 8.1   Circuit of capital and West Indies cricket.

formats which are the traditional five-day Test match and the fifty-over One Day International (ODI). This can be illustrated in the number of countries playing the game as well as the number of competitions across the world. For instance, while the International Cricket Council recognizes ten countries as qualified to play Test cricket and twenty to play ODIs, eighty-five are eligible to play the T20 format.[14] In addition, while there are no ODI or Test match leagues across the cricketing world (the World Test Championships do not strictly qualify as a league), there are now at least twelve such T20 leagues around the world, notably in Australia, England, South Africa, India, Pakistan, Bangladesh, and the Caribbean.[15] What is also noteworthy is that these leagues have all emerged only within the last seventeen years since the formation of the first such league in England in 2003.[16]

The T20 format was first introduced to the Caribbean region by former American billionaire Allen Stanford in 2006 as only the second such league in the world. It was called the Stanford 20/20 tournament and featured nineteen teams in its first season and twenty-one in its second, from the English, Dutch, and American Caribbean, who competed for the prize of US $1 million.[17] In addition, in a one-off game between the Stanford All Star team and England, the winner received US

$20 million.[18] The league folded in 2009, after just two seasons in 2006 and 2008, following Stanford's indictment in the USA for carrying out a Ponzi scheme valued at around US $8 billion. He was subsequently convicted in 2012 on thirteen charges of fraud and sentenced to 112 years in prison.[19]

In an attempt to fill the void created by the League's collapse, the West Indian Cricket Board (WICB) introduced its own T20 league in 2010.[20] This league, however, was much smaller as it consisted of eight teams, but unlike the Stanford League, it included a non-Caribbean team—that is, Canada. In addition, it was not as well resourced as Stanford's, for the winning team received US $25,000 compared to US $1 million prize money for the Stanford league.[21] Nevertheless, like its predecessor, the WICB T20 league was short-lived, ending in 2012 after just three years.[22]

These temporary attempts at organizing a national T20 league were followed by the launch of the CPL in 2013. The inaugural season, consisting of six teams, yielded a profit of US $4.5 million for the WICB.[23] The number of teams increased to seven in 2015 but was reduced to six in 2019 (Table 8.1).[24] For the period of this study, these teams included the Barbados Tridents, Guyana Amazon Warriors, Jamaican Tallawahs, St Kitts and Nevis Patriots, St Lucia Zouks, and Trinidad and Tobago Knight Riders. Apart from the smaller number of teams, the CPL differed from its forerunners in two major related ways: its franchise character and the composition of its teams. In term of its franchise character, the League was firmly based on the American sport model and, as a result, introduced the player draft for the first time in Caribbean sport. Secondly, consistent with the franchise model, the teams were free to select players who were not native to the particular island, since they were not national teams in its usual legal or political sense. In this regard, both the Stanford 20/20 and WICB T20 formats were based on the traditional model of international sport. In the CPL, however, teams consisted of three sets of players: players born in the country with which the team is associated, regional players from other countries in the Caribbean, and 'overseas' players from cricketing nations outside of the Caribbean (Table 8.1). The CPL therefore was based on this triumvirate of national, regional, and global players whose numbers varied from team to team.

The Triumvirate in the CPL: National, Regional, and Global

Tables 8.1 to 8.7 delineate the distribution of players in the CPL by country of origin. The three major types, sources, or levels of the triumvirate of players can also be referred to as tendencies, streams, or trends. These tendencies are examined in terms of how strong or weak they were. The determination or characterization of the strength of a particular tendency was based on three major considerations: the proportion of players in each stream, the number of seasons over which a particular pattern was consistent, and the margin of difference between certain streams. These proportions and their associated strength were as follows: very weak (0–29 per cent), weak (30–49 per cent), strong (50–59 per cent), very strong (60–69 per cent), and extremely strong (70 per cent or more). Additionally, the assessment of the nature of the nationalist tendency involved looking at the total number of non-nationals on each team. This number consisted of Caribbean nationals who were not citizens of the country with which their team was associated and foreign or overseas players. The use of numbers to make inferences about nationalist or non-nationalist tendencies in sport is not new. For instance, the size of crowd attendance at a sport competition as well as television viewership have historically been used as markers or barometers of national support for teams or athletes in sport. However, what might be different is this attempt to describe these various tendencies as either weak or strong based on descriptive statistical distributions or frequencies which might also be considered arbitrary. For the League as a whole, the triumvirate of player streams or tendencies was distributed as follows in Table 8.1.

Table 8.1 Distribution of players in the Caribbean Premier T20 League by country/region of origin

Year	Teams	Total players	National	Global	Regional (Caribbean)	Total non-national
2013	6	90	46.7% (42)	21.1% (19)	32.2% (29)	53.3% (48)
2015	7	98	40.8% (40)	28.6% (28)	30.6% (30)	59.2% (58)
2017	7	108	26.9% (29)	37.0% (40)	36.1% (39)	73.1% (79)
2019	6	114	39.5% (45)	31.6% (36)	28.9% (33)	60.5% (59)

1. **National/nationalist tendency or stream.** This describes or represents those who played for teams associated with the island of their birth or citizenship. They represented a varying minority of players which ranged from 26.9 per cent to 46.7 per cent in the period examined between 2013 and 2019. As a result, based on the classificatory scheme used, this tendency falls within the categories of weak or very weak. However, the annual figures or breakdown of cricketers in this category show the national tendency to be statistically greater than the other tendencies for three of the four seasons examined (2013: 46.7 per cent; 2015: 40.8 per cent; 2019: 39.5 per cent). In 2017, it was weaker than the other tendencies for it represented around a quarter of players (26.9 per cent) compared to 37 per cent for the global and 36.1 per cent for the regional tendency. Therefore, while the nationalist tendency was statistically greater than the other tendencies for much of the period examined, it was still in the weak category.

2. **Regional/regionalist tendency or stream.** This describes or represents players who were born in the Caribbean or were citizens of a Caribbean country but played for a team that was not associated with their Caribbean country of birth or citizenship. This tendency varied between 28.9 per cent and 36.1 per cent in the period examined and also fell within the categories of weak or very weak.

3. **Global tendency/stream.** This tendency or stream consists of overseas players from across the cricketing world who were neither born in nor were citizens of any Caribbean country. This tendency varied between 21 per cent and 37 per cent and, similar to the nationalist and regionalist tendencies, it also fell within the weak and very weak categories.

   It is interesting to note therefore that the three major player streams or tendencies in the CPL as a whole are either weak or very weak. Although the national tendency was relatively stronger than the other tendencies, it was still found to be weaker than the non-national tendency.

4. **Non-national tendency/stream.** When combined, the strengths of regional and global streams or players were greater than the national stream's in all of the seasons examined as they varied between

53.3 per cent and 73.1 per cent, compared to the national stream which ranged between 26.9 per cent and 46.7 per cent. Relatedly, the non-national stream was in the categories of strong in 2013 (53.3 per cent) and 2015 (59.2 per cent), very strong in 2019 (60.5 per cent), and extremely strong in 2017 (73.1 per cent), while declining by 13 per cent in 2019. Viewed from this perspective, the nationalist tendency or stream in West Indian cricket could be seen as being totally subdued by or subordinated to the combination of non-nationalist or counter-regional and global streams.

However, a much more nuanced and variegated picture of player distribution as well as the triumvirate of tendencies in the League emerges on individual examination of the trends for each team. In this regard, in general terms, while all the teams were found to have the same basic mixed tendencies or triumvirate of national, regional, and global players, the trends varied from team to team. For each tendency, there was a further subdivision or subgrouping of teams depending on its strength or weakness.

Category 1: Nationalist Tendency

1a: Very Strong Nationalist Tendency

The teams in this category were the Jamaica Tallawahs and the Trinidad and Tobago Knight Riders but the figures for both teams reveal variations in the nature of their nationalist tendency across the seasons studied. For the Tallawahs (Table 8.4), it varied from weak in one year (31.6 per cent in 2017) to strong in another (55 per cent in 2019) and extremely strong in 2013 (73.3 per cent) and 2015 (75 per cent). Conversely, the proportion of non-Jamaican nationals was generally in the minority across three seasons, varying between 25 per cent and 45 per cent except for 2017, when they represented the majority or 68.4 per cent, outnumbering Jamaican nationals (31.6 per cent) by some 36.8 per cent. However, since Jamaicans outnumbered non-Jamaicans both collectively and individually for three out of four seasons by proportions ranging from 55 per cent to 75 per cent, their nationalist tendency was considered very strong. The nationalist tendency for the Trinidad and Tobago Knight Riders (Table 8.7) also varied from weak in 2017 (44.4 per cent) to strong in 2013 (53.3 per cent) and very strong in both 2015 (62.5 per cent) and 2019 (66.6 per cent). Conversely, non-Trinidad and Tobago nationals were in the minority across three seasons, ranging between 33.3 per cent and 46.7 per cent except for 2017 when they amounted to 55.6 per cent and outnumbered Trinidad and Tobago nationals (44.4 per cent), though by 11.2 per cent. As a result, since Trinidad and Tobago nationals outnumbered its non-nationals collectively for three out of the four seasons examined and also outnumbered them individually by proportions ranging between 53 per cent and 67 per cent, Trinidad and Tobago is also characterized as having a very strong national or nationalist tendency.

1b: Weak Nationalist Tendency

The Barbados Tridents (Table 8.2) and the Guyana Amazon Warriors (Table 8.3) were in this category. The nationalist tendency of the Tridents varied from very weak in 2017 (23.5 per cent) to weak in 2015 (37.5 per cent), and strong in both 2013 (53.3 per cent) and 2019 (52.6 per cent). However, Barbados' non-nationals were in the majority in both 2015 (62.5 per cent) and 2017 (76.5 per cent), outnumbering its nationals by large margins of 25 per cent and 53 per cent, respectively. This tendency is generally considered weak because Barbadian players were in the majority for only two out of four seasons and not by large majorities, while Barbados' non-nationals outnumbered its nationals by relatively large margins for two of the four seasons (2015 and 2017). At best, the Barbadian Tridents reflect a mix of weak and moderately strong nationalist tendencies but more in the direction of the former. In relation to the Amazon Warriors, its nationalist tendency was weak for every season as it ranged between 33.3 per cent and 47 per cent. As a related consequence, its non-nationals were in the majority for every season as they ranged between 53 per cent and 67 per cent, which surpassed nationals by margins varying between 5.9 per cent and 33.4 per cent. For both the Tridents and the Warriors, therefore, the nationalist tendency was generally weak and much less prominent than the non-nationalist tendency.

1c: Very Weak Nationalist Tendency

The two teams in this category were the St Kitts and Nevis Patriots (Table 8.5) and the St Lucian Zouks (Table 8.7). The national tendency for both these teams was very weak for every season as the number of native players for the Patriots amounted to 12.5 per cent in 2015, and 5.5 per cent in both 2017 and 2019 while for the Zouks, it ranged between 13 per cent and 22.2 per cent. Invariably, non-nationals outnumbered nationals on these teams by large majorities and margins. In the case of the Patriots, these majorities amounted to 87.5 per cent and 94.4 per cent, while the margins amounted to 75 per cent and 88.9 per cent. For the Zouks, the majorities ranged between 78 per cent and 88 per cent, while the margins ranged between 56 per cent and 74 per cent. In interpreting these figures, however, one must recognize the fact that the very small number of nationals on these teams was probably a result of the limited number of players of international standard in the countries, which might be linked to the size of their populations and the smaller number of males on the island from which to draw. Recent figures for 2020 put the population of St Kitts and Nevis at 53,356 and that of St Lucia at 183,975.[25] In that context, they have to rely heavily on regional and foreign players, unlike the teams from Jamaica and Trinidad and Tobago where more than half the teams have consisted of native-born players or nationals because they have access to a greater pool of talent, which might also be linked to their relatively larger population size (over 2.9 million in the case of Jamaica and 1.4 million in the case of Trinidad and Tobago),[26] as well as their cricket history.

Category 2: Regionalist Tendency

2a: (Very) Strong Regionalist Tendency

The two teams that had the weakest nationalist tendency or presence, the St Kitts and Nevis Patriots and St Lucia Zouks, were the ones with the strongest regionalist tendency. For instance, in the case of the Patriots, the extent of its regionalist tendency was strong in 2015 (56.2 per cent), very strong in 2017 (61.1 per cent), and extremely strong in 2019 (72.2 per cent) as regional players made up the majority of the team which had increased continuously from 2015 to 2019. In the case of the Zouks, the extent/strength of its regional tendency was more mixed, for while it was strong in 2013 (53.3 per cent) and 2015 (56.2 per cent), it was weak in 2017 (38.9 per cent) and 2019 (45.4 per cent). Again, the relatively high proportion of regional players in these teams can be explained in terms of the limited player pools in these countries, which leads them to depend more on other countries as sources for their supply of players.

2b: (Very) Weak Regionalist Tendency

Teams other than the Patriots and the Zouks reflected a generally weak or very weak regionalist tendency or presence. The teams that were very weak in this regard were Jamaica and Trinidad and Tobago where the proportion of regional players varied between 5.5 per cent and 26.7 per cent in the case of the latter and 0 per cent to 31.6 per cent in the case of the former. The teams which had relatively more regional players compared to the Tallawahs and the Knight Riders but whose regional tendency can still be classified as very weak, weak, or both were the Guyana Amazon Warriors and the Barbados Tridents. In the case of Tridents, their regional stream was very weak in both 2013 (26.7 per cent) and 2019 (5.3 per cent), while in 2015 (31.2 per cent) and 2017 (41.2 per cent) it was still weak, though higher compared to 2013 and 2019. For the Amazon Warriors, its regional tendency was very weak in 2015 (22.2 per cent), 2017 (27.8 per cent), and 2019 (23.5 per cent) and weak in 2013 (40 per cent). For both the Tridents and Warriors, therefore, their regional stream was either weak or very weak.

Category 3: Global Tendency

3a: Very Weak/Weak

The global tendency among all the teams, across all the seasons examined, was found to be either weak or very weak or both, although there were slight variations across the teams. For instance, the teams which reflected a blend of a weak and very weak global presence included the

Jamaica Tallawahs where the number of foreign players varied between 19 per cent and 37 per cent; Guyana Amazon Warriors, between 20 per cent and 39 per cent; St Kitts and Nevis Patriots, between 22 per cent and 33 per cent; Trinidad and Tobago Knight Riders, between 20 per cent and 39 per cent; and St Lucia Zouks, between 27 per cent and 41 per cent. In the case of the Tridents, this tendency was just weak as opposed to very weak as the number of foreign players ranged between 31 per cent and 41 per cent. The weak nature of this global tendency as far as team composition is concerned could be partially explained by the limits that are placed on the number of foreign players that any team can recruit or have. Their presence, however, is still significant and important since they contribute to the number of non-nationals on each team, which was found to be greater than nationals on several teams.

However, the number of foreign players in a team is misleading as a barometer of globalization since other important markers must include the nature of team ownership as well as the media broadcast of the League and the global TV audience. With respect to team ownership, all of the six teams are owned by Indian companies or businessmen.[27] In relation to the media, both broadcast and digital platforms (e.g. YouTube and Facebook), the League was televised to forty countries around the world. The latter has involved partnerships with broadcasters in the UK (such as Sky Sports and Dave/UKTV), the USA (One World Sports), New Zealand (Sky), Australia (Fox Sports), EcoNet/KweseTV (sub-Saharan Africa), and OSN (Middle East), as well as India (Sony Six). In this context, the estimated size of the global cumulative media audience for the CPL increased from 36 million in its inaugural year in 2013 to 312 million in 2019 and to 523 million for the 2020 edition of the tournament.[28] The League therefore can be considered a global event and an expression of the global circuit of economic capital, although foreign players make up a minority of the teams.

A different picture emerges when we compare the findings for the league as a whole to the findings of the individual teams. Firstly, based on player origins, the nationalist tendency or symbolic political capital across most of the teams (four out of six) is weak or very weak, which is consistent with the league as a whole except in the case of the Jamaica Tallawahs and the Trinidad and Tobago Knight Riders where it is strong or very strong. Secondly, the regional and global tendencies were also found to be generally weak across the majority of teams consistent with the League as a

Table 8.2 Barbados Tridents: distribution of players by country (%)

Year	Total players	Barbados	Other Caribbean	Foreign	Total non-Bajans
2013	15	53.3	26.7	33.3	47.7
2015	16	37.5	31.2	31.2	62.5
2017	17	23.5	41.2	35.3	76.5
2019	19	52.6	5.3	42.1	47.4

Table 8.3 Guyana Amazon Warriors: distribution of players by country

Year	Total players	Guyana	Other Caribbean	Foreign	Total non-Guyanese
2013	15	40	40	20	60
2015	18	44.4	22.2	33.3	55.5
2017	18	33.3	27.8	38.9	66.7
2019	17	47.0	23.5	29.4	52.9

Table 8.4 Jamaica Tallawahs: distribution of players by country

Year	Total players	Jamaica	Other Caribbean	Foreign	Total non-Jamaican
2013	15	73.3	0	26.6	26.6
2015	16	75	6.2	18.7	25
2017	19	31.6	31.6	36.8	68.4
2019	20	55.0	20.0	25.0	45.0

Table 8.5 St Kitts/Nevis: distribution of players by country

Year	Total players	St Kitts/ Nevis	Other Caribbean	Foreign	Total non-Kittians/ Nevisians
2013	0	0	0	0	0
2015	16	12.5	56.2	31.2	87.5
2017	18	5.5	61.1	33.3	94.4
2019	18	5.5	72.2	22.2	94.4

Note: The St Kitts and Nevis Patriots did not play in the inaugural season in 2013.

Table 8.6 St Lucia Zouks: distribution of players by country

Year	Total players	St Lucia	Other Caribbean	Foreign	Total non-Lucian
2013	15	20	53.3	26.6	80
2015	16	13.3	56.2	31.2	87.7
2017	17	22.2	38.9	38.9	77.8
2019	22	13.6	45.4	40.9	86.4

Table 8.7 Trinidad and Tobago Knight Riders: distribution of players by country

Year	Total players	Trinidad-Tobago	Other Caribbean	Foreign	Total non-Trinidad and Tobago
2013	15	53.3	26.7	20	46.7
2015	16	62.5	12.5	25	37.5
2017	18	44.4	16.7	38.9	55.6
2019	18	66.6	5.5	27.8	33.3

whole. However, the use of player origins or numbers does not accurately capture the extent to which the CPL is integrated with global finance capital through team ownership, global media coverage, and viewership. On the contrary, based on these markers, global economic capital seems to trump symbolic political capital or nationalism in the CPL. In addition, the global character of the League is also evident from the fact that it involves players from thirteen countries drawn from Africa, Asia, Europe, Oceania, and North America. Nevertheless, while nationalism may generally appear, at best, to be on the back foot in at least four out of the six teams (i.e. Tridents, Zouks, Warriors, and Patriots) and, in the League as a whole, based on sheer player numbers as well as team ownership, the numbers by themselves do not sufficiently capture the extent to which the CPL has served to activate, reflect, and reinforce nationalist sentiments or tendencies in the region, despite its apparent subordination to global capital. This comes into sharp focus when examining other political and cultural markers of nationalism linked to the marketing strategy of the CPL.

Nationalism, Commercialism, and the CPL

The CPL's Americanized franchise model reflects a curious blend of nationalism and commercialism or economic capital and symbolic political capital due to five major factors:

1. The naming of the teams after particular Caribbean countries together with their peculiar franchise name (e.g. Guyana Amazon Warriors, Barbados Tridents, Trinidad and Tobago Knight Riders, St Kitts and Nevis Patriots, St Lucia Zouks).
2. The use of the colours of the national flag of the island nation with which a team is associated as part of the team's uniform as well as the associated team merchandise (e.g. hats, T-shirts) and even facial paint.
3. The use of the particular Caribbean country with which the team is associated as the team's home base or home ground.
4. The general appointment of team captains who were citizens of the country with which the team was associated. The only general exceptions to this practice included the appointment of a player from Trinidad and Tobago to captain the Barbados Tridents which lasted five years and players from Jamaica, Trinidad and Tobago, Barbados, and even South Africa to captain the St Kitts Nevis Patriots.[29]
5. The use of music or singers associated with a particular island during matches which can include, for example, the playing of reggae music in Jamaica and *soca* or *soca chutney* music in Trinidad and Tobago or Barbados and the other islands involved.

Because of these factors (national colours, songs, home base, country name, team captain), the teams and the competition retained their symbolic national or nationalist character and appeal *de facto*, although *de jure* they were not representative national teams consistent with the franchise model. In the original franchise model or concept, teams carry the name of cities, states, or regions within a country but not the country itself. In the CPL, however, this is clearly not the case as all teams carry the name of a particular country as opposed to a city like the Kingston Tallawahs, the Bridgetown Tridents, the Port of Spain Knight Riders, or the Castries Zouks. This approach to naming was driven by marketing and economic considerations linked to the creation of team loyalty and a ready-made fan base both for TV viewing and local attendance at the games. The naming of the teams, therefore, reflected a modification of the original franchise concept to suit not just the small size or demographic limitations of the Caribbean but also the requirements of capital accumulation or economic capital. More generally, the use of national symbolic political capital (national colours, songs) was still intimately connected to the requirements of economic capital and, more so, global economic capital expressed through the franchise model of sport.

In addition, apart from the commercialized and professionalized nature of the League, another layer of economic capital pertained to the League's general economic impact in the region and particularly in relation to tourism (especially sport tourism) on which most islands heavily depend.[30] As regards its general economic impact on the region, measured in terms of employment, tourist spending, organizer spending, and accommodation, this increased from US $105 million in 2013 to US $136 million in 2019 with some annual fluctuations.[31] In relation to the development of sport tourism and state support for the league, a former minister of sport from Trinidad and Tobago stated that 'The Government of Trinidad and Tobago is pleased to continue on our Sports Tourism drive with the hosting the CPL semi-final and final for the next 3 years [2018–2020] at the brand new Brian Lara Cricket Academy.'[32] Relatedly, after an Indian-owned company purchased the St Lucian Zouks, the St Lucian prime minister reportedly stated, 'Saint Lucians continue to root for the Zouks and . . . The Government of Saint Lucia looks forward to working closely with the new owners to create a team we can all be proud of.'[33] The more fundamental significance of these statements has been the general role of the state in the Caribbean, as political capital, in facilitating economic capital through the CPL due to its socio-economic benefits for the region, particularly in the vital tourism sector.

T20 Cricket, the West Indies Team, and the Circuit of Capital

The relationship between T20 cricket, economic capital, symbolic capital, and symbolic political capital, however, expressed itself in a much more confrontational manner in relation to the West Indies cricket team. The root of this clash or conflict lies in the historical construction of West Indian cricketers and the West Indies team as symbols of nationalism, regionalism, and anti-imperialism as part of a process of self-empowerment and political resistance against British imperialism or, in short, as symbolic political capital.[34] Additionally, it may also lie in the British-derived middle-class-based amateur-gentleman ideology, as well as the related Coubertinian notion of playing sport for honour and glory, which gave sport its primary value as symbolic capital.[35]

This clash between cricket as symbolic political capital and economic capital in West Indies cricket predated the arrival of T20 cricket in the region in the first decade of the new millennium. The two most notable antecedents were the participation of West Indian cricketers in Kerry Packer's World Series cricket (1976–1977) and in South African domestic cricket at the height of the struggle against apartheid.[36] These early attempts to convert symbolic capital into economic capital took place before the sport was sufficiently commercialized to be transformed into a major industry. The transformation of sport into economic capital may have started with the 1984 Los Angeles Olympics which accelerated in the 1990s, and manifested itself in the growth of professional sport, media sport, sponsorship, endorsement deals, and concerns with image rights.[37] Inevitably, these developments expressed themselves in West Indies cricket.

As a consequence, from the second half of the 1990s, long before the advent of T20 cricket in the West Indies through Allen Stanford in 2006, cricket had started to experience regular convulsions through conflict between its players and the WICB. For instance, between 1996 and 2012, the West Indies Players Union (WIPA) filed and won all of the fifteen lawsuits against the WICB over issues relating to their share of sponsorship money, player endorsements, player fees, and the general treatment of players. In one of these disputes, in 2004, the then chief executive officer of the Federation of International Cricketers' Associations (FICA), Tim May, made the following comment in support of the West Indies Players Union: 'It is ridiculous to suggest that players should agree to give away the right for third parties to use their image and attributes for advertising and promotional purposes without any financial consideration.'[38]

This period was marked by what Beckles describes as 'cricket's divorce from nationalism and the abandonment of nationalist sentiment', though he never really examines whether the nature of the marriage or the nationalist courting of players, might have had anything to do with the supposed 'divorce' in the first place.[39] Against this background, the advent of T20 cricket in the new millennium served to intensify or exacerbate the conflicts and supposed 'divorce' between economic capital and cricket's symbolic political function in the West Indies. In this regard, players were accused of having a 'cash consciousness' and placing 'cash before country' as the deeper political and ideological importance of the game for the people of the region appeared to have been subordinated to their own material self-interests.[40]

In the fifteen-year period spanning 1980 to 1995, the West Indies were the leading team in world cricket, winning twenty-nine successive Test (world) cricket series against the likes of England, Australia, India, and Pakistan. Up until that time, no team had ever achieved this feat. Since 1995, however, they have experienced a sharp and steady decline and, up to March 2020, were positioned eighth out of twelve Test-playing countries in the Test cricket rankings.[41] The decline of the West Indies in world cricket was even attributed to T20 cricket as '[t]he whole sale migration of senior players into the T20 bounty has produced disastrous Test results for Windies'.[42] In short, the argument was that materialism (economic capital) seems to have trumped nationalism (symbolic political capital) among West Indian players.

Discussion and Conclusion

This chapter demonstrates that T20 cricket in the West Indies and particularly the Caribbean Premier League has had several mixed and contradictory economic and political implications for this region and the development of cricket. It has also shown the dynamic nature of economic, symbolic, and political capital as part of the interconnected circuit or figuration of capital which framed the study. While the CPL is based on a triumvirate of three major tendencies or streams—the national, regional, and global—their strength and related positioning varied significantly. In the latter regard, the nationalist tendency in particular was found to be generally weak or not prominent based on an examination of players' country of origin. In this context, it seems reasonable to suggest that the CPL has facilitated a process of denationalization within West Indian cricket, which bears an affinity to a similar process in the wider economy associated with neoliberalism through foreign ownership in certain sectors of the economy that include, notably, telecommunications, electricity provision, postal services, and oil and gas production.[43]

This process of denationalization was also facilitated by global player streams and investment capital. Although the global player stream was also weak, it was still sufficient to create some semblance of cosmopolitanism in the League. This would have aided the process of commercialization or capital accumulation by helping to broaden its global media reach or audience through having players from countries such as Australia, New Zealand, and South Africa. Relatedly, this denationalization was also evident in the foreign nature of the League and team ownership or global economic capital. In speaking to global capital flows, therefore, as a marker of economic capital and denationalization, there is a need to distinguish between the globalization of players or human capital in sport which was very limited or weak and the globalization of investment capital which was very strong or dominant. It is important to note, however, that the economic capital generated by the CPL (income, revenues, profits) did not just accrue to the League owners, team owners, and players but also to the local economies and particularly their stakeholders in tourism in general and sport tourism in particular. In addition, the generation of economic capital in these respects was facilitated by the holders of political capital or the leaders of Caribbean states through their support for the League since they recognized its national, economic, and sporting value for the development of the game in the region. Political capital therefore served directly to facilitate economic capital at all levels (owners, organizers, players, coaches, and tourist stakeholders). States in the Caribbean therefore became a site that reflected the workings of economic, political, and symbolic capital.

While the cosmopolitanism-driven globalization in the CPL has contributed to the process of denationalization and the conversion of symbolic player capital into economic capital, it has also facilitated island nationalism through configuring or constructing teams in such a way as to reflect particular symbols of nationalism or national identify (i.e. use of national colours, country name, etc.). In this way, symbolic political capital served (global) economic capital or capital accumulation. This contradictory impact of globalization on West Indian cricket, through disrupting as well as reinvigorating and reflecting nation(alism), is further evidence that globalization did not spell the end of the state or nationalist feeling but gave it more visibility and vigour.[44] It may have placed cricket nationalism on the 'back foot' but it is surely not out.

The case of the CPL helps to demonstrate the interrelated nature of Bourdieu's circuit of capital, showing how economic capital facilitated and helped to undermine symbolic political capital (nationalism) which also aided economic capital at a global, regional, and local level. Relatedly, political capital (holders of state power) facilitated economic capital through the support of the Caribbean states for the League. In the West Indies, therefore, nationalism has been surrounded by three sets of pressures: cosmopolitanism, commercialism, and globalization. And while it may appear to be on the back foot or very weak on one marker (i.e. the proportion of nationals in the league), on another (i.e. the trappings of symbolic political capital like national colours, music, naming, and even crowd support), it appears to be very much still in the game.

Outside the CPL, the participation of players who represent the West Indies cricket team in T20 competitions was also examined to illustrate the connection between economic capital and symbolic capital. However, this connection was more oppositional and contentious as many players, including some leading ones, tried to convert their symbolic capital into economic capital which was seen as anathema to or compromising their historical nationalist, regionalist, and anti-imperialist political symbolisms. While this attempted conversion was not new, the context of T20 cricket and the greater commercialization and globalization of the game were. The symbolic political value or functions of the West Indies cricket team are even more acute because the team does not represent a single nation-state like other teams in international competition but at least ten small island states who form part of the former British West Indies. However, while the West Indies team does not represent a singular nation-state, the nationalist and regionalist feelings towards the team are no less potent. In this context, the team has been historically seen as a symbol of an elusive West Indian nation or regionalism and consequently has formed part of the collective West Indian political imagination.[45] Consequently, the economic capital which T20 and professional cricket generally represent was seen as disrupting if not destroying this important political symbolism although, at the same time, they have also served to reflect and reinforce it. Drawing on Anderson's notion of the nation as an imagined political community, a dominant theme in the literature is the role sport teams play in bringing this imagined nation to life.[46] In the context of the West Indies cricket team, this role is even more crucial since the nation it represents basically does not exist except in the collective imagination.

However, since the recent change in the administrative leadership of West Indies cricket with the 2019 election of a new president and executive team, we have seen a kind of rapprochement or more accommodating approach to West Indian players who participate in T20 leagues across the world, many of whom now qualify and play for the team after being disqualified by the previous Windies Board.[47] This has now provided the conditions for the easier conversion of the players' symbolic political capital into economic capital, both of which are needed for the development of the players and the game in the region.

Notes

1. C.L.R. James, *Beyond a Boundary* (London: Hutchinson, 1963); Hilary Beckles, *The Development of West Indies Cricket, Vol. I: The Age of Nationalism* (London: Pluto Press, 1998).

2. Hilary Beckles, *Cricket without a Cause: Fall and Rise of the Mighty West Indian Test Cricketers* (Kingston: Ian Randle Publishers, 2017).

3. Pierre Bourdieu, 'The forms of capital', in *Handbook of Theory and Research for the Sociology of Education*, ed. J.G. Richardson (New York: Greenwood Press, 1986), 243.

4. Bourdieu, 'The forms of capital', 248–252; Richard Giulianotti, 'Civilizing games: Norbert Elias and the sociology of sport', in *Sport and Modern Social Theorists*, ed. Richard Giulianotti (New York: Palgrave Macmillan, 2004), 157.

5. Bourdieu, 'The forms of capital', 243–248; Pierre Bourdieu, *Distinction: A Social Critique of the Judgment of Taste* (Paris: Les Editions de Minuit, 1979), 291.

6. Bourdieu, *Practical Reason* (Cambridge: Polity Press, 1994/1998), 41.

7. Ibid., 47–49.

8. Ibid., 47.

9. Ibid.

10. Roy McCree, 'The death of a female boxer: Media, sport, nationalism, and gender'. *Journal of Sport and Social Issues* 35, no. 4 (2011): 327.

11. Philip White and Brian Wilson, 'Distinctions in the stands: An investigation of Bourdieu's "habitus", socioeconomic status and sport spectatorship in Canada', *International Review for Sociology of Sport* 34, no. 3 (1999): 245–264; Thomas Wilson, 'The paradox of social class and sports involvement: The roles of cultural and economic capital', *International Review for Sociology of Sport* 37, no. 1 (2002): 5–16; Alan Tomlinson, 'Pierre Bourdieu and the sociological study of sport: Habitus, capital and field', in *Sport and Modern Social Theorists*, ed. Richard Giulianotti (New York: Palgrave Macmillan, 2004), 161–162; Carl Stempel, 'Adult participation sports as cultural capital: A test of Bourdieu's theory of the field of sports', *International Review for Sociology of Sport* 40, no. 4 (2005): 411–432; Alan Warde, 'Cultural capital and the place of sport', *Cultural Trends* 15, nos. 2 and 3 (2006): 107–122; David Purdue and David Howe, 'Plotting a paralympic field: An elite disability sport competition viewed through Bourdieu's sociological lens', *International Review for Sociology of Sport* 50, no. 1 (2015): 83–97.

12. Jonathan Sullivan, Simon Chadwick, and Michael Gow, 'China's football dream: Sport, citizenship, symbolic power, and civic spaces', *Journal of Sport and Social Issues* 43, no. 6 (2019): 493–514.

13. Norbert Elias, *The Sociology of Individuals* (Oxford: Blackwell, 1987).

14. www.icc-cricket.com/rankings/mens/overview.

15. 'Popular T20 cricket leagues in the world', www.mykhel.com/cricket/t20-leagues. accessed 12 November 2020.

16. Paul Maidment, 'Cricket dreams crash with Stanford's fall', 17 February 2009, www.forbes.com/2009/02/17/allan-stanford-cricket-business-sports_0217_s tanford_cricket.html?sh=626e8abbfc37, accessed 19 November 2020.

17. Mark Pouchet, 'Big bucks on the line in Stanford final', ESPNcricinfo, 13 August 2006, www.espncricinfo.com/story/_/id/22993336/all-play-stanford-finals, acces sed 13 November 2020; www.espncricinfo.com/stanford/engine/series/228881. html?view=records, accessed 13 November 2020.

18. Paul Kitchin, 'Sponsorship management in cricket: A case study of the Stanford Super Series, the West Indian Cricket Board and Digicel', *Birkbeck Sport Business Centre Case Study Paper Series* 1, no. 1 (2009): 2–32, www.researchgate.net/publ ication/275947123_Sponsorship_Management_in_Cricket_A_Case_Study_ of_the_Stanford_Super_Series_the_West_Indian_Cricket_Board_and_Digicel; Maidment, 'Cricket dreams crash with Stanford's fall'.

19. Maidment, 'Cricket dreams crash with Stanford's fall'; Kitchin, 'Sponsorship management in cricket'.

20. WICB, 'Fantastic ticket prices for Caribbean T20', 7 July 2010, https://www.crick etworld.com/fantastic-ticket-prices-for-caribbean-t20/24796 htm, accessed 14 November 2020.

21. WICB, 'WICB Caribbean T20 trophy: The big prize!', 21 July 2010, www.crick etworld.com/wicb-caribbean-t20-trophy-the-big-prize-/24966.htm, accessed 29 November 2010.

22. Vinode Mamchan, 'WICB needs to bring back regional T20', *The Guardian*, 23 May 2015, www.guardian.co.tt/article-6.2.364729.f35a3844e5, accessed 16 November 2020.

23. Mamchan, 'WICB needs to bring back regional T20'; *Jamaican Observer*, 'WICB to earn US$4.5 million from CPL', 15 May 2013, www.jamaicaobserver.com/sport/WICB-to-earn-US-4-5-million-from-CPL_14266073&template=Mobile Article, accessed 16 November 2020.

24. Having just six teams or a small number of teams was consistent with the size of the other major T20 leagues around the world which have varied between five and eight teams. www.mykhel.com/cricket/t20-leagues, accessed 12 November 2020. In addition, it should be noted that of the six teams, two have undergone name changes. These are the St Lucian Zouks whose name was changed to St Lucian Stars in 2017 then to the St Lucian Kings in 2021 and the Barbados Tridents, whose name was changed to the Barbados Royals in 2021 (The Cricketer, 'CPL franchise St Lucia Zouks renamed as St Lucia Kings', https://www.thecricketer. com/Topics/cpl/cpl_franchise_st_lucia_zouks_renamed_st_lucia_kings.html, accessed 13 April 2024; CPL, 'Barbados Franchise Rebrands as the Royals', https:// www.cplt20.com/barbados-franchise-rebrands-royals, https://www.cplt20.com/barbados-franchise-rebrands-royals, accessed 13 April 2024.). In addition, for the 2024 CPL, the Jamaican Tallawahs were replaced by the Antigua and Barbuda Falcons (CPL, 'Antigua & Barbuda Falcons Unveiled as New Franchise', https:// www.cplt20.com/antigua-barbuda-falcons-unveiled-new-franchise#:~:text= The%20newest%20franchise%20in%20the,Title%20Sponsor%20of%20the%20t eam, accessed April 13, 2024.).

25. www.worldometers.info/world-population/saint-kitts-and-nevis-population; www.worldometers.info/world-population/saint-lucia-population.

26. www.worldometers.info/world-population/trinidad-and-tobago-population; www.worldometers.info/world-population/jamaica-population.

27. Vijay Tagore, 'All Caribbean Premier League teams now have Indian owners', 6 February 2019, https://mumbaimirror.indiatimes.com/sport/cricket/west-ind ian-league/articleshow/67857576.cms, accessed 25 November 2020.

28. Shweta Agnihotri, 'CPL viewership up by 56%, 312 mn watch 2019 edition', 6 February 2020, www.insidesport.co/cpl-viewership-up-by-56-312-mn-watch-2019-edition, accessed 25 November 2020; CPL, 'Massive increase in hero CPL viewership', n.d., www.cplt20.com/massive-increase-hero-cpl-viewership, acces sed 22 November 2020.

29. CPL, 'Pollard ready for the new challenge at the St Lucia stars', n.d., www.cplt20. com/magazine-team-news/pollard-ready-new-challenge-st-lucia-stars-0, acces sed 23 November 2020; ESPNcricinfo, 'List of captains', https://stats.espncricinfo. com/ci/engine/records/individual/list_captains.html?class=6;id=5543;type= team, accessed 13 November 2020.

30. Sherma Roberts, Mechelle Best, and Acolla Cameron, *Contemporary Caribbean Tourism: Concepts and Cases* (Kingston: Ian Randle, 2014).

31. Leighton Levey, 'Hero CPL had record economic impact of US$136m across the region', 24 January 2020, https://www.sportsmax.tv/index.php/cricket/cricket-regional/item/56297-2019-hero-cpl-had-record-economic-impact-of-us-136m-across-the-region#:~:text=CPL-, accessed 24 November 2020.

32. Barnacle News, 'Hero CPL finals to be in Trinidad & Tobago from 2018–2020', 5 March 2018, www.thebarnaclenews.com/hero-cpl-finals-trinidad-tobago-2018-2020, accessed 15 November 2020.

33. Caribbean Camera Inc., 'St Lucia CPL cricket franchise sold to Indian company', 19 February 2020, https://thecaribbeancamera.com/st-lucia-cpl-cricket-franch ise-sold-to-indian-company, accessed 25 November 2020.

34. James, *Beyond a Boundary*; Beckles, *The Development of West Indies Cricket, Vol. I*.

35. Adrian Smith and Dilwyn Porter, *Amateurs and Professionals in Post-War British Sport* (London: Psychology Press, 2000); Ernest Cashmore, *Making Sense of Sport* (London: Routledge, 2012).

36. Ashley Gray, *The Unforgiven: Missionaries or Mercenaries? The Tragic Story of the Rebel West Indian Cricketers Who Toured Apartheid South* (Worthing: Pitch Publishing, 2020).

37. Christopher Hill, *Olympics Politics: Athens to Atlanta 1896–1996* (Manchester: Manchester University Press, 1996); Cashmore, *Making Sense of Sport*; Jay Coakley, *Sports in Society: Issues and Controversies*, 12th ed. (New York: McGraw-Hill Education, 2016).

38. *Trinidad and Tobago Newsday*, 27 November 2004; Wisden cricinfo, 'The contracts dispute-explained', 25 November 2004, https://www.espncricinfo.com/story/the-contracts-dispute-explained-136045, accessed 13 April 2024.

39. Beckles, *Cricket without a Cause*, 106.

40. Ibid., 11–19.

41. www.icc-cricket.com/rankings/mens/team-rankings/test, accessed 11 November 2020.

42. Beckles, *Cricket without a Cause*, 14.

43. Richard Bernal and Leslie Winsome, 'Privatization in the English speaking Caribbean: An assessment', *Policy Papers on the Americas, Volume X, Study 7* (Washington, DC: CSIS, 1999).

44. David Held and Anthony McGrew, *The Global Transformations Reader* (Cambridge: Polity Press, 2004); Richard Giulianotti and Roland Robertson, 'Sport and globalization: Transnational dimensions', *Global Networks* 7, no. 2 (2007): 107–112.

45. C.L.R. James, 'The birth of a nation', in *Contemporary Caribbean: A Sociological Reader, Volume I*, ed. Susan Craig (St Joseph, Trinidad: College Press, 1981), 3–38.

46. Joseph Maguire, *Global Sport: Identity, Societies, Civilizations* (Cambridge: Polity Press, 1999); Alan Bairner, *Sport, Nationalism and Globalization* (Albany, NY: State University of New York Press, 2001).

47. *Trinidad Guardian*, 25 March 2019.

Index